Pre-Publication Comments on *Jesus, Politics, and Society*

"I welcome Fr. Cassidy's fresh approach to the Gospel of Luke. Two features in particular give me pleasure. One is his recognition that Luke's distinctive outlook and emphasis do not at all diminish his right to be regarded as an accurate historian. The other is his demonstration that Luke does not accommodate Jesus' teaching to Roman imperial interests; rather, while making it plain that Jesus and the Zealots were poles apart, he shows that his teaching was so essentially revolutionary as to pose a greater threat to the principles of Roman rule than the Zealot policy could ever do."

F. F. Bruce, *Rylands Professor of Biblical Criticism and Exegesis,*
University of Manchester

"I am particularly impressed by Fr. Cassidy's consistent effort to extricate Jesus from the limited categories that have variously been used to interpret his impact on history. Fr. Cassidy's use of Luke's acknowledged acquaintance with imperial matters and affairs as a methodological starting point is eminently sound."

Frederick W. Danker, *Department of Exegetical Theology,*
Christ Seminary—Seminex

"Dr. Cassidy's work offers a balanced survey of the religious, political, and economic milieu of New Testament times. His account of Luke's portrait of Jesus' social attitude is clearly the result of meticulous research and serious reflection."

David Daube, *Emeritus Regius Professor of Civil Law,*
University of Oxford

"Cassidy's study is marked by an admirable combination of careful historical and theological scholarship on the one hand and concern for the mission of the church on the other. He challenges the common view that Jesus' outlook was essentially nonpolitical and concludes, to the contrary, that he posed a real threat to Roman rule. I take pleasure in warmly commending *Jesus, Politics, and Society* to every serious student of the New Testament and to those who are concerned with the church's mission in today's world."

W. Ward Gasque, *Associate Professor of New Testament,*
Regent College

"The contemporary debate has polarized into two diametrically opposed positions which view Jesus respectively as carrying a Zealot portfolio and, on the other side, being opposed totally to any direct involvement in Palestinian politics. Fr. Cassidy's treatment serves a useful purpose in indicating that both these extreme positions leave something to be desired and hardly tally with the full data of the Gospel record, particularly the third Gospel. While he does not accept in full the so-called Zealot hypothesis, by which Jesus was caught up in the anti-Roman revolutionary movement, he does show that Jesus had a distinctive attitude to the economic conditions of his day and advocated a type of passive resistance that Cassidy well illustrates from the life of Mahatma Gandhi in India. This is a novel contribution and will appeal to all New Testament students who are concerned to place the life setting of Jesus in the contemporary ethos of his times."

Ralph P. Martin, *Professor of New Testament,*
Fuller Theological Seminary

"Cassidy, who has had experience with groups working for social change and who takes into account recent critical analyses of the Third Gospel, provides in this book a thoughtful and incisive account of Jesus' political and social stance as set forth in Luke's Gospel."

Bruce M. Metzger, *Professor of New Testament Language and Literature,*
Princeton Theological Seminary

"I welcome the appearance in print of Fr. Cassidy's clearly written study of the social and political stance of our Lord according to St. Luke. The book is patiently and lucidly written, and comes across as an informed study, cautious in its thesis, and faithful to the biblical text. It will contribute to the growing clarity that is emerging as to where Jesus stood in the social and political situation of his day, and where we should be standing in ours."

Clark H. Pinnock, *Associate Professor, Divinity College,*
McMaster University

Jesus, Politics, and Society

A Study of Luke's Gospel

Richard J. Cassidy

ORBIS BOOKS
Maryknoll, New York 10545

The Catholic Foreign Mission Society of America (Maryknoll) recruits and trains people for overseas missionary service. Through Orbis Books Maryknoll aims to foster the international dialogue which is essential to mission. The books published, however, reflect the opinions of their authors and are not meant to represent the official position of the Society.

Library of Congress Cataloging in Publication Data

Cassidy, Richard J
   Jesus, politics, and society: a study of Luke's gospel.

   Bibliography: p.
   1. Bible. N.T. Luke—Criticism, interpretation,
etc. I. Title.
BS2595.2.C37   226'.4'06   78-735
ISBN 0-88344-237-X

To My Parents

Contents

Preface

The further I proceeded in efforts for social renewal and the further I proceeded in my study of theology and Scripture, the more it became apparent to me that a systematic analysis of the gospel reports concerning Jesus' social and political stance needed to be undertaken. In both areas, questions about the meaning and implications of various gospel passages were constantly emerging and I was unable to find any work that addressed all of the factors involved. As a result I decided to undertake a study that would analyze the existing social and political conditions and then analyze Luke's reports concerning Jesus' own stance.

The pages that follow represent the fruits of these concerns and efforts. The material here presented in Appendices I, II, and III attempts a reconstruction of the social and political context. Chapters Two through Six analyze the reports that Luke gives regarding Jesus' stance. I hope that both parts will serve to make an appropriate contribution and that the reader will derive something of the satisfaction that I experienced myself as the work progressed.

Throughout this period my family and many good friends, particularly several friends from an informal three-year seminar at the North American College in Rome, have been supportive in a great variety of ways. Cardinal John F. Dearden and many others affiliated with the Archdiocese of Detroit have also provided a great deal of encouragement. In addition the archdiocese has provided the financial support necessary for this period of study.

My sincere thanks also go to Professor Edward C. Hobbs, the chairperson of my dissertation committee at the Graduate Theological Union in Berkeley, to Professor John C. Bennett, the co-chairperson, and to Professors David Daube, J. Warren Holleran, Herman C. Waetjen, and Mark K. Juergensmeyer. Professor Hobbs and the other committee members have provided me with steady encouragement and have allowed me to benefit freely from their respective areas of expertise. It goes without saying that the analyses and arguments presented in the following pages are not necessarily their own.

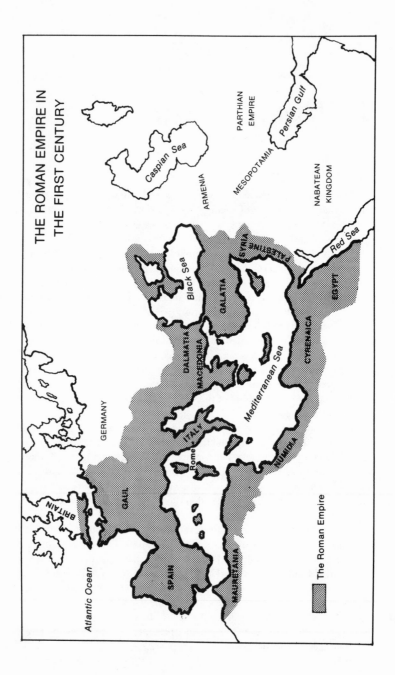

THE ROMAN EMPIRE IN
THE FIRST CENTURY

The Roman Empire

CHAPTER ONE

Luke, Theologian and Empire Historian

Before we enter into an assessment of Luke's work as a theologian and historian, it is desirable to familiarize ourselves with the New Testament discipline called redaction criticism and to consider several important questions regarding the circumstances in which Luke wrote.

1. REDACTION CRITICISM

In New Testament studies, it is now commonly held that when he wrote his gospel (and later when he wrote the Acts of the Apostles),[1] Luke made use of a number of sources. Virtually all New Testament scholars now agree that Luke possessed a copy of Mark's gospel;[2] and, in addition, the majority of scholars hold that Luke had access to another source, "Q," which he shared with Matthew. Further, he may well have had sources peculiar to him alone.[3]

Our knowledge that Luke made use of various sources should not, however, lead us to conclude that he simply combined selected passages in a "scissors and paste" manner. On the contrary, Luke handled his sources in an extremely creative manner and very definitely left his personal stamp upon the final account. This can be clearly seen simply by comparing Luke's final product

1

with that given us by Mark.[4] Our appreciation for Luke's work is even further enhanced when we give consideration to the findings that have recently emerged in connection with what is called "redaction criticism."

Redaction criticism is the New Testament discipline that systematically treats the process to which we have just adverted, that is, the process by which the various New Testament writings, particularly the gospels, were composed.[5] At the first stage of their investigations, scholars use redaction criticism to determine the kinds of sources that a given New Testament writer made use of. If it is clear that the writer made significant modifications in a particular source, then the redaction critics seek to understand the rationale for the changes and to determine what the particular modifications reveal about the author's overall theology. What general outlook toward God does each evangelist have? How do their respective presentations of Jesus' teaching compare? Their presentations about his death? These are typical of the questions that redaction critics ask at this stage of their study.

As redaction criticism has moved forward, scholars have developed procedures for investigating the composition process of the gospels.[6] These procedures are not applicable in the same degree to the other New Testament writings; but because we know that Luke made use of Mark, Luke's gospel is one of the works on which they can be used most effectively.[7] Thus, at the outset of our study, it is well that we pause to familiarize ourselves with the most important of these procedures.

The first step that redaction criticism follows with respect to Luke's gospel is to identify and analyze the definite changes (whether they consist of additions, alterations, or omissions) that Luke has introduced into Mark's account. It can be presumed that when Luke altered one of Mark's accounts he did so because he wanted to place greater emphasis upon particular elements that he saw within Mark's account or because he wished to take account of factors to which Mark had not adverted. This being the case, these Lukan alterations are a good starting point from which to investigate Luke's theology. An analysis of them will not give us the overall outline of his thought or even indicate all of his concerns; however, it will indicate a number of his particular interests and emphases, and these will serve as mosaic pieces to be fitted and integrated with findings that are achieved by other procedures. Second, not only are the alterations that Luke introduces into Mark's account significant; the instances in which he uses Mark's passages without changing them are also of considerable importance. In these cases it can be assumed that Luke found the language used by Mark useful for his purposes, and efforts to determine the meaning of the passage in Luke's gospel can then proceed. Following this, we can determine just how the meaning of the particular passage under consideration fits with the meaning of other passages in the gospel.

This second principle, that is, that we are able to learn about Luke's theology even when he does nothing more than take Mark's passages directly into hs own account, has not always been fully appreciated by scholars who have commented upon Luke's gospel. Nevertheless, as Earle Ellis and Stephen Wilson have both pointed out, such a conclusion is a logical consequence of the freedom with which Luke approaches Mark and his other sources. The fact that Luke so frequently altered Mark suggests that he felt free not to include in his final draft elements or passages that did not fully serve his purposes. This being the case, there is a strong presumption that all the passages that are included in Luke's finished account are congruent with his overall understanding and represent aspects of his overall vision.[8]

Third, as noted above, the majority of New Testament scholars believe that in addition to having Mark as a source Luke also had access to another source, "Q," and perhaps others. Thus it would seem logical to analyze the alterations that Luke has made in each of these sources in the same way that we analyze his modifications in Mark. However, the difficulty is that even if the material in these two sources actually existed in written form we do not now have access to it. Thus, before we can embark upon an analysis of the changes that Luke may have made in the material that came down to him by way of these sources, we first have to reconstruct these two sources by attempting to see beneath the surfaces of the final accounts given by Matthew and Luke. This is an exceedingly difficult task; and while definite gains can be achieved, the results are far less certain then those that can be obtained from a study of Luke's alterations of Mark.

Finally, we should recognize that a given passage in the gospels (or in the other scriptural writings) may contain several dimensions of meaning. For example, a particular passage might indicate what Luke thought about the subject of Christ's second coming; however, it might also give an indication of the approach that Luke thought the early Christians should follow with respect to political rule by the Romans. Or similarly, a given passage might indicate how Luke viewed the role of the Holy Spirit, but it might also indicate how he interpreted the situation of Gentile converts to Christianity.

2. QUESTIONS SURROUNDING THE WRITING OF LUKE-ACTS

As we have noted above, it is virtually certain that the same person wrote both the gospel of Luke and the Acts of the Apostles. "Luke" is the traditional name for this person. On the basis of considerations such as the reference in Acts 1:1 to the preceding volume and the mention of Theophilus in the dedications of both works, it is generally held that the two books were conceived as a single work.[9] Nevertheless, the gospel can be considered to constitute a unity in itself.[10]

Except for the fact that Luke possessed a copy of Mark (and so must necessarily be assigned a date of composition later than Mark), little that is definite can be said regarding Luke's date of composition. Dates have been put forward ranging from A.D. 60 to A.D. 150. Arguing on the basis of Luke's rendering of Jesus' prophecy concerning the destruction of Jerusalem, some scholars hold that the gospel must have been written later than A.D. 70,[11] many of them opting for a time somewhere around the end of the first century. However, earlier as well as later dates are argued for. It seems clear from the prologue to the gospel that Luke was not an eyewitness to the events of Jesus' ministry, but whether or not he was an eyewitness to some of the events recorded in the Acts of the Apostles is still a debated issue.[12]

An analysis of Luke's style as a writer and his proficiency in Greek indicates that he had the benefit of a Greek education and suggests that he may have come from a Gentile rather than a Jewish family and background. The familiarity with the city of Antioch that is evidenced in the book of Acts has given rise to the theory that Antioch was his home city; however, this is only one possibility among a number of others.[13]

As for the general situation of the Christian communities at the time Luke wrote, it is important to make at least a tentative effort to position Christianity with respect to Judaism and the Roman Empire. Even if we set the limits for the period in which Luke wrote quite far apart, for example, between A.D. 65 and 110, we are still faced with the conclusion that Luke would necessarily have been writing at a time when the Roman Empire was at its high tide. Thus the fundamental political reality of Luke's situation was Roman rule, and all the implications that that rule carried with it in terms of taxation, law, religion, and so forth.

Without attempting to take a definite position on the question of how the Christians of Luke's day fared under Roman rule, we might still indicate several of the factors that were very likely at work in the overall situation. On the one hand, it seems as though Christianity was able to spread relatively rapidly within the Empire; this "free passage" suggests that it was not generally (at least at the outset) perceived as a threat to the Roman order. On the other hand, we do know that perhaps as early as A.D. 64 (during the reign of Nero) and certainly in A.D. 94 (during the reign of Domitian), Christians were persecuted by the Roman emperors.[14]

Also the fact that Christianity was closely intertwined with Judaism for a considerable part of the period with which we are concerned is extremely important. From the time of Julius Caesar on, Judaism had been accorded special privileges within the territory ruled by Rome.[15] Thus, the fact that the early Christians were frequently considered to be a "party" within Judaism probably initially worked to their advantage, allowing them to be covered by the concessions that had been granted to the Jews.[16] Later on, however, their same status as a Jewish "party" may have worked to their disadvantage. It is safe to presume that the hostility and bitterness generated by the Jewish War of A.D. 66 adversely affected the standing of the Jews dispersed throughout the empire as well as those in Judea; to the degree that this was the case, the Christians themselves (particularly Jewish-born Christians) may well have come under suspicion.[17]

Thus, Judaism influenced the Christianity of Luke's day not only because Christian self-identity had been clarified only after a long period of dialogue and controversy over such matters as the observance of the Mosaic law; it exercised a considerable influence also upon the way in which Christianity spread throughout the Roman empire.

As a conclusion to the present section, a few observations are called for with respect to the audience Luke envisioned for his work. Since the prologues to the gospel and to Acts both shed light upon the question of Luke's audience, it is appropriate to cite them in their entirety:[18]

Inasmuch as many have undertaken to compile a narrative of the things which have been accomplished among us, just as they were delivered to us by those who from the beginning were eyewitnesses and ministers of the word, it seemed good to me also, having followed all things closely for some time past, to write an orderly account for you, most excellent Theophilus, that you may know the truth concerning the things of which you have been informed [Luke 1:1–4].

In the first book, O Theophilus, I have dealt with all that Jesus began to do and teach until the day when he was taken up after he had given commandment through the Holy Spirit to the apostles whom he had chosen [Acts 1:1–2].

In a first reading of these prologues, an element that immediately comes to the fore is that both of them make mention of a person named Theophilus. Various interpretations have been put forward regarding Theophilus' identity, among them that he was a Gentile Christian who had asked Luke for information about Christ, that he was a Roman official interested in becoming a Christian,[19] that he was Roman official who had received unfavorable reports about the activities of Christians,[20] or , less likely, that he was simply Luke's publisher.[21] Nevertheless, interesting as the question of Theophilus' identity is, it would be a mistake for us to approach our study on the assumption that Luke intended his work only for an audience of one.[22] Rather, it is much more likely that Luke envisioned a large audience for his work. While he probably hoped that it would be read by educated pagans, his primary concern may well have been to provide the Christian communities throughout the empire with important information regarding the events of Jesus' life.[23] Since illiteracy was common throughout much of the ancient world and since the majority of the early Christians came from the lower classes, some commentators hold that Luke intended his work primarily for educated pagans.[24] However, this view does not sufficiently take into account the close community life of the early Christians and the likelihood that, particularly in the context of the liturgy, literate members of the community would have read Luke's accounts for the benefit of all.[25]

One additional consideration that bears upon the question of Luke's audience is that Luke's personal faith in Christ undoubtedly was a factor motivating him to write.[26] Thus, Luke may well have written for both the Christian communities and pagans, but his work was also an expression of his own commitment to Christ.

3. LUKE, THE THEOLOGIAN

Working according to the procedures of redaction criticism that we described above, New Testament scholars have made considerable progress in understanding Luke's overall theology. Given the complex nature of the gospel and the book of Acts, it cannot be said that biblical scholarship has yet succeeded in grasping the full scope of Luke's vision. However, a number of concerns and emphases that are proper to Luke have been identified, and it is clear that any comprehensive statement of Luke's theology will have to take these into consideration.

In the chapters that follow our primary concern will be to analyze the social and political stance that Luke attributes to Jesus. This will require us to deal with Hans Conzelmann's position that a "political apologetic" was a definite element in Luke's theology. As a prelude to these tasks we first need to understand how Conzelmann sees Luke relating eschatology and political apology.

Conzelmann argues that the main problem that Luke addresses was the "delay" in Christ's second coming.[27] Conzelmann sees the expectation that Christ was soon to return as one of the main elements in the outlook of the early Christians who had preceded Luke or were his contemporaries. Thus, as the years had lengthened into decades and the second coming did not occur, an increasing degree of anxiety had begun to develop within the Christian community.

In Conzelmann's interpretation, Luke responds to this situation by reinterpreting the prevalent understanding of redemptive history, dividing it into three stages: the period of Israel, the period of Christ, and the period of the church.[28] The advantage of this approach, Conzelmann believes, was that Luke could emphasize the importance of the "present" time, the time of the church, the time in which the Christians were then living.

Luke was thus able to assure the Christian community that God's plan of salvation had an extended time dimension and thereby dispel their anxiety regarding Christ's return. In addition, Conzelmann believes that the prominence of the Holy Spirit in Luke's writing is at least partially explained by Luke's desire to assure his hearers that God had provided them with a source of wisdom and strength for their continuing lives in the world.[29]

After ascertaining Luke's solution for enabling the Christian men and women of his time to go about their lives without anxiety, Conzelmann then asks: What recommendations did Luke give regarding how the Christians ought to conduct themselves toward the Roman state? In Conzelmann's analysis, Luke's answer is that since Jesus himself was not in conflict with the existing political order during his ministry, his followers should follow a similar course and seek to act in harmony with the Roman order.[30]

Since this position was undoubtedly one that would have commended itself to any Roman officials who read Luke's work, Conzelmann implies that Luke was motivated to make such a presentation as a means of enhancing Christianity's opportunities within the empire. Thus, in Conzelmann's view, the result was that Luke entered upon a full-blown political apologetic as an extension of his eschatology, and both elements are important components of his overall theology.[31]

Since Conzelmann's *The Theology of St. Luke* came to be regarded as a landmark in Lukan studies almost immediately after it was published in 1953, a number of subsequent commentators have taken up Conzelmann's main arguments regarding Luke's eschatology and have developed them or, in some instances, criticized them.[32] The result has been that much of the recent discussion regarding Luke's theology has centered on the question of his eschatology. However, to sharpen our appreciation for the magnitude of Luke's theological vision, we should look at some of the other elements that scholars believe he expressed in his writings. Luke's universalism has frequently been commented upon,[33] and a number of studies noted the great concern for the poor, the socially outcast, women, and Gentiles that Luke attributes to Jesus.[34] Second, not only Conzelmann but a number of other scholars as well have commented upon the special emphasis that Luke gives to the activity of the Holy Spirit.[35] This is in turn often related to another of Luke's particular emphases: prayer.[36] Finally, we should note the recent suggestion that throughout his work Luke was also engaging in a broad polemic against the heresy of Gnosticism.[37]

The intention of this section on Luke's role as a theologian has been to enhance our sensitivity to the various dimensions of meaning involved in Luke's writings. It should be clear at this point that the task of determining exactly what Luke was saying in a particular passage (or throughout the entire gospel) is not an easy one. Redaction criticism, particularly through the comparisons that it initiates with Mark's gospel, can aid us in this process. But the conclusion that emerges from redaction criticism, namely, that Luke was a highly creative theologian, carries with it a new series of questions related to Luke's reliability as a historian.

4. LUKE'S ACCURACY AS A HISTORIAN

The very modifications that Luke introduces into Mark's gospel indicate that he was not concerned with providing a reliable historical account of Jesus' teachings or activities, for if Luke were concerned with presenting a historically accurate report, he would have been obligated to show greater respect for his sources: So runs the argument of those who feel that Luke cannot be considered a historian in the modern sense of that term.[38]

A second argument against Luke's reliability begins from the premise that Luke's sources were themselves unreliable. In discussing Luke's sources above, we did not discuss the process by which these sources themselves emerged. The prevailing opinion among New Testament scholars is that the individual passages or "pericopes" in all of Luke's sources (including those in Mark's gospel) had themselves passed through the hands of a number of Christian communities before they were variously collected and ordered as a "source."[39]

Those who hold that Luke's sources are unreliable maintain that during the long period that intervened between Jesus' death and the time when the gospels began to be written down, the reports of Jesus' teachings and activities could not fail to have been modified. The gospels themselves, it is argued, provide evidence that the early communities shaped (and ultimately distorted) the reports of Jesus' teaching and deeds to meet their own concrete needs. Thus, even if Luke had been committed to following his sources closely, he still would not have been able to produce an account that was historically reliable. Too much time, and too many hands, had intervened between the time of Jesus' death and the time of Luke's writing.

To these two "in principle" arguments against Luke's accuracy is added a third, extremely concrete criticism: Luke's writings do, in fact, contain a significant number of errors and misrepresentations. Two different types of failings are alleged to be present in Luke's writings: First, errors of geographical, cultural, and political fact; and second, important inaccuracies with respect to the description (and interpretation) of persons, issues, and events.

The two principal examples of Luke's inaccuracy with respect to political facts are the passage in the gospel referring to the census ordered by Caesar Augustus and the passage in Acts in which Gamaliel refers to two political uprisings. The census passage is as follows:

In those days a decree went out from Caesar Augustus that all the world should be enrolled. This was the first enrollment, when Quirinius was governor of Syria. And all went to be enrolled, each to his own city. And Joseph also went up from Galilee, from the city of Nazareth, to Judea, to the city of David, which is called Bethlehem, because he was of the house and lineage of David, to be enrolled with Mary, his betrothed, who was with child [Luke 2:1-5].

Any number of arguments have been brought against the accuracy of this account, but it will be sufficient for our purposes to indicate several of the principal ones.[40] It has been alleged that Augustus never ordered such a general enrollment; that even if there had been such a census, there would have been no need for Joseph (and Mary) to go up to Bethlehem to register for it; and third, that Quirinius was not governor of Syria at the time when the census was supposed to have taken place, that is, during the lifetime of Herod the Great. (That Herod the Great was living at the time of Jesus' birth follows from the reference in Luke 1:5. There is also the witness of Matthew's gospel that Jesus was born during Herod the Great's reign.)

Luke's report of the census does have some basis in history, Luke's critics believe. Josephus, the Jewish historian, does record that a Roman census took place in Judea in A.D. 6-7.[41] But what has happened, they assert, is that Luke either confused the facts or else had apologetic reasons for wanting to show that Joseph was loyal to the Roman census decree.[42]

The pertinent section of Gamaliel's speech in Acts is as follows:

And he said to them, "Men of Israel, take care what you do with these men. For before these days Theudas arose, giving himself out to be somebody, and a number of men, about four hundred, joined him; but he was slain and all who followed him were dispersed and came to nothing. After him Judas the Galilean arose in the days of the census and drew away some of the people after him; he also perished, and all who followed him were scattered" [Acts 5:35–37].

Here it is alleged that Luke simply confused the true historical sequence and placed the uprising of Judas after that of Theudas when in fact the insurrection led by Judas actually took place well before the events with which Theudas was connected. Possibly, Luke's critics contend, Luke read Josephus' report of the two uprisings somewhat carelessly and reversed their correct sequence.[43]

The charges brought against Luke's reliability with respect to his description (and thus interpretation) of persons, issues, and events are well expressed in the works of Ernst Haenchen and S.G.F. Brandon. In his essay, "The Book of Acts as Source

Material for the History of Early Christianity," Haenchen brings together a long series of misrepresentations and distortions that, in his estimation, Luke has promulgated in Acts.[44] Haenchen's overall position is that Luke is more a "fascinating narrator" than he is a historian in our modern sense of the term.[45] He believes that Luke misrepresents the situation of the early church in Jerusalem,[46] misrepresents the nature of the original mission to the Gentiles,[47] and distorts Paul's theology (as expressed in Paul's epistles) regarding the Jewish law.[48]

Haenchen also finds that Luke inaccurately reports several of the events that transpired on Paul's missionary journey.[49] And, while he does believe that Acts preserves certain reports that are historically correct and thus can provide source material for early Christian history, he holds that its main purpose was to edify the early Christian communities, which did not call for rigorous historical accuracy.[50]

Although Brandon writes from a perspective that is different from Haenchen's, his conclusions regarding Luke's reliability are remarkably similar. Brandon has written extensively about the trial and death of Jesus, and in his opinion Luke's version of these events (and also the versions given by the other evangelists) is essentially unreliable.[51]

On the basis of his own research Brandon has concluded that the Romans had primary responsibility for Jesus' death. Not only does he find the gospel accounts at variance with this position, he also detects signs of a conscious effort to downplay Roman involvement and emphasize Jewish responsibility for Jesus' death.[52] In Luke's gospel he finds a clear indication of this tendency in the fact that Luke has Pilate three times pronounce Jesus innocent.[53] The reason for this bias, he argues, is that Christianity wanted to be able to spread peacefully throughout the Roman empire and thus had to obscure the fact that Jesus, the founder of Christianity, had been judged dangerous to the Roman order and put to death by the Roman governor of Judea.[54]

Luke's Reliability as Empire Historian. While another study might try to respond to the arguments advanced against Luke's reliability, it is not within the limits of our own study to do so. Our question is not whether Luke's description of Jesus' socio-political stance is reliable; rather we want to determine what kind of social and political stance Luke actually attributes to Jesus. Our question is thus prior to the question of Luke's historical accuracy. Before it can be determined whether or not Luke's description is reliable, it first has to be determined what that description actually is.

Although we will not treat the issue of Luke's overall reliability as a historian, we do want to make one important qualification in our general position: We believe that Luke is reliable when touching upon matters pertaining to "empire history." We use the term "empire history" to refer to the situations, procedures, persons, and events mentioned in Luke's writings that would have been of particular interest to Luke's readers throughout the empire and of which his readers may be presumed to have had some prior knowledge.[55] In the main, the items encompassed would fall within the broad category of political affairs and would include such things as the description of rulers and officials, the description of administrative and judicial procedures, and the dating of specific events in relation to other events more widely known throughout the empire. It is our contention that when Luke touches upon such matters as these, he gives an extremely accurate presentation.

If we go back for a moment to the claim that Luke makes in the prologue to his work, we can begin to see why a high level of accuracy would be extremely necessary to his purposes. In the prologue Luke indicates that he writes, "having followed all things closely for some time past," that he intends to present "an orderly account," and that his reason for doing this is that Theophilus "may know the truth concerning the things" of which he has been informed.

Luke's claim could not have been more apparent to his readers. He is going to present them with an account on which they may rely with confidence. It is possible to dispute the precise meaning of each of the three phrases that we have quoted; but appearing together within the space of a brief paragraph, their overall meaning is clear: Luke is announcing his intention to write a reliable account and he is doing this in no uncertain terms.

Luke's readers lived under Roman rule. It follows that they, especially the pagans, would relate Luke's account to their own experience of events, rulers, and procedures known to them as a result of their own familiarity with the Roman order. Thus, regardless of his own specific theological concerns, if Luke was to establish his credibility with these readers, he would have to strive for an accurate presentation of matters of empire history that he included in his account.

In comparison with Mark and Matthew, Luke includes such references in his gospel to a remarkable degree.[56] We have noted that Luke locates Jesus' birth during the time of the census ordered by Caesar Augustus. He follows a similar path in the way he locates the second principal event in Jesus' life, the beginning of his public ministry. The section introducing John the Baptist (and Jesus' entry into public life) begins in the following way:

In the fifteenth year of the reign of Tiberius Caesar, Pontius Pilate being governor of Judea, and Herod being tetrarch of Galilee, and his brother Philip tetrarch of the region of Ituraea and Trachonitis, and Lysanias tetrarch of Abilene, in the high-priesthood of Annas and Caiaphas, the word of God came to John the son of Zechariah in the wilderness [Luke 3:1–3].

In his description of Jesus' preaching and public ministry, Luke also provides his readers with certain political notices pertaining to empire history. They are told, for instance, that Jesus knew of Pilate's slaughter of some Galileans (13:1–3) and that Jesus engaged in serious controversy with Herod Antipas (13:31–34). Finally, in his description of Jesus' trial, Luke provides a detailed listing of the charges that were brought against him (23:2–5) and describes the way in which Herod Antipas entered the proceedings at Pilate's request (23:6–12). It is significant that all four of the above instances are proper to Luke alone; they are not paralleled in either Mark's or Matthew's accounts.

All of these references were potential trouble spots for Luke's credibility with his readers. If, for instance, he described the interchange between Pilate and Herod Antipas in such a way that his readers—familiar with Roman trial procedures and with the political relationship between a Roman governor and the tetrarch of a neighboring semi-independent territory—would have found the description improbable, then his credibility would have been adversely affected. Similarly, if his report about Pilate's slaughter of the Galileans would have struck his informed readers as implausible or contrary to fact, then Luke would have been foolish to include it. Thus Luke's opening statement that he intended to write an accurate account, coupled with the general knowledge that his educated readers would have had, undoubtedly provided him with a strong motivation for reporting as accurately as possible any matters pertaining to empire history that he chose to include.

Not only was it in Luke's own interest to be accurate with respect to subjects with which his educated readers throughout the empire would be familiar; it has also been strongly argued that Luke is, *in fact*, amazingly reliable when he identifies political rulers, presents judicial proceedings, describes socio-political issues, and so forth.

A. N. Sherwin-White is strongly committed to such a position. By profession a Roman historian, Sherwin-White has also written on the political procedures that are described in the gospels and other New Testament writings.[57] After an extended analysis of the judicial procedures that Luke describes in Acts, he concludes: "The accounts of these trials in Acts are so technically correct that Roman historians since Mommsen have often used them as the best illustration of Roman provincial jurisdiction in this particular period."[58] His estimation of the reliability of Luke's description of Roman citizenship is similarly high.[59]

The Census and the Uprisings. Before direct reference to Luke's text in order to demonstrate his accuracy with regard to empire history, it is necessary to frame the general outlines of a response to the criticisms that have been levelled against the census passage and the chronology of the two uprisings referred to in Acts.

The general perspective with which we approach these two passages is of fundamental importance. If Luke's reports are considered generally suspect, then the burden of proof is on Luke's defenders, and they have to bring forward conclusive evidence of Luke's accuracy. On the other hand, if the initial premise is that Luke's writings generally evidence a remarkable accuracy in matters pertaining to empire history and deserve to be given the benefit of the doubt in particular cases, then the burden of proof falls upon Luke's critics.

On the basis of the analysis that we have made in the preceding pages and particularly in light of the instances (to be discussed below) in which Luke alters Mark in the interests of greater accuracy, our own conclusion is that there is far greater justification for adopting the second of the two perspectives. Luke has demonstrated a remarkable accuracy in matters pertaining to empire history; thus, in our estimation, the burden of proof lies with those who hold that the census described by Luke did not take place (or did not take place as Luke describes it) and with those who hold that Judas' uprising did not follow one led by a person named Theudas.

We indicated earlier that many New Testament scholars have objected to Luke's description of the census and his assertion that it took place while Quirinius was governor of Syria; in fact most of the evidence presently available supports these scholars. On the one hand, there is evidence that Quirinius was not the governor of Syria when Luke asserts the census took place; on the other, available information regarding Roman administrative procedures generally contradicts Luke's statements that the census took place in Herod the Great's territories and that the heads of families were required to return to their home cities. In addition, if there had been such a general census, we might expect to have some record of it preserved by one of the early historians, by various inscriptions, or other data; but there is no mention of it.[60]

We have argued that Luke should be given the benefit of the doubt until substantial evidence to the contrary is brought forward. We are therefore faced with deciding whether the existing evidence substantially establishes that the census could not have taken place as Luke says. This question is particularly acute with respect to the evidence that delineates Quirinius' career as a Roman official.

The evidence that Quirinius was not governor of Syria at the approximate time of the census comes to us primarily from Josephus and Tacitus; it consists of biographical information about Quirinius as well as references to the various persons who served terms as the Roman governors of Syria. When the references from these and other sources are pieced together, the resulting composite places Quirinius in office at a time too late for Luke's census.

But as Jack Finegan and A. N. Sherwin-White have pointed out, the evidence does not preclude the possibility that Quirinius also served as governor in 3 B.C., which would fit Luke's description.[61] There is no evidence that Quirinius actually served two terms as governor, but Finegan and Sherwin-White indicate that we do not have enough information about Quirinius' career on the one hand or the chronology of the Roman governors of Syria on the other to rule out that this might have happened.

In his commentary on Luke's gospel, Joseph Schmid provides an extremely helpful excursus on this and the other objections that have been raised against the census account.[62] In each instance (i.e., its occurrence in Herod's territories and the stipulation requiring Joseph to travel to Bethlehem), Schmid's analyses result in conclusions similar to that we have reached with reference to the time of Quirinius' governorship. Schmid cites the evidence against the various points in Luke's account, but his conclusion is that it does not preclude the possibility that the census took place as Luke says.

With respect to the Acts passage in which Luke indicates that the uprising of Theudas took place before that led by Judas, the primary question again is whether or not Luke should be given the benefit of the doubt. Since Josephus places Judas' uprising in A.D. 6–7 and one by Theudas in A.D. 44–46, it has been supposed that Luke is in error when he reverses the sequence. However, the fact that we do not now have any historical records of an earlier uprising by another person named Theudas does not mean that such an uprising could not have taken place, though it does lessen its historical probability.

In support of this possibility, F. F. Bruce points out that "Theudas" was a name commonly in use during this period and that a number of uprisings took place around the time of Herod the Great's death.[63] These considerations do not, of course, establish that a person named Theudas actually led such an uprising; but they do leave open such a possibility.

Luke's Changes for Accuracy. We have already established the significance of any modifications that Luke introduces into Mark's account; it is, therefore, appropriate to conclude our argument for Luke's reliability with a consideration of three such changes. All three concern political "identifications" and all three were made for the sake of greater accuracy.

In the section about the concern of Herod Antipas that Jesus might be John the Baptist risen from the dead (6:14–16), Mark gives Herod the title "king." Since Antipas' father, Herod the Great, had had this title, and since it was a title not always used precisely, Mark's use of the term is not inappropriate. Luke, though, in his parallel passage (9:7–9), calls Herod "tetrarch," which is the technically precise term. At the death of Herod the Great, the territory he ruled had been divided among his sons, and Herod Antipas was given jurisdiction over the tetrarchy of Galilee and Perea.[64]

Second, in his listing of the twelve called by Jesus (3:13–19), Mark describes Simon with the Greek term *ton Kananaion*, a term usually translated, "the Canaanean." However, Oscar Cullmann has argued persuasively that rather than referring to the land of Canaan, the term actually is a Greek rendering of the Aramaic word for "Zealot." Thus, he argues, the root meaning of Mark's designation is not Simon the Canaanean, but rather Simon the Zealot.[65]

In his parallel account (6:12–16), Luke gives Simon the designation, *ton kaloumenon Zeloten*, a phrase which is translated "who was called the Zealot." Luke is thus much more explicit about Simon's political background than Mark is, and it is fair to suppose that Luke evaluated Mark's indication of Simon's background as being too obscure for his own readers in the empire. Thus, he changed Mark's *ton Kananaion* into a Greek term, *ton kaloumenon Zeloten*, that his readers would be sure to understand.

In the third instance, Luke does not make a specific correction in a passage taken over from Mark; rather his concern is to clearly identify Pilate as the Roman governor of Judea well before the time of Jesus' trial.

We are so familiar with Pilate's role in Jesus' trial that it may come as a surprise to learn that Mark never actually tells his readers who Pilate is. In fact the first time that Pilate is even mentioned is in Chapter 15 when the chief priests and other Sanhedrin members have Jesus bound and hand him over "to Pilate." This "Pilate" then interrogates Jesus as a Roman governor might well be expected to do, and it is clear that he is a person of high authority; but even in the trial narrative itself Mark never explicitly tells his readers that Pilate is, in fact, the Roman governor of Judea.

Luke, on the contrary, introduces Pilate at the very beginning of Jesus' public ministry (3:1) and clearly indicates that he is the governor of Judea. In addition, although he does not mention him by name, Luke also indicates Pilate's office and authority in his narration of the tribute passage (20:20–26). There Luke states that the scribes and chief priests intended to entrap Jesus "so as to deliver him up to the authority and jurisdiction of the governor." Thus, well in advance of the time of Jesus' trial, Luke's readers know who Pilate is and what authority he holds. In the trial itself Luke simply refers to him as "Pilate," but after his earlier descriptions, that is all that is necessary.

As we turn now to a study of the social stance of Jesus, our judgment in favor of Luke's accuracy with respect to empire history will help us significantly in our efforts to understand his description of Jesus' social and political stance.

CHAPTER TWO

The Social Stance of Jesus (I)

When we refer to Jesus' "social stance," we mean the response that Jesus made, through his teachings and conduct, to the question of how persons and groups ought to live together. In our use of the term "political," we include, for example, the form of government, the various political authorities, and governmental policies such as taxation. In referring to Jesus' social *and* political stance, our intention is to emphasize that Jesus responded not only to the social situation of the poor, the infirm, and the oppressed, but also to the policies and practices of the political leaders of his time.

Here it is important to remember that we cannot treat all the elements in Luke's gospel that bear upon our central theme. What Luke tells his readers concerning Jesus' identity,[1] whether Luke's Jesus expected an early coming of "the final days,"[2] and the degree to which he shows Jesus relying upon future rewards and punishments are all factors that bear upon Luke's presentation of Jesus' social and political stance. In order to keep our study within reasonable limits, however, we will have to abstract from much of Luke's information on such subjects.

Our approach will familiarize us with the chief characteristics of Jesus' social and political stance and enable us to see how the various elements, taken together, constitute a vision of a new order of social relationships.[3] Relying on Luke's description throughout,[4] we will initially consider the social groups for which

Jesus expressed concern, and then enter into an extended analysis of his stance toward the poor and the rich and toward surplus possessions.

1. JESUS' CONCERN FOR THE POOR, THE INFIRM, WOMEN, AND PAGANS

In his opening chapters Luke portrays Mary, Jesus' mother, and John the Baptist, his cousin, as having definite sympathies for the poor and oppressed.[5] Thus, in response to Elizabeth's greeting Mary echoes the prayer prayed by Hannah (1 Sam. 2:1–10); she recalls God's greatness and that

he has put down the mighty from their thrones, and exalted those of low degree, he has filled the hungry with good things, and the rich he has sent empty away (1:52–53).

Similarly, when John is questioned regarding the concrete implications of his teaching and his baptism, part of his reply is, "He who has two coats, let him share with him who has none; and he who has food, let him do likewise" (3:11). Luke also indicates that because John criticized Herod for marrying his brother's wife and "for all the evil things that Herod had done" (3:19), John earned the enmity of Herod, and, as a result, Herod had John imprisoned.

After Jesus was baptized and tempted in the desert,[6] Luke tells us that he taught and was favorably received in the synagogues of Galilee. Then, in describing Jesus' visit to his home town of Nazareth, Luke indicates the content of Jesus' teaching.[7] Attending the synagogue service, Jesus was given the opportunity to participate in the service by reading aloud from the Scriptures. He read from the writings of Isaiah and then announced to the congregation: "Today this scripture has been fulfilled in your hearing" (4:21).

At first, Jesus seems to have gained the approval of those who were present; but then a striking change of mood occurred and the congregation became antagonistic.[8] Rebuking them, Jesus said that no prophet is acceptable in his own country and to their displeasure recalled instances in which the prophets Elijah and

Elisha worked miracles for pagans when many Jews were equally in need of help. These words so enraged his audience that they attempted to throw Jesus to his death and would have done so if he had not escaped by passing through their midst.

Because Luke gives little explanation for the rapid changes in the attitudes of Jesus and his hearers, and because the words that he portrays Jesus as reading do not follow the exact sequence of Isaiah's verses, the passage presents us with a number of difficulties.[9] Let us concentrate upon two points that are clearly contained within the passage. First, Luke depicts Jesus as associating himself with important social themes drawn from Isaiah.[10] Second, he indicates that Gentiles as well as Jews are included in Jesus' vision and concern.

What were the words from Isaiah that Jesus read and associated himself with? In Luke's report they are as follows:

The Spirit of the Lord is upon me, because he has anointed me to preach good news to the poor. He has sent me to proclaim release to the captives and recovering of sight to the blind, to set at liberty those who are oppressed, to proclaim the acceptable year of the Lord [4:18–19].

The poor, captives, the blind, the oppressed: These are the groups listed in this passage. In the light of the meaning of these verses in their original context, there are good grounds for holding that it is the literally poor and literally blind who are designated.[11] Reference to several other passages in Luke's account also leads us to believe that when Luke refers to the poor, the blind, and so forth, he means those who are literally poor and literally blind.[12]

In his sixth chapter, Luke presents an account of a "Great Sermon" that Jesus addressed to his disciples.[13] He had just come down from the hills to a plain, and a large crowd had gathered to hear and to be healed of their diseases. Jesus began with these words:

Blessed are you poor, for yours is the kingdom of God. Blessed are you that hunger now, for you shall be satisfied. Blessed are you that weep now, for you shall laugh [6:20–21].

Because Luke's version of Jesus' sermon includes much material also found in Matthew's "Sermon on the Mount," the two sermons have frequently been compared.[14] While there are many similarities there are also important differences; one is particularly significant for our study. In contrast with Luke, Matthew describes Jesus as directing his "blessings" to those who are "poor *in spirit*" and to "those who hunger *and thirst for righteousness.*"

According to Matthew's version, Jesus' blessings might be taken to apply to those who were actually rich in possessions as long as they were poor "in spirit." This is not the case with Luke. For not only does Luke's version name the poor and the hungry without any qualifications; Luke also includes a series of "woes" addressed to the rich and the comfortable that contrast with the preceding blessings of the poor and the hungry. The overall effect is that those who are actually poor and actually hungry are the ones to whom the blessings are addressed.

But woe to you who are rich, for you have received your consolation. Woe to you that are full now, for you shall hunger. Woe to you that laugh now, for you shall mourn and weep [6:24–25].

The point to be noted here is that Luke describes Jesus as having definite sympathy and concern for those who are poor and hungry.

Luke also indicates that Jesus responded with compassion to the *sick and the infirm.* In his description of Jesus' public ministry, Luke indicates that Jesus worked many cures,[15] and he frequently includes summary statements concerning Jesus' healing activities.[16] He also describes Jesus' reference to these cures in his response to John the Baptist. As John's disciples approached, Jesus cured a large number of people from "diseases and plagues and evil spirits" (7:21). Jesus then responds to John's messengers:

Go and tell John what you have seen and heard: the blind receive their sight, the lame walk, lepers are cleansed, and the deaf hear, the dead are raised up, the poor have good news preached to them. And blessed is he who takes no offense at me [7:22–23].

Jesus' reply recalls the words from Isaiah which Jesus used in the synagogue at Nazareth. Here Jesus again refers to the poor; and, in addition to the blind, he also mentions those who suffer from lameness, deafness, and leprosy.

Luke indicates that *Gentiles* were among those who benefited from Jesus' healing activity,[17] and this provides concrete reinforcement for Jesus' rebuke of the townspeople of Nazareth after they rejected him. Here, as well as in such matters as the use of surplus possessions and the use of violence, there is a remarkable congruence in Luke between what Jesus teaches and what he practices.

Jesus also healed a relatively large number of *women*. Luke indicates that Jesus healed Simon's mother-in law of a fever (4:38–39), that he aided a widow by raising her son to life (7:11–17), that he cured a woman who had long been afflicted with a hemorrhage (8:43–48), and that he healed a woman who had been beset by a spirit that rendered her infirm for eighteen years (13:10–13).[18] Luke also says that Jesus healed a number of other women from "evil spirits and infirmities" (8:2).

Jesus' healings, as well as the forgiveness that he extended toward a woman who was a public outcast (7:36–50), establish Jesus' concern for women.

Although Luke's Jesus expressed a definite concern for the poor, the infirm, women, and Gentiles, it is also clear that Jesus is not portrayed as unconcerned about those not falling within these groups. Rather, *universalism* is a striking feature of Jesus' social stance. Luke describes him as including persons from a wide range of backgrounds among his disciples,[19] and shows him accepting dinner invitations and hospitality from men who were wealthy.[20] On occasion, Jesus' cures and healings also benefited the rich and the powerful.[21]

Nevertheless, the universalism that Luke attributes to Jesus does not imply an acceptance of the status quo. Jesus visits the rich and accepts hospitality from them; but he also calls upon them to divest themselves of their wealth. Similarly, Luke presents Jesus in extremely close association with the twelve; but he also shows him consistently reprimanding them for their ambition and their inclination to violence.[22] According to Luke, Jesus' position is one of concern and compassion for people from all walks of life, but he does not passively accept values or practices that run counter to his own vision regarding healthy social relationships.

2. JESUS' STANCE REGARDING RICHES AND THE RICH

Luke provides us with relatively extensive information on Jesus' stance toward riches and the rich.

Opposition to the Accumulation of Possessions. In Luke 12, Jesus teaches about the place of possessions in human living. Although we will not consider all these teachings here, the parable we include provides a good starting point for our analysis of Jesus' stance with regard to surplus possessions.[23] Someone in the crowd asked Jesus' help in obtaining a share of an inheritance. Refusing the request, Jesus stated to those who were gathered:

Take heed, and beware of all covetousness; for a man's life does not consist in the abundance of his possessions [12:15].

He then developed this line of thought in the following parable:

And he told them a parable, saying, "The land of a rich man brought forth plentifully; and he thought to himself, 'What shall I do, for I have nowhere to store my crops?' And he said, 'I will do this: I will pull down my barns, and build larger ones; and there I will store all my grain and my goods. And I will say to my soul, Soul, you have ample goods laid up for many years; take your ease, eat, drink, and be merry.' But God said to him, 'Fool! This night your soul is required of you; and the things you have prepared, whose will they be?' So is he who lays up treasure for himself, and is not rich toward God" [12:15–21].

It is important to recognize that the parable focuses upon the accumulation of additional goods by those who already have enough for their needs.[24] The landowner to whom Jesus refers does not seem to have come by his additional grain unfairly; the parable does not state that there was any dishonesty connected with his actions. Rather, the surprising criticism made against him is simply that he kept the additional goods for himself and did not use them to be "rich toward God." He seemingly broke no law, and his harvesting and storing of the extra yield did not diminish the supply of food normally available to those around him. Yet, by holding on to more possessions than he needed, he proved himself a fool in the sight of God.

Counsel to Live Simply. Luke reports that Jesus followed the parable with a series of teachings that sketch an approach to living characterized by a greater simplicity and a lessened anxiety toward possessions (12:22–34). These teachings provide a context for the position that Jesus has just taken in opposing the accumulation of surplus goods. Luke also presents Jesus as calling for simplicity when he sends the twelve to preach the kingdom of God. On that occasion, Jesus' words were, "Take nothing for your journey, no staff nor bag, nor money; and do not have two tunics" (9:3). Similarly, when he sent seventy disciples on ahead of him to the towns and places he was going to visit, Jesus instructed them to "carry no purse, no bag, no sandals" (10:4).[25]

Where Luke touches upon Jesus' own lifestyle, he portrays it as consistent with Jesus' teachings on excess possessions and simplicity. The daily events, the journeys, and the celebrations in which Jesus participated with the disciples were characterized by simplicity.[26] On one occasion Jesus stressed the relatively spare nature of his own living circumstances by emphasizing to a potential disciple that "foxes have holes and birds of the air have nests; but the Son of man has nowhere to lay his head" (9:58).[27] As to how Jesus and the twelve obtained their livelihood, the only information that Luke provides us is that several women disciples accompanied them and "provided for them out of their means" (8:3).

The Rich Admonished to Give to the Poor. Jesus' stance regarding riches extended beyond the warnings that he gave about covetousness and the accumulation of surplus possessions.

And a ruler asked him, "Good Teacher, what shall I do to inherit eternal life?" And Jesus said to him, "Why do you call me good? No one is good but God alone. You know the commandments: 'Do not commit adultery, Do not kill, Do not steal, Do not bear false witness, Honor your father and mother.' " And he said, "All these I have observed from my youth." And when Jesus heard it, he said to him, "One thing you still lack. Sell all that you have and distribute to the poor, and you will have treasure in heaven; and come, follow me." But when he heard this he became sad, for he was very rich (18:18–23).[28]

The radical nature of the call that Jesus addressed to the ruler has frequently been noted, but it has been frequently overlooked that the particularly disconcerting element, "sell all that you have and distribute to the poor," is not a stray note that finds its way into Luke's description of Jesus only in this one instance. Rather, it is thoroughly consistent with Luke's general description of Jesus.

In this passage, the person whom Jesus addresses very likely belonged to the richest segment of society; but Luke also depicts Jesus as giving similar teachings to those who were not nearly so rich. In the setting of the Great Sermon, Jesus bids his hearers to "give to everyone who begs from you" (6:30) and to lend, expecting nothing in return (6:35). Similarly, after he has recounted the parable of the rich fool, Jesus instructs the disciples as follows:

Sell your possessions and give alms; provide yourselves with purses that do not grow old, with a treasure in the heavens which does not fail, where no thief approaches and no moth destroys. For where your treasure is, there will your heart be also [12:32–34].

At first sight, the parable of the unjust steward (Luke 16:1–9) does not seem to pertain particularly to selling one's possessions to benefit the poor; indeed the parable seems to emphasize the importance of astuteness in managing one's affairs.[29] However, in his comments following the parable, Jesus draws an application that is related to the theme of surplus possessions. The steward of the parable shows his ability to provide for his own future position, and Jesus urges his disciples to make similarly astute preparations:

And I tell you, make friends for yourselves by means of unrighteous mammon, so that when it fails they may receive you into the eternal habitations (16:9).

In our interpretation, Jesus' reference to "unrighteous mammon" is a reference to surplus possessions;[30] by advising the disciples to use it to make friends for themselves, Jesus is encouraging them to be responsible with their possessions. If they are truly responsible, they will use these extra goods for the sake of the poor. Jesus' subsequent words, "You cannot serve God and mammon"

(16:13), emphasize that the disciples' decision in this regard is radical.

Jesus' Criticism of the Rich. Since Luke's Jesus accepts hospitality from persons of means and works cures that benefit the rich and the powerful, the degree to which he also criticizes the rich may initially seem surprising to us. However, if we regard the criticism in relation to Jesus' overall stance, then its forcefulness and frequency is not quite so startling.

We indicated that the juxtaposition of the blessings and the woes in the Great Sermon meant that the literally poor were being addressed in the blessing. The converse is also true: It is the literally rich (in our interpretation those who hold surplus possessions) who are being addressed in the woes. Thus in the statement, "But woe to you that are rich, for you have received your consolation," Luke presents Jesus as making a generalized criticism of the rich.

The second instance in which Jesus speaks adversely of the rich occurs in Jesus' explanation of the parable of the sower and the seed (8:4–15).[31] The reference to those who are "choked by the cares and riches and pleasures of life" (8:14) is not nearly as direct or general a criticism as that which Jesus tendered in the woe; but it is, nevertheless, a reminder that in Jesus' view the patterns and practices common to the rich are not happy ones.

Luke 16 presents a series of Jesus' teachings relative to riches and the rich in addition to the parable of the "unjust" steward. Luke tells us that after Jesus had completed the initial parable and his comments on it, "the Pharisees, who were lovers of money, heard all this, and they scoffed at him" (16:14). Jesus responds:

But he said to them, "You are those who justify yourselves before men, but God knows your hearts; for what is exalted among men is an abomination in the sight of God" [16:15].[32]

In our view, Jesus' words are addressed to these Pharisees precisely because they are "lovers of money" and do not want to take seriously his teaching that surplus possessions are to be used to benefit the poor. In effect, he tells them that while they may have standing before their peers (because of their wealth?), they do not have it before God.

Jesus follows his rebuke to the money-loving Pharisees with three succinct statements regarding the kingdom, the law, and the indissolubility of marriage; but Jesus immediately returned to the subject of riches and wealth by telling a parable about a rich man and a poor beggar.

There was a rich man, who was clothed in purple and fine linen and who feasted sumptuously every day. And at his gate lay a poor man named Lazarus, full of sores, who desired to be fed with what fell from the rich man's table; moreover the dogs came and licked his sores. The poor man died and was carried by the angels to Abraham's bosom. The rich man also died and was buried; and in Hades, being in torment, he lifted up his eyes, and saw Abraham far off and Lazarus in his bosom. And he called out, "Father Abraham, have mercy upon me, and send Lazarus to dip the end of his finger in water and cool my tongue; for I am in anguish in this flame." But Abraham said, "Son, remember that you in your lifetime received your good things, and Lazarus in like manner evil things; but now he is comforted here, and you are in anguish. And besides all this, between us and you a great chasm has been fixed, in order that those who would pass from here to you may not be able, and none may cross from there to us." And he said, "Then I beg you, father, to send him to my father's house, for I have five brothers, so that he may warn them, lest they also come into this place of torment." But Abraham said, "They have Moses and the prophets; let them hear them." And he said, "No, father Abraham; but if some one goes to them from the dead, they will repent." He said to him, "If they do not hear Moses and the prophets, neither will they be convinced if some one should rise from the dead" [16:19–31].

The parable contains a number of elements that pertain to our subject, but we will limit ourselves to two. It should be noted first that Jesus' detailed description of the rich man's life of luxury and ease has the effect of holding specific practices up for criticism. Second, although the parable does not explicitly state that there was a causal relationship between the rich man's fate and his refusal to share his possessions, such a relationship is clearly implied.[33] This second point is of particular importance. For the first time we have an implied explanation for Jesus' criticism of the rich: They have not shared their surplus possessions with the poor.

Two other comments that Luke's Jesus makes about the rich also suggest that their surplus possessions are a crucial factor in his estimation of them. Jesus makes the first when he notices the rich contributing to the temple treasury and at the same time sees a poor widow doing so. He praises the gift given by the widow; but, on the grounds that they are contributing only from their abundance, he discounts the offerings made by the rich.[34]

He looked up and saw the rich putting their gifts into the treasury; and he saw a poor widow put in two copper coins. And he said, "Truly I tell you, this poor widow has put in more than all of them; for they all contributed out of their abundance, but she out of her poverty put in all the living that she had" [21:1–4].

When we cited Jesus' words to the rich ruler we did not take account of his words after it became apparent that the ruler found the teaching extremely difficult to accept:

Jesus looking at him said, "How hard it is for those who have riches to enter the kingdom of God! For it is easier for a camel to go through the eye of a needle than for a rich man to enter the kingdom of God" [18:24–25].

On the basis of our analysis we are now in a position to offer an explanation for Jesus' surprising statement. Luke has elsewhere described Jesus' insistence that surplus possessions be used for the poor, and he has also indicated Jesus' awareness of the attachment that the rich have for their possessions. Thus Jesus' words here represent a practical assessment of the real difficulties that the rich have in giving up their surplus possessions.[35]

Praise for Those Who Give Up Their Possessions. Although Jesus criticizes those who refuse to give up their surplus possessions, he is full of praise for those who do take this step and strive to live simply. Luke reports that Jesus' words to the rich ruler and his comment about the difficulty the rich encounter in trying to enter the kingdom of God engendered great controversy. He then goes on to tell us that Jesus commended Peter and the others for the commitment that they themselves had undertaken:

Those who heard it said, "Then who can be saved?" But he said, "What is impossible with men is possible with God." And Peter said, "Lo, we have left our homes and followed you." And he said to them, "Truly, I say to you, there is no man who has left house or wife or brothers or parents or children, for the sake of the kingdom of God, who will not receive manifold more in this time, and in the age to come eternal life" [18:26–30].[36]

Jesus' praise for those who use their resources for the sake of the needy is expressed in the parable of the good Samaritan (10:30–37), and his commendation for those who adopt a simple way of living is contained in his endorsement of John the Baptist's austerity:

What then did you go out to see? A man clothed in soft raiment? Behold those who are gorgeously appareled and live in luxury are in kings' courts [7:25].[37]

It is, however, in Jesus' encounter with Zaccheus that we find the best example of his attitude toward those who have embraced his teachings regarding surplus possessions (19:1–10).[38] Luke tells us that Zaccheus climbed a tree in order to see Jesus and that Jesus disregarded the murmuring of those around him as he availed himself of Zaccheus' hospitality. Then the following conversation took place:

And Zaccheus stood and said to the Lord, "Behold, Lord, the half of my goods I give to the poor, and if I have defrauded any one of anything, I restore it fourfold." And Jesus said to him, "Today salvation has come to this house, since he also is a son of Abraham. For the Son of man came to seek and save the lost" [19:8–10].

Here a rich man receives Jesus' high praise. However, the point that must not be overlooked is that Zaccheus has taken a substantial step toward putting Jesus' teachings into practice by making reparation to those he had defrauded and by giving half of his possessions to the poor. In contrast to the rich ruler who had such difficulty in accepting Jesus' teachings regarding possessions, Zaccheus has moved decisively. He is thus no longer among those to whom Jesus said, "Woe to you that are rich" and those whom he described in the parable of the rich man and Lazarus. Instead, Zaccheus has joined the ranks of Jesus' faithful disciples, those who have heard Jesus' words and put them into practice.

3. PERSPECTIVES ON JESUS' STANCE

Why were the poor of Jesus' day poor? Was it because resources of Galilee and Judea were not adequate for the needs of the total population? Or did the explanation lie in the social conditions under which agricultural production took place? Was the land farmed inefficiently as a result of the unenlightened policies of the landowners, or did they appropriate for themselves so much of what was produced that there was not enough left for the rest of the population?

Although Luke's Jesus is strongly concerned about the poor, he does not offer any explicit analysis of why they were poor. At first, this might not seem to be the case, given the frequency with which Jesus criticizes the rich and admonishes them to give up their surplus possessions. However, when we reflect over the full range of Luke's reports, we see that there is scarcely an instance in which Jesus has charged the rich with exploiting the poor or has indicated that their actions have helped to maintain or create poverty.[39] To be sure, Jesus challenges the rich to use their surplus possessions to provide for the poor and implies that they are negligent if they do not, but he does not assign to them any responsibility for the fact that the poor are poor.

If we ask whether Luke's Jesus has any program to overcome poverty, we have to be careful about the meaning of the term "program."[40] Since Jesus did advocate that specific steps be taken to benefit the poor, however, we may respond to this question in the affirmative.

What were these steps? We saw that Jesus manifested a strong and consistent concern for the poor; in effect, this concern was the underlying premise for the approach that Jesus followed. We have also seen that Luke's Jesus frequently called upon those with surplus possessions to use them to benefit the poor. This is the second point in Jesus' program.

Jesus' program can also be said to include a third element. This derives from Jesus' recommendation to the disciples that they find ways to enable the poor (and the infirm) to participate fully in the ongoing life of the community.

We find one of the most powerful expressions of this in Luke's fourteenth chapter, where Jesus teaches concerning various types of social conduct. Jesus presents these teachings in terms of the behavior proper for those who are attending or giving banquets, but it is clear that the patterns of conduct he recommends have application in other circumstances as well.[41]

He said also to the man who had invited him, "When you give a dinner or a banquet, do not invite your friends or your brothers or your kinsmen or rich neighbors, lest they also invite you in return, and you be repaid. But when you give a feast, invite the poor, the maimed, the lame, the blind, and you will be blessed, because they cannot repay you. You will be repaid at the resurrection of the just" [14:12–14].

This passage emphasizes that Jesus' followers should strive to include the poor and the infirm within the life of the community. It can also be argued that Jesus adopts a similar position toward "tax collectors and sinners" and other outcasts.[42] This theme of an inclusive community or society is an important feature of Jesus' general response to the social suffering taking place around him. Coupled with his recommendation that the rich use their surplus possessions to aid the poor, it can be said to constitute his response to poverty.[43]

CHAPTER THREE

The Social Stance
of Jesus (II)

In this chapter we will investigate Jesus' response to oppression and injustice. Then we will see that Jesus' general social stance is best described as an espousal of a new social order based on service and humility. Third, we will consider his approach toward violence. Finally, we will make brief reference to several other themes recognizable in Jesus' social stance.

1. JESUS' RESPONSE TO OPPRESSION AND INJUSTICE

With regard to abuses in the judicial process, Luke indicates that Jesus twice spoke of the difficulties that widows experienced in trying to gain just treatment, but both are phrased in such a way that the issue of injustice does not receive unalloyed emphasis. The first occurs in a list of Jesus' criticisms of the scribes. In addition to criticizing their love of public salutations and the best seats in the synagogues, Jesus censured them as those "who devour widows' houses" (20:47).[1]

In the second instance, Jesus tells a parable concerning a widow who persistently pleaded with the judge for justice against her adversary (18:1–5).[2] The woman eventually wore down the judge's indifference and obtained justice. In a comment on the parable Jesus states that God will eventually provide justice for those who cry out to him all the day long. While the theme of redressing injustice is thus present in both the parable and Jesus' elaboration on it, so also is the theme of persevering in prayer. In fact, Luke's introduction to the parable particularly highlights this point: "He told them a parable to the effect that they ought always to pray and not lose heart" (18:1).

Beyond these two instances, the main socio-economic abuse to which Jesus responds in Luke occurred at the Jerusalem temple.[3] Luke describes Jesus' "protest" in the following way:

And he entered the temple and began to drive out those who sold, saying to them, "It is written, 'My house shall be a house of prayer'; but you have made it a den of robbers" [20:45–46].

Luke shows Jesus acting against "those who sold" and accusing the traffickers of having made the temple a "den of robbers." The chief priests exercised tight control over all temple activities and very likely derived a portion of their personal incomes from the buying and selling that took place within temple precincts. In the passage above, Luke does not explicitly state that Jesus' actions actually placed him in conflict with the chief priests; but it does clearly portray Jesus as acting against the prevailing economic practices.[4]

Since he makes reference to a passage from Isaiah, "My house shall be a house of prayer," as he began to drive out those who sold, it is likely that Jesus' action is directed against a religious abuse or religious oppression as well as against economic oppression. On this point, we should also make mention of the numerous instances in which Luke depicts Jesus disregarding or reinterpreting specific points of Jewish law and criticizing the Pharisees for their excessive legalism.[5] The parable of the wicked tenants (20:9–19) should also be mentioned under the heading of Jesus' criticism of religious abuses.

An additional important feature of Jesus' response to injustice and oppression is his extremely progressive stance toward women's role and status. We have already indicated that women figured in a significant number of Jesus' healings, that he praised the generosity of a poor widow, and that he was concerned that widows not be deprived of legal rights. We will consider three of Luke's other reports regarding Jesus' stance toward women.

In the first of these, Luke states Jesus' teaching regarding divorce and remarriage:

Everyone who divorces his wife and marries another commits adultery, and he who marries a woman divorced from her husband commits adultery [16:18].

Luke does not have Jesus elaborate on this, but in itself it contained important implications for the status of women in Jesus' day. The prevailing patterns enabled a man to divorce his wife and take another at his own discretion and did not necessarily require him to provide his wife with a writ of divorce. In contrast, Luke has shown Jesus as equating divorce and remarriage with adultery.[6] If such a teaching had become widely accepted and practiced, women throughout Palestine would have received increased security and a new status.

The second of Luke's reports describes Jesus' visit to Mary and Martha (10:38–42).[7] The passage has become well known because of Jesus' reply to Martha's request that he reprimand Mary for not helping with the serving; but what we are interested in is that Luke describes Jesus as being at home and at ease in the company of Martha and Mary. At the time, it probably was not usual for women to take the initiative in providing hospitality for men. Moreover, Jesus appears to have been on particularly good terms with them. Martha's question and Jesus' response both suggest that a degree of familiarity and friendship existed between them.

The final passage occurs at the beginning of Luke 8. After telling his readers that Jesus granted forgiveness of sins to the woman who had anointed his feet Luke continues:

Soon afterward he went on through the cities and villages, preaching and bringing the good news of the kingdom of God. And the twelve were with him, and also some women who had been healed of evil spirits and infirmities: Mary, called Magdalene, from whom seven demons had gone out, and Joanna, the wife of Chusa, Herod's steward, and Susanna and many others, who provided for them out of their means [8:1–3].

Three points are of interest to us here. First, Luke repeats what he has included elsewhere, namely, that Jesus had cured a number of women from evil spirits and infirmities. Second, some of these women, who apparently were not related to them by marriage or family, travelled as a group with Jesus and the twelve.[8] Third, and even more remarkable, some of these women provided for the group out of their own resources.

Taken together, these three aspects of Luke's description indicate that Jesus had adopted a pattern of behavior that implicitly opened the way to new personal identity and social standing for women. By implication, their social roles were to be broadened appreciably, and they were to be participants in community life as independent persons.

2. JESUS' CALL FOR SOCIAL RELATIONSHIPS BASED ON SERVICE

In assessing Luke's presentation of Jesus' stance toward poverty and toward the social situation of women, we have twice reached the conclusion that radically new patterns of social relationships would be required if Jesus' teachings were to be adopted and if his conduct were to serve as a model for the conduct of his disciples. Here let us emphasize that Luke does not use the phrase "new patterns of social relationships" to describe Jesus' social stance, nor does he anywhere explicitly state that Jesus proposed to constitute these relationships on the basis of service and humility. However, we shall see that Luke portrays Jesus as strongly emphasizing the importance of humility and dedicated service. We shall also see that the domination practiced by the existing political rulers could have no place within the service-oriented relationships that Jesus advocated.

Near the end of his ninth chapter, Luke reports that many were marvelling at Jesus' deeds. Possibly because things were going so well, an argument arose among the disciples as to which of them was the greatest. Their dispute is in sharp contrast to Jesus' statement to them that he was ultimately going to be delivered into the hands of his enemies. Jesus responds to their quarrel:

But when Jesus perceived the thoughts of their hearts, he took a child and put him by his side, and said to them, "Whoever receives this child in my name receives me, and whoever receives me receives him who sent me; for he who is least among you all is the one who is great" [9:47–48].[9]

Jesus admonishes the disciples not to strive after that "greatness" based on rank or position. Rather, he intimates that true greatness accrues from being able to recognize the worth and importance of those members of society frequently considered to be least important. While he does not use the terms "humility" or "service," they are clearly accurate words for the approach Jesus is here commending to the disciples.

These themes, particularly that of humility, are also very much present in the parable Jesus addressed to those choosing the places of honor at a banquet:

Now he told a parable to those who were invited, when he marked how they chose the places of honor, saying to them, "When you are invited by anyone to a marriage feast, do not sit down in a place of honor, lest a more eminent man than you be invited by him; and he who invited you both will come and say to you, 'Give place to this man,' and then you will begin with shame to take the lowest place. But when you are invited, go and sit in the lowest place, so that when your host comes he may say to you, 'Friend, go up higher'; then you will be honored in the presence of all who sit at table with you. For everyone who exalts himself will be humbled, and he who humbles himself will be exalted" [14:7–11].[10]

According to Luke, Jesus' most explicit statement on dedicated service is as follows:

Will any one of you, who has a servant plowing or keeping sheep, say to him when he has come in from the field, "Come at once and sit down at table"? Will he not rather say to him, "Prepare supper for me, and gird yourself and serve me, till I eat and drink; and afterward you shall eat and drink"? Does he thank the servant because he did what was commanded? So you also, when you have done all that is commanded you, say, "We are unworthy servants; we have only done what was our duty" [17:7–10].[11]

It is clear that Jesus stressed humility and a spirit of service and encouraged his followers to emphasize these qualities in their own social relationships. They were to hold all persons as "great" and were not to be concerned about social rank or social position. They were to fulfill their various responsibilities as dedicated servants. However, in addition to his support for a style of acting and living based upon humility and service, Luke's Jesus also criticizes certain practices and patterns as inconsistent with such values. In one instance, Jesus criticizes some of the Pharisees for wanting "the best seat in the synagogues and salutations in the market places" (11:43).[12] Later on, Jesus lists other marks of "greatness" that the scribes seek and warns the disciples not to follow their example.

Beware of the scribes, who like to go about in long robes, and love salutations in the market places and the best seats in the synagogues and the places of honor at feasts, who devour widows' houses and for a pretense make long prayers. They will receive the greater condemnation [20:46–47].[13]

Humility and service also are Jesus' presuppositions for criticizing political relationships of domination and oppression. Jesus describes "the kings of the Gentiles" as dominating their subjects and indicates that this is contrary to the approach he is advocating. In particular, Jesus' use of the term "benefactors" emphasizes this contrast between his own approach and that of the pagan rulers. He uses it sarcastically; for if they were truly seeking to be benefactors, the rulers would cease to act as lords and to dominate and subjugate others:

A dispute also arose among them, which of them was to be regarded as the greatest. And he said to them, "The kings of the Gentiles exercise lordship over them; and those in authority over them are called benefactors. But not so with you; rather let the greatest among you become as the youngest, and the leader as one who serves. For which is the greater, one who sits at table, or one who serves? Is it not the one who sits at table? But I am among you as one who serves" (22:24–27).[14]

The above passage shows that if Jesus' call to establish social relationships based upon service and humility were widely accepted, extensive changes in the existing political patterns would be required. By implication, we can conclude that, to the extent that they were not premised upon humility and service, far-reaching changes would also be required in the other social patterns then prevailing. For if the concept of social relationships based upon service can be used to criticize political patterns, it also can be used to criticize other harmful social patterns.

The themes of service and humility thus provide the key to an understanding of Jesus' social and political stance. What convictions underpin Jesus' attitudes and actions toward the poor, toward the infirm, toward the rich, and toward women? Judging from Luke's reports, the answer is to be found in Jesus' conviction about social relationships based upon service and humility.

3. JESUS AND VIOLENCE

We have noted that the Zealot movement was active at the time of Jesus' ministry and that, as a consequence, the question of whether violence should be used to achieve social reform was prominent (see Appendix III). We now want to determine what approach Jesus adopts toward violence. Luke does not explicitly utilize the concepts of "nonresistance" or "nonviolence" in his description of Jesus' stance, but an understanding of what these categories involve and the differences between them will help us gain a better understanding of Jesus' approach.[15]

Persons committed to nonresistance and nonviolence attempt to bring the power of love into human affairs in a radical and creative way. Proponents of both approaches argue that doing physical violence to persons is a serious obstacle to the creation of a society that is lastingly free from injustice and oppression. For this reason, both reject particular actions or general strategies that involve violence. There is, however, a difference between these two approaches, a difference arising from their respective responses to the violence (and other evils) that already exist in a given situation.

Adherents of nonresistance not only reject actions that would involve them in doing physical violence to others, but they also refrain from directly confronting those responsible for existing evils. Instead, they seek solidarity with those who are suffering from these evils, offering no defense if they themselves are subjected to violence by those who have power. Their hope is that their own commitment and example will eventually inspire changes in the attitudes and actions of others.

In contrast, those who adopt the position of nonviolence believe that challenges to and confrontations with those responsible for the existing social evils may serve as an effective means of bringing about a change in their behavior. They hold that as long as such challenges are made within the context of love and truth, and as long as they avoid violence to persons, these challenges can serve as a creative means of initiating a dialogue that may eventually result in a favorable change of behavior.

The general thrust of Luke's descriptions shows Jesus within the camp of those who adhere to nonviolence. There is one passage (6:27–31) in which Jesus appears to adopt a position bordering on nonresistance, but most of Luke's descriptions show Jesus vigorously challenging those responsible for the existing social patterns. Often he presents Jesus as doing this through his teaching; but, on one important occasion, he also shows him doing so by his actions.

In fact, Luke presents Jesus as teaching and acting so aggressively and assertively that some scholars have concluded that Luke actually presents him as sanctioning the use of violence. It is clear that Jesus sharply criticized the rich and several of the political rulers of his day. It is also clear that he foresees divisions arising as a consequence of his teachings. Nevertheless, Luke does not indicate that Jesus ever supported the use of physical violence against persons. Rather, Jesus consistently rejects the inclinations of some of his followers to utilize such violence.

According to Luke, Jesus was familiar with the violent measures that his immediate political rulers employed to accomplish their purposes. Luke indicates that Jesus knew that Herod Antipas had imprisoned John the Baptist and implies that he knew of John's execution.[16] Luke relates that Jesus received a report concerning "the Galileans whose blood Pilate had mingled with their sacrifices" (13:1), and, most important, he reports that Jesus received a warning from some Pharisees that Herod Antipas was seeking to kill *him* (13:31).[17] Further, several of the parables recounted by Jesus also demonstrate that he was aware of the role that power and physical coercion played in the normal course of Palestinian life.[18]

In this context it should also be recalled that one of the twelve,

Simon, had a Zealot background. By noting this, Luke suggests that Jesus was at least familiar with the main characteristics of the Zealots' program, particularly their commitment to overthrow Roman rule by force of arms.

Against this background the passages in Luke's account that describe Jesus' response to violence take on heightened significance. In particular, the passage below indicates the striking contrast between Jesus' approach and that adopted by many of his contemporaries. Indeed, taken apart from Luke's other reports, the following passage from Jesus' "Great Sermon" would indicate that his stance was one of nonresistance:

> But I say to you that hear, love your enemies, do good to those who hate you, bless those who curse you, pray for those who abuse you. To him who strikes you on the cheek, offer the other also; and from him who takes away your coat do not withhold even your shirt. Give to everyone who begs from you; and of him who takes away your goods, do not ask them again. And as you wish that men would do to you, do so to them [6:27–31].

It is significant that the injunction, "To him who strikes you on the cheek, offer the other also," is presented within the context of love for one's enemies.[19] Although the attempt to suffer violence without responding in kind still requires the highest imaginable degree of self-transcendence, the proposal is more plausible within the context of a general appeal to love one's enemies. It is important that we do not attempt to analyze Luke's description of Jesus' approach to violence in isolation from Luke's descriptions of other features in Jesus' social stance.

Jesus' teachings on forgiveness also help to supply a context for his approach to violence. The words in the Lord's Prayer, "and forgive us our sins, for we ourselves forgive everyone who is indebted to us" (11:4), emphasize from a slightly different perspective that Jesus' disciples should seek to be reconciled with all those around them.[20] A similar notion is found in Jesus' extended teaching regarding forgiveness:

> Take heed for yourselves; if your brother sins, rebuke him, and if he repents, forgive him; and if he sins against you seven times in the day, and

turns to you seven times, and says, "I repent," you must forgive him [17:3–4].[21]

It is also important that we view Jesus' harsh and divisive words within the context of his teachings regarding love of enemies and regarding forgiveness. Jesus engages in heated controversy with various groups, and in the following passage he reflects the startling divisions resulting from his ministry. Considered apart from Jesus' other words and actions, this passage might suggest that he acquiesced in whatever strife and conflict his ministry caused, perhaps even to the point of violence. On the other hand, however, his words can also constitute a recognition of the serious strife his teachings are engendering, without representing any endorsement for the use of harsh measures by his disciples. Given Jesus' other teachings regarding forgiveness and love for enemies, this latter interpretation is to be preferred.

I came to cast fire upon the earth; and would that it were already kindled! I have a baptism to be baptized with; and how I am constrained until it is accomplished! Do you think that I have come to give peace on earth? No, I tell you, but rather division; for henceforth in one house there will be five divided, three against two and two against three; they shall be divided, father against son and son against father; mother against daughter and daughter against her mother, mother-in-law against her daughter-in-law and daughter-in-law against her mother-in-law [12:49–53].[22]

Not only does Jesus sometimes speak extremely fiery words in Luke; he also acts decisively and aggressively. The events that Luke describes near the end of his ninth chapter occur after Jesus and his disciples embarked on a journey toward Jerusalem.[23] Because Jerusalem was their destination, a Samaritan village refused them hospitality,[24] and James and John proposed to Jesus that they call down fire to destroy the villagers. Luke describes Jesus' response as extremely definite: Jesus "turned and rebuked them"(9:55).[25] Thus by the time Jesus enters the temple in Jerusalem, not only has he taught forgiveness and love of one's enemies to the point of turning the other cheek, but he has also explicitly rejected a proposal that would have resulted in physical violence to persons.

Prior to his description of Jesus' actions at the temple, Luke describes the feelings that Jesus experienced as he drew near to Jerusalem. Coming within sight of the city, Jesus wept over it and uttered the following rueful, prophetic words:

Would that even today you knew the things that make for peace! But now they are hid from your eyes. For the days shall come upon you, when your enemies will cast up a bank about you and surround you, and hem you in on every side, and dash you to the ground, and they will not leave one stone upon another in you; because you did not know the time of your visitation [19:42–44].

There is an element of reproach in Jesus' grief-stricken prophecy. To some degree, at least, he rebukes Jerusalem's inhabitants for not having fostered peace.[26] We are, however, primarily concerned with Jesus' actions once he had entered the temple.

And he entered the temple and began to drive out those who sold, saying to them, "It is written, 'My house shall be a house of prayer'; but you have made it a den of robbers" [19:45–46].

When we previously considered this passage, we noted that Jesus' actions were directed against the economic practices that he saw taking place. Here our concern is to note that, while Luke indicates that Jesus acted aggressively and suggests that he acted with passion, he does not indicate that Jesus did bodily harm to those who were responsible for what was going on.

Without close attention to what Luke's description actually states, it is possible to make an "imaginative reconstruction" of the situation, a reconstruction in which Jesus physically pummels and whips the merchants as a means of driving them from their posts.[27] Luke's text does not, however, support such an interpretation.

Ekballein, the Greek word that Luke uses to describe Jesus' action, is translated by the Revised Standard Version as "(began) to drive out." So translated, Luke's description stops short of indicating that Jesus pummelled or whipped anyone; and *ekballein* itself actually favors the interpretation that the "driving out" was achieved by shouts and gestures rather than by physical coercion.

Thus, while the text does not explicitly state that Jesus accomplished his demonstration without inflicting physical harm upon any of those he acted against, it does lean in that direction.²⁸ Conversely, to state that Jesus' actions involved the use of violence against persons is to go beyond the sense of the text.

We make a full analysis of Jesus' arrest and trial in Chapter Five; here, as a conclusion to our study of Jesus' stance toward violence, it will be helpful to consider briefly three of Luke's reports regarding events that transpired during Jesus' final days. Two of these reports are of particular concern to us. In one, Luke indicates that Jesus strongly rebuked the disciples for their tendencies toward violence. In the other, which we shall take up first, the meaning of the words that Jesus addresses to the disciples is not as clear.²⁹

And he said to them, "When I sent you out with no purse or bag or sandals, did you lack anything?" They said, "Nothing." He said to them, "But now, let him who has a purse take it, and likewise a bag. And let him who has no sword sell his mantle and buy one. For I tell you that this scripture must be fulfilled in me, 'And he was reckoned with transgressors'; for what is written about me has its fulfillment." And they said, "Look, Lord, here are two swords." And he said to them, "It is enough" (22:35–38).

Do Jesus' words, "And let him who has no sword sell his mantle and buy one," mean that, at the conclusion of the Last Supper, Jesus literally instructed the disciples to take up arms? That is the question evoked by the foregoing passage. Moreover, by stating that the disciples actually produced two swords, Luke indicates that they understood Jesus' words to have this meaning.

There are, however, two other considerations that argue against such an interpretation. First, Jesus' words *hikanon estin* indicate disapproval for the disciples' response. Second, Jesus' rebuke of the disciples for their inclinations toward violence on two other occasions lends weight to the premise that such was his response in this instance too.³⁰

The Revised Standard Version translates *hikanon estin* as "It is enough," but a more accurate rendering would be "Enough of this." As several commentators have pointed out, the sense of this phrase is that, frustrated with the disciples' lack of comprehension, Jesus wishes to break off the discussion.³¹ What he had intended to communicate to them in his words about buying a sword was that they would need to strengthen their commitments for the time of difficulty that was approaching.[32] He did not intend that they should actually procure swords; but, just as James and John had acted contrary to the spirit of his teaching in seeking to call down fire upon the Samaritan village, the disciples are again shown as misunderstanding the meaning of Jesus' teachings.

Jesus' words and deeds at the time of his arrest also support this interpretation of his words regarding the need for swords. Once again, Luke's description delineates a sequence of events in which the disciples propose to rely on violence, seek Jesus' approval for what they propose, and instead earn his rebuke.

While he was still speaking, there came a crowd, and the man called Judas, one of the twelve, was leading them. He drew near to Jesus to kiss him; but Jesus said to him, "Judas, would you betray the Son of man with a kiss?" And when those who were about him saw what would follow, they said, "Lord, shall we strike with the sword?" And one of them struck the slave of the high priest and cut off his right ear. But Jesus said, "No more of this!" And he touched his ear and healed him [22:47–51].[33]

The fact that Jesus replied so emphatically to the disciples' question and the action that one of them took is in itself sufficient to indicate that his position against violence was firm.[34] However, as Luke describes the situation, Jesus took a further step that illustrated how violence was to be met not with counterviolence, but with love.

By showing him healing the wound of the high priest's servant, Luke presents Jesus concretizing and summarizing the approach toward violence and toward one's enemies that he has been espousing throughout his ministry. Jesus had previously stressed love for enemies as an alternative to responding toward them with violence, and Luke now shows him observing this teaching in the breach. Responding with love and forgiveness, rather than with violence, Jesus heals the wound of one who had come out against him as an enemy.

We will conclude our study of Jesus' stance with respect to violence with a reference to Jesus' words at the time of his crucifixion. The passage is among the best known in Luke's gospel:

"Father, forgive them, for they know not what they do" (23:34).[35] We noted earlier that Jesus' teaching regarding forgiveness constituted an important element in his general position with respect to violence. We now find Jesus himself practicing this teaching in a most radical way. Throughout Luke's gospel, Jesus' teaching and actions relative to violence are thoroughly consistent. In particular circumstances Jesus acts and speaks aggressively, but he always does so without doing or sanctioning violence to persons, and he continually witnesses to overriding love and forgiveness.

4. OTHER FACTORS IN JESUS' SOCIAL STANCE

At the beginning of Chapter Two we indicated that, in order to keep our study within limits, we would have to refrain from treating all the elements present in Luke's full description of Jesus' stance toward the world around him. Our concern is to analyze the aspects of Luke's description that pertain most directly to the subject of Jesus' social and political stance; and, to that end, we have abstracted from other elements in Luke's presentation. These elements did have relevance for a comprehensive interpretation of Jesus' social and political stance; but to attempt to treat all of them would have required a far more extensive effort than was possible or indeed was necessary.

Since we have uncovered the general lines of the social stance that Luke attributes to Jesus, it is appropriate that we briefly advert to several of the features in Luke's other descriptions of Jesus that supply a context for the social positions that he ascribes to him. These features do not contravene any of the points that we have established above. Rather, in several respects they help to make them more understandable.

In our preceding analysis, we noted the concern for the poor, the infirm, and for women and pagans that Luke attributes to Jesus. We also saw that Jesus asked the rich to divest themselves of their surplus possessions, and that he counterposed an emphasis upon humility and service to the domination being practiced by the political rulers of his day. Taking all of these factors into consideration, we argued that the most accurate way of describing Jesus' social stance was to say that he espoused a new order of social relationships. Finally, we concluded that, although Jesus acted assertively upon occasion, he rejected the use of violence against persons. The point that we now wish to emphasize is that Luke places these social positions of Jesus within the context of Jesus' deep belief in God and his frequent advertence to God's purposes and the nature of God's kingdom.

At the outset of Chapter Two we noted the difficulty of treating every facet in Luke's description of Jesus. Nevertheless three additional elements must here be noted, at least briefly. First, Luke describes Jesus as having a deep faith that all of life and all of human endeavor take place under God. This is the basis on which Jesus prays the "Our Father," and the basis on which he elsewhere refers to God as the "Lord of heaven and earth" (10:21).

Second, Luke also indicates that Jesus adopted many of the social positions that he did precisely because of what he conceived God's purposes to be. On the question of love for one's enemies, Jesus justified the teaching that he gave by referring to God's kindness to the ungrateful and the selfish (6:35). Similarly, in asking the disciples to lessen their concern for possessions, Jesus referred to God's care for the lilies and the birds and stated that God's care for people was much greater (12:22–32). In addition to these specific references to God's actions and purposes, Luke also shows Jesus relating his ministry as a whole to the theme of the kingdom of God.[36]

Third, consistent with what he tells us about Jesus' belief in God, Luke also indicates that Jesus prayed frequently and, in particular, at important junctures in his ministry.[37] As we have noted above, Jesus also counselled the disciples to pray and not to lose heart (18:1).

The significance of all these considerations is that they indicate how strongly a religious foundation undergirded the social and political stance that Jesus adopted. Indeed, Jesus' social stance cannot really be adequately grasped without reference to his faith in God and his understanding of God's purposes.

Throughout our study, our primary concern has been to analyze the content of Jesus' social stance. We have concentrated our analysis on Jesus' response to the social situation around him and the positions he adopted on the leading social-political questions of his day. In Luke's gospel, however, Jesus continually adverts to God's involvement in human affairs, and his social stance is always ultimately related to his belief in God and his judgment about God's concerns. It is, therefore, fitting that, before proceeding further with our analysis, we strongly emphasize this point.

CHAPTER FOUR

Jesus and His Political Rulers

By the time of Jesus' ministry, the Romans had placed Judea under the direct rule of a Roman governor, but had allowed Herod Antipas to continue as tetrarch of Galilee and Perea.[1] The Roman governors serving in Judea had entrusted a great deal of responsibility for daily administration to the Jerusalem sanhedrin, so that the chief priests, as leading members of the sanhedrin, possessed considerable political power. Here we shall note Luke's portrayal of Jesus' response to these political conditions and rulers.

We will begin with Jesus' response to Herod Antipas, and the chief priests, but our primary concern will be Jesus' approach to the Roman social order and to the Roman officials responsible for that order.

1. JESUS AND HEROD ANTIPAS

Herod Antipas first appears in Luke's account when Luke reports that Herod imprisoned John the Baptist. Several chapters later, Luke reports that Herod had beheaded John, and that Herod was disconcerted by Jesus' actions and "sought to see him" (9:9).

Before Jesus' trial, Luke makes only one further mention of Herod, but the reference is extremely important for it provides valuable information relative to Jesus' outlook toward his political rulers. In this passage, Herod's attitude has become much more ominous. Now it is no longer a question of being curious about what Jesus is doing. Rather, he desires to kill him.

At that very hour some Pharisees came, and said to him, "Get away from here, for Herod wants to kill you." And he said to them, "Go and tell that fox, 'Behold, I cast out demons and perform cures today and tomorrow, and the third day I finish my course. Nevertheless I must go on my way today and tomorrow and the day following; for it cannot be that a prophet should perish away from Jerusalem' " [13:31–33].[2]

Three elements in the above passage are particularly important. First, Jesus accepts the Pharisees' report about Herod's intentions as plausible; that is, he finds it believable that Herod is seeking to kill him. Luke does not tell us why Jesus took the Pharisees' report as seriously as he did, and we are left to conjecture that Jesus saw himself proceeding along lines similar to John and knew that Herod had killed John. We can also conjecture that Jesus realized that his stance toward the poor and the rich and toward the role of women was generating controversy and that he knew Herod would not tolerate such views and such turbulence.[3] Jesus does not, however, question the accuracy of the Pharisees' report or impugn their motives for bringing it. He does not reply, as he conceivably could have, that the Pharisees were hypocrites trying to engender mistrust where there was no basis for it.[4]

Second, Jesus indicates that he will not alter the course of his ministry as a consequence of any steps that Herod may be contemplating against him.[5] Jesus declares that he intends to "cast out demons and perform cures" until he finishes his appointed course, regardless of what Herod plans to do. Even though Herod is the political ruler with direct jurisdiction over him, Jesus will not alter his conduct to placate him. He will not attempt to work out some form of accommodation that will enable him to continue his ministry free from Herod's hostility.

Third, Jesus also explicitly criticizes Herod, terming him "that fox." This indicates that Jesus viewed Herod's role as destructive and suggests that he had an appreciation for Herod's position as a political ruler of secondary standing.[6] As Jesus used it in this passage, the term "fox" also expresses a certain scorn.[7] Far from deferring to Herod as the tetrarch of Galilee and its most important person, Jesus refers to him deprecatingly.

2. JESUS AND THE CHIEF PRIESTS

In Luke's account, the Pharisees and their scribes frequently dispute with Jesus during his ministry in Galilee.[8] However, from the time that Jesus enters Jerusalem the Pharisees depart from the scene, and the chief priests and their allies come forward as Jesus' principal adversaries.[9] Indeed, as Luke's narrative goes forward it becomes clear that the chief priests are much more dangerous opponents of Jesus than the Pharisees or Herod Antipas ever were.

Immediately after recounting Jesus' protest at the temple, Luke states:

And he was teaching daily in the temple. The chief priests and the scribes and the principal men of the people sought to destroy him; but they could not find anything they could do for all the people hung upon his words [19:47].

Luke does not explicitly state that the chief priests decided to destroy Jesus because of his protest against the merchants in the temple; but his positioning this report immediately after this description of Jesus' actions suggests such a causal relationship.[10] There are two other considerations that argue for this meaning. First, since Luke has not indicated that Jesus had any previous contact with the chief priests, his protest is, seemingly, the only thing that could have earned him their hostility. Second, his actions in driving out the merchants very likely constituted a threat to the chief priests' authority and to their ability to continue the economic practices that they found personally remunerative.[11]

After they had determined to get rid of Jesus, the chief priests and their allies sought to undermine his position with a series of potentially dangerous questions. They themselves asked the first question about the source of his authority. Then they sent spies to ask his opinion on whether it was lawful to pay tribute to Rome.[12] Third, a group of Sadducees approached him with a case of seven brothers who had successively wed the same woman.

Although we will consider Jesus' response to the tribute question later, here we nevertheless want to note a feature common to all three of Jesus' replies: Jesus does not give a direct answer to the question originally addressed to him.

In the first instance, the question addressed to Jesus was: "Tell us by what authority you do these things, or who it is that gave you this authority" (20:2). Jesus replied with a counter-question about John's baptism, and when they chose not to answer his question, he refused to answer theirs.

In the third instance, the Sadducees posed a hypothetical problem in which, as a result of a succession of deaths, one woman had been married to seven brothers at different times in her life. They then asked: "In the resurrection, therefore, whose wife will the woman be?" (20:33).[13] Jesus replies by drawing a contrast between life in the present age and life in the resurrection. Instead of giving the Sadducees a direct answer that they can use to discredit him, he says that those who rise from the dead "neither marry nor are given in marriage . . . because they are equal to angels." His response undercuts the original question by showing that it is based on false assumptions, on relationships that obtain only in the present age.[14]

Luke reports that Jesus disconcerted his adversaries by his skillful replies (20:26 and 20:39–40), and, of even more interest to us, that after his first reply Jesus went on to attack the chief priests as irresponsible and murderous stewards with his parable about wicked tenants. The context and Luke's concluding comment make it clear that Jesus was speaking about the chief priests and their allies. The parable itself reads as follows:

A man planted a vineyard, and let it out to tenants, and went into another country for a long while. When the time came, he sent a servant to the tenants, that they should give him some of the fruit of the vineyard, but the tenants beat him, and sent him away empty-handed. And he sent another servant; him also they beat and treated shamefully, and sent him away empty-handed. And he sent yet a third; this one they wounded and cast out. Then the owner of the vineyard said, "What shall I do? I will send my beloved son; it may be that they will respect him." But when the tenants saw him, they said to themselves, "This is the heir; let us kill him, that the inheritance may be ours." And they cast him out of the vineyard and killed him. What then will the owner of the vineyard do to them? He will come and destroy those tenants, and give the vineyard to others [20:9–16a].[15]

After Jesus concluded the parable, the chief priests expressed shock, and Jesus responded by citing a passage from Psalm 118. Luke then emphasizes that the parable was directed against the priests:

When they heard this, they said "God forbid!" But he looked at them and said, "What then is this that is written: 'The very stone which the builders rejected has become the head of the corner'? Every one who falls on that stone will be broken to pieces; but when it falls on any one it will crush him." The scribes and the chief priests tried to lay hands on him at that very hour, but they feared the people; for they perceived that he had told this parable against them [20:16b–19].

Jesus' actions at the temple, this parable, and his replies to the questions together establish beyond any doubt that he did not allow the wishes and policies of the chief priests to determine his course of action. That they controlled the temple and held important positions on the sanhedrin did not deter him from challenging their economic practices. When they asked him to justify his conduct, he refused to do so and proceeded to attack them vigorously.

We can conclude that Jesus shows virtually no deference to Herod Antipas, his own immediate political ruler in Galilee, or to the Jerusalem chief priests. Indeed, Jesus was outspokenly critical of Herod and clearly questioned the stewardship of the chief priests. But if this was his stance toward rulers who were essentially Roman vassals, what approach did he take toward the Roman authorities themselves?

3. JESUS AND ROMAN PATTERNS

The Romans, by virtue of their military power and their political control, possessed a high degree of responsibility for the social practices and patterns that were characteristic of Palestinian life in Jesus' day. This does not imply that the Romans possessed total responsibility for these practices and does not deny that many of them antedated Roman rule. Rather, it emphasizes the Romans' discretion to change practices that they considered detrimental, or with which they did not fully agree.

By way of illustration, let us consider the prevailing legal and judicial practices. If there were patterned abuses in this area and the Romans tolerated them after they came to power, then they became heir to a part of the responsibility for them.[16] In addition to implicitly endorsing many of the existing patterns, the Romans brought their own practices and made them part of daily life in Judea and the surrounding territories. The Roman commitment to violence to further their interests and the Roman practice of siphoning off the material wealth of the provinces are cases in point. It is not an exaggeration to say that the fundamental premise on which the Roman empire rested was that other peoples were to be subjugated and controlled by force. Similarly, Roman rule in Judea and elsewhere rested upon the concept that the strong and the powerful should use their superior resources to further enrich themselves.

In these assumptions and in the practices that resulted from them, the Romans were not strikingly different from the rulers and the empires that preceded and followed them. Our purpose is thus not to compare the Romans and their counterparts in other times and other places. It is, however, extremely important that we fully appreciate the character of the patterns that the Romans were supporting, because it was precisely in this context that Jesus espoused radically different ones.

We have already considered Luke's description of how Jesus acted to accord women a new social standing and to make it possible for them to enter into new public roles; he did this in the context of oppressive patterns affirmed and supported by the Romans. Similarly, Jesus' rejection of violence against persons contrasts with the Roman practice of using violence to destroy and subjugate. Finally, Jesus' teaching that material possessions were to be shared rather than accumulated contradicted the usual Roman practice of self-enrichment at the expense of subject peoples.

4. TRIBUTE AND ROMAN OFFICIALS

As early as Chapter 13 of his gospel, Luke indicates that Jesus knows that Pilate has massacred some Galileans.[17] It is not until after Jesus reaches Jerusalem, though, that he teaches with direct reference to Roman rule.

During his ministry in Jerusalem, Jesus enunciated three teachings that touched upon the subject of Roman rule in one way or another. The first came in his response to the question of the chief priests' spies in reference to tribute:

They asked him, "Teacher, we know that you speak and teach rightly, and show no partiality, but truly teach the way of God. Is it lawful for us to give tribute to Caesar, or not?" [20:21–22]

The question was indeed artfully phrased and well suited to discrediting Jesus.[18] Noting that Jesus perceived their craftiness, Luke gives his response:

"Show me a coin. Whose likeness and inscription has it?" They said, "Caesar's." He said to them, "Then render to Caesar the things that are Caesar's, and to God the things that are God's" [20:23–25].

Although there are minor differences between Jesus' response in Luke and those in Mark and Matthew, the three passages are on the whole extremely similar.[19] Indeed, the central element in Jesus' reply, "Render to Caesar . . . and to God" is virtually the same in all three.

Many New Testament scholars have advanced interpretations regarding the meaning of Jesus' words. The majority believe that Jesus was advocating support for the Roman order, but they differ over how strongly he affirmed such support in comparison with his emphasis on the things of God.[20] There is a minority of scholars who maintain that Jesus opposed the payment of taxes.[21] There have also been scholars who took the position that Jesus was stating that all of the earth's kingdoms were soon to pass away.[22]

While worthwhile insights have emerged from the attention given this passage, it is our opinion that none of these interpretations adequately expresses the meaning of Jesus' words. The principal failing is that the scholars have not paid enough attention to the other reports that the evangelists give concerning Jesus' approach to the Roman social order and the political authorities who had a part in that order.

The assumption has all too frequently been that this passage is the only report in the gospel traditions that indicates Jesus' attitude toward the Roman state. Consequently, much time has been devoted to analyzing its internal form and structure, while relatively little effort has been given to assessing its relationship to the other gospel statements about Jesus' social and political stance.

Because readers of the tribute passage are frequently preconditioned to expect that a closer examination of it will tell whether or not Jesus paid Roman taxes, we should state at the outset that, in our estimation, Jesus' words do not reveal what action he took. At first such a conclusion may seem somewhat disconcerting, but further analysis will substantiate its plausibility.

First we should note that Jesus' request that his questioners show him a coin may have had the effect of putting them in a bad light. According to the Greek text, Jesus asked them for a *denarius*, a Roman coin that bore the image and inscription of the emperor.[23] If dedicated Jews refused to handle such coins on the grounds that the likenesses and inscriptions on them violated the Mosaic prohibitions against images, then Jesus' opponents were probably publicly embarrassed for handling such a coin.[24] They pretended to be seriously concerned about the observance of the law—they had asked whether it was *lawful* to give tribute to Caesar—and yet they obviously did not take the law seriously enough to observe its prohibitions against images.

Regardless of whether the first part of Jesus' reponse illumined the bad faith of his questioners, we are still faced with interpreting the second part of his reply:

Then render to Caesar the things that are Caesar's and to God the things that are God's.[25]

Because the saying divides into two similarly patterned clauses joined by the conjunction "and," many scholars have been led to hold that Jesus was identifying two parallel sets of obligations and teaching that both were to be fulfilled. Jesus is stating, it is argued, that both temporal and religious obligations are important and need to be met. Ethelbert Stauffer even goes so far as to hold that the admonition to render the things of God is an admonition to pay the annual temple tax. In Stauffer's interpretation, Jesus is counselling the payment of tribute to Caesar and the temple tax to God.[26]

Similarly, although they do not take Jesus' words about rendering to God as an endorsement for the temple tax, numerous other scholars accept that Jesus was positing a separation between the things of Caesar and the things of God and stating that obligations were to be met in each area. Regardless of whether they maintain that Jesus was emphasizing that the things of God were more important than the things of Caesar, or whether they hold that Jesus was affirming that God was to be rendered to at the same time as Caesar, these scholars tend to agree that Jesus was counselling the fulfillment of obligations in both spheres.[27]

Almost invariably, interpreters who make the initial assumption that Jesus' words envisioned two different spheres and two kinds of obligations also conclude that Jesus was counselling the payment of tribute.[28] Such a conclusion follows logically once it is assumed that Caesar's demands are to be met. But what if the assumption that Jesus was designating two separate sets of obligations is itself challenged? What meaning do Jesus' words have if we deny the assumption that he was dualistically separating human activity into a temporal realm and a spiritual realm?

Our interpretation is that, instead of positing the existence of two separate realms, Caesar's and God's, Jesus really taught and acted in terms of only one realm: *God's*. Far from having any kind of independent existence of its own, Caesar's realm, the social order of the Roman empire, was in Jesus' view a part of the larger order of creation, whose only author was God.[29] Therefore the Romans' social patterns were to be evaluated against the standard of the social patterns desired by God, and supported or not on that basis.

In our view, then, the meaning of the first clause of Jesus' answer was the following: Render to Caesar the things that are Caesar's. But what things are Caesar's? For Caesar does not possess anything autonomously from God. Thus, the only areas in which Caesar can expect allegiance are those in which his patterns are in conformity with God's desired patterns.

The second clause in Jesus' response repeats and intensifies this teaching: Render to God the things that are God's. But everything belongs to God, and there is no area in which God's desires can rightfully be neglected. Indeed, God must be rendered to even if to do so requires a rejection of the practices that the Caesars themselves have set in place.

Such an interpretation fits well with what we have established as Jesus' stance in Luke toward the social practices and the various political authorities of his day. Jesus is not at all intimidated by a particular social order or by the rulers who hold high offices within it. He does not hesitate to advocate substantially different social patterns, and he does not defer to the established rulers or hesitate to criticize them.

In our reading, then, Jesus was indicating how the Roman social order was to be critically evaluated. It was not to be supported and submitted to simply because it was firmly established and because the Romans possessed a high degree of military power and political organization. On the contrary, its policies and practices were to be evaluated and responded to from the standpoint of the social patterns that God desired.

We remarked that Jesus did not give a direct answer to any of the three questions presented to him. The original tribute question that the spies put to him was, "Is it lawful for us to give tribute to Caesar or not?" Jesus has not answered this question, but rather indicated that two other questions have first to be met: What social patterns and practices are in accord with God's designs? How do the patterns of the Roman order look by comparison?

Did Jesus himself pay Roman taxes? Our own position is that Jesus did not include this information in his response. The spies' question was designed to force him to make such a declaration; but as we have noted Jesus did not respond to the question as they had asked it. His answer had to do with tribute, but it was not an answer to the question originally addressed to him.

It is also our opinion that this particular question cannot be resolved on the basis of the information that Luke gives us in the rest of his gospel. It is possible to use various passages and themes of the gospel to argue affirmatively or negatively, but in our judgment the evidence is not conclusive, or even heavily weighted in one direction or the other.[30]

Although Luke does not provide us with an answer on this point, we should not, however, be blind to the answers that he does make available to us. While we do not know whether Jesus paid the Roman taxes, we do know a great deal about the way in which he assessed the Roman social order. Luke's description of Jesus' response to the tribute question has been extremely helpful in this regard, and we will now take up two other Lukan passages that shed light upon this subject.

In Chapter Three we considered Luke's report of the teaching regarding service that Jesus gave to the disciples at the Last Supper. We saw then that Jesus used the concept of service as a basis for criticizing relationships based upon domination; here we will note the parallels between the tribute passage and the Last Supper teaching again cited here:

A dispute also arose among them, which of them was to be regarded as the greatest. And he said to them, "The kings of the Gentiles exercise lordship over them; and those in authority are called benefactors. But not so with you; rather let the greatest among you become as the youngest, and the leader as one who serves. For which is the greater, one who sits at table, or one who serves? Is it not the one who sits at table? But I am among you as one who serves" [22:24–27].

In both instances Jesus has provided a frame of reference to evaluate social patterns and practices. How should the dominating practices of the kings of the Gentiles be evaluated? On the basis of Jesus' teaching on service and humility. How should the Roman order be evaluated? On the basis of the social patterns desired by God.

In addition to providing us with a second instance in which Jesus draws a contrast between two types of social patterns, the above passage is also noteworthy because of Jesus' clear criticism of Gentile rulers. Here it is reasonable to suppose that the Roman officials would have been included under the designation, "the kings of the Gentiles"; and if Joseph Schmid is correct in saying that the Roman emperors used the term "benefactor" to describe themselves, then Jesus' criticism is that much more specific.[31]

In addition to the tribute passage and the passage on the Gentile rulers, Luke also includes a third passage in which Jesus expressed himself in reference to Roman officials and the Roman order they represented. In it Jesus warns his disciples that they can expect to be brought before kings and governors. Earlier in his ministry, Jesus had told the disciples that they would have to stand before "synagogues and the rulers and the authorities" (12:11–12).[32] On the first occasion, Jesus did not refer explicitly to Roman governors, but Luke indicates that he refers to them now:

But before all this they will lay their hands on you and persecute you, delivering you up to the synagogues and prisons, and you will be brought before kings and governors for my name's sake. This will be a time for you to bear testimony. Settle it therefore in your minds not to meditate beforehand how to answer; for I will give you a mouth and wisdom, which none of your adversaries will be able to withstand or contradict [21:12–15].[33]

In addition to standing as a warning, Jesus' words also have the character of a prediction. For reasons that he does not explicitly indicate, Luke's Jesus has reached the conclusion that his disciples will find themselves in conflict with *kings* and *governors*.[34]

Jesus does not in any way suggest that the disciples seek to avoid such confrontations. They are not to turn from their course to remain on good terms with the authorities. On the contrary, they are to stand firm, and Jesus will give them the wisdom that they need to maintain their witness.

5. PERSPECTIVES ON JESUS' STANCE

Luke's reports in the three passages we have considered are consistent with one another and also with the information concerning Jesus' social stance given in other parts of his gospel. The common theme running through each of these passages, a theme which finds expression throughout Luke's gospel, is that there is nothing sacrosanct about the Roman social order. Jesus himself does not show deference to the officials who oversee this order. Whether they are officials of the stature of Herod Antipas or the Jerusalem chief priests, and even if they have the more exalted title of Benefactor, Jesus criticizes them freely. Moreover, Jesus does not submit to the social patterns and practices to which the Romans and their allies are committed. He rejects the violence and exploitation that they accept as a normal part of living, and his teachings and conduct run counter to many of the other patterns that they accept and endorse.

When the various elements present in Luke's description are related, Jesus is shown to be no particular friend of the Roman order. On the contrary, the social practices he espouses were profoundly at variance with those of the Roman order.

CHAPTER FIVE

The Trial and Death of Jesus

In this chapter our principal concern will be to analyze Luke's reports concerning the actions and interactions of the major figures present at Jesus' trial: the chief priests, Pontius Pilate, Herod Antipas, and Jesus himself. We will treat Jesus' responses to each of these authorities and try to reconstruct the motives that Luke ascribes to each of these four. Finally, we will analyze the verdicts that Pilate and Herod reach.

To the degree that it is possible for us to do so, we will also try to reconstruct the motives that Luke ascribes to each of these four principal persons and groups. We remarked earlier that Luke frequently describes what happened without giving a great deal of explanation about why it happened, and we will find that this is very much the case throughout his trial narrative.[1] While Luke's description of the chief priests' actions does not create any particular difficulties, this is not true for his description of Jesus' responses to Herod and Pilate and his description of their responses to him.

1. JESUS' ARREST AND THE HEARING BEFORE THE SANHEDRIN

We saw that the chief priests and their allies had decided to get rid of Jesus, and Luke subsequently tells us that they were glad when Judas approached them with his proposal to betray Jesus.[2] Luke next reports that after Jesus had celebrated the Last Supper with his disciples and had retired to the Mount of Olives to pray, Judas approached with a group that included the captain of the temple and other chief priests, the elders, and at least one of the high priest's servants. They seized Jesus and took him to the courtyard of the high priest's house where they kept him until daybreak, beating him and mocking him during the night hours. At daybreak the chief priests and scribes convened a session of the sanhedrin.

Luke's version of Jesus' arraignment before the sanhedrin differs considerably from Mark's and Matthew's, and a number of scholars believe that Luke relied substantially on personal sources for his account of this event and for his trial narrative as a whole.[3] In Luke the focus of the hearing is whether or not Jesus claimed to be the messiah; Luke does not mention a charge that Mark and Matthew emphasize, that Jesus boasted of destroying and rebuilding the temple.[4] Luke describes the council member's questions and Jesus' answers:

And they said, "If you are the Christ, tell us." But he said to them, "If I tell you, you will not believe; and if I ask you, you will not answer. But from now on the Son of man shall be seated at the right hand of the Power of God." And they all said, "Are you the Son of God, then?" And he said to them, "You say that I am." And they said, "What further testimony do we need? We have heard it ourselves from his own lips." Then the whole company of them arose, and brought him before Pilate [22:66–23:1].

Jesus' answer to their first question is searing. He first tells them that they are not capable of engaging in normal conversation, and then implies that he will ultimately receive vindication from God.[5] They challenge this by asking him whether he thinks that he is the Son of God;[6] his response is terse and noncommittal: "You say that I am."[7]

Although Jesus' replies (seemingly) did not suffice to establish a case against him, this does not appear to have mattered to the sanhedrin members. They claim they have the evidence they need, and they hurry him off to Pilate.[8]

2. JESUS BEFORE PILATE

On reaching Pilate, the sanhedrin members first indicate the charges they are bringing against Jesus:

And they began to accuse him, saying, "We found this man perverting our nation, and forbidding us to give tribute to Caesar, and saying that he himself is Christ a king" [23:2].[9]

In the light of the information that Luke has already given us about Jesus' teachings and ministry, how should we view these charges? Are all three true? Are all three false? Are one or two true and the remainder false?

Most commentators on Luke's gospel believe that the charges are false; we substantially concur.[10] The three charges represent serious distortions of Jesus' positions. Like all distortions, there is a degree of plausibility to each of them; but individually and collectively they do not give an accurate description of Jesus' specific positions and his overall stance.

The basic thrust of the charges is that Jesus had adopted a stance similar to the Zealots. He was, the sanhedrin members assert, seeking to throw off Roman rule and establish himself as king over the Jews of Palestine.[11] To see the distortion that these charges involved, it is helpful to view each of them in the context of what Luke has already told us about Jesus' social and political stance.

Had Jesus been "perverting" (or "misleading") the nation?[12] In the sense of calling for an armed revolution against Rome, the answer is no. He had been calling for radically new social patterns, and he had freely criticized the existing patterns and the authorities who maintained them, but he had not accepted the Zealots' position that Roman rule should be resisted by force of arms.

Had Jesus been forbidding the payment of tribute? We have already concluded that, while indicating the steps that should be followed in making such a decision, and while allowing for the possibility that tribute might be refused, Jesus did not explicitly commit himself to either tax payment or tax resistance.

Had Jesus been claiming to be "Christ a king?" While we have not systematically addressed the question of whether Jesus claimed that he was the Christ, it is clear that Jesus did not see himself as a kingly messiah and did not aspire to rule over Palestine in place of the Romans. Rather than seeking to establish a kingdom of his own, Luke's Jesus espouses social patterns and practices based on service and humility and does not take a definite position with regard to any of the existing forms of government.

According to Luke's description of the proceedings, after Pilate had heard the charges brought by the council members, he questioned Jesus about the third charge: "Are you the king of the Jews?" (23:3) The question was straightforward enough and since Pilate held life and death power over him, Jesus might have been expected to reply directly and courteously.[13] However, as Luke reports it, his reply was noncommittal and showed no particular deference. He gave approximately the same reply that he had given to the sanhedrin members' second question: "You have said so" (23:3).[14]

What was Pilate's next step? Luke records no further interrogation, nor does he indicate that Pilate paused to weigh the various factors involved. Instead, Pilate turns to the chief priests and the multitudes and announces his conclusion: "I find no crime in this man" (23:4).[15]

In summary we present the entire passage that we have considered in this section. We would again emphasize the character of Luke's trial descriptions, that is, that he frequently tells us how persons and groups acted without indicating their motivations for doing so:

And Pilate asked him, "Are you the King of the Jews?" And he answered him, "You have said so." And Pilate said to the chief priests and the multitudes, "I find no crime in this man." But they were urgent, saying, "He stirs up the people, teaching throughout all Judea, from Galilee even to this place. When Pilate heard this, he asked whether the man was a Galilean. And when he learned that he belonged to Herod's jurisdiction, he sent him over to Herod, who was himself in Jerusalem at that time [23:2–7].

3. THE HEARING BEFORE HEROD ANTIPAS

In the concluding verse of the passage above Luke implies that since Jesus was a Galilean Herod possessed some jurisdiction over him. This point is subsequently strengthened when Pilate comments (after Herod has sent Jesus back to him) that Herod did not find Jesus guilty of any of the charges against him. Pilate seems to assume that Herod could have rendered a verdict of guilty if he had chosen to do so. However, Luke's description does not go beyond this; it does not give us any information regarding the official Roman guidelines that governed such situations. Even though Luke does not indicate what would have happened if Herod had returned a verdict of guilty, the sense of his account is that Herod's interrogation of Jesus was of considerable importance.

Against such a background, how does Luke depict Jesus before Herod? The following passage describes the interaction:

When Herod saw Jesus, he was very glad, for he had long desired to see him, because he had heard about him and he was hoping to see some sign done by him. So he questioned him at some length; but he made no answer. The chief priests and the scribes stood by, vehemently accusing him. And Herod and his soldiers treated him with contempt and mocked him; then, arraying him in gorgeous apparel, he sent him back to Pilate. And Herod and Pilate became friends with each other that very day, for before this they had been at enmity with each other [23:8–12].[16]

Earlier Luke had indicated that Herod was seeking to kill Jesus; now, however, he is eager to see Jesus do some sign.[17] Since Herod held at least some power over Jesus and his verdict had some influence over whether Jesus lived or died, it is striking that Jesus refuses to cooperate with him; he refuses to answer any of his questions.

Luke does not tell us here why Jesus refused to cooperate with Herod; accordingly, any interpretation of Jesus' silence has to be based on other passages in Luke or on information derived from other, independent sources. In our view, the most appropriate starting point for any interpretation is the other passages in Luke's gospel that record Jesus' interaction with various political authorities. The interpretations of commentators who have not taken account of these other reports do not provide fully satisfactory explanations.[18]

We would also note here that the chief priests and the scribes have been present, vigorously pressing their case against Jesus. This element in Luke's description of the hearing before Herod is frequently overlooked, but it is of considerable importance.[19] The scene has shifted from Pilate's quarters to Herod's, but here again are the chief priests, relentlessly hammering their accusations against Jesus.

4. JESUS AGAIN BEFORE PILATE

The next part of Jesus' trial takes place before Pilate:

Pilate then called together the chief priests and the rulers and the people, and said to them, "You brought me this man as one who was perverting the people; and after examining him before you, behold, I did not find this man guilty of any of your charges against him; neither did Herod, for he sent him back to us. Behold, nothing deserving death has been done by him; I will therefore chastise him and release him" [23:13–16].

Here there are three points that we should briefly take account of. First, Pilate's exoneration of Jesus is complete. He states that Jesus is not guilty "of any of your charges against him." Second, Pilate indicates that this is Herod's judgment as well. Our third point is implicit in the second, for in making reference to Herod's findings, Pilate implies that he regards Herod as qualified to judge whether Jesus is dangerous to Roman rule or not. Whatever their previous differences may have been, Pilate still regards Herod as a Roman ally, competent to judge concerning Rome's interests.[20]

We now come to the passage in Luke's trial narrative that New Testament scholars have frequently focused on in advancing the argument that Luke wanted to develop a "political apologetic" for Christianity. Luke twice describes Pilate as reaffirming his initial decision—within the space of six verses. This strong affirmation of Jesus' innocence, supporters of the political apologetic position maintain, is due to Luke's concern about the hearing Christianity would receive within the Roman empire.[21] By showing Pilate, the Roman governor, so emphatically affirming Jesus' innocence, Luke was striving to make it clear that the Roman empire had nothing to fear from Jesus or any of his followers.

Before presenting our own interpretation, let us first cite Luke's next six verses, which immediately follow Pilate's declaration that he will chastise Jesus and release him:

> But they all cried out together, "Away with this man, and release to us Barabbas"—a man who had been thrown into prison for an insurrection started in the city, and for murder. Pilate addressed them once more, desiring to release Jesus, but they shouted out, "Crucify, crucify him!" A third time he said to them, "Why, what evil has he done? I will therefore chastise him and release him." But they were urgent, demanding with loud cries that he should be crucified. And their voices prevailed [23:18–23].

Our own view is that Luke's concern is not to establish Jesus' loyalty and submissiveness to the Roman empire, but rather to indicate in unmistakable terms that the chief priests and their allies were the ones primarily responsible for Jesus' ultimate fate. There is much to support such an interpretation, not only in the passage above, but also in the rest of Luke's account.

Consider what Luke has thus far told us about the chief priests' motives for wanting to destroy Jesus and their efforts to do so. The chief priests initially decide to kill Jesus after his protest at the temple,[22] and Jesus' attack on them in the parable of the wicked tenants subsequently confirms their resolve.[23] They formulate a plan to denounce Jesus to the Roman governor, and they send spies to entrap him with a question on the payment of tribute.[24] They are not immediately successful, but they are happy when a new opportunity presents itself in the person of Judas.[25] They organize and participate in Jesus' arrest,[26] and they are responsible for the beating he receives in the high priest's courtyard.[27] As the leading members of the sanhedrin,[28] they interrogate Jesus and hand him over to Pilate just as they had planned to do all along.[29]

In the trial before Pilate they assume the role of prosecutors.[30] They bring charges against Jesus and reiterate them when Pilate's initial inclination is to find Jesus innocent.[31] Not willing to have Herod make an independent examination, the chief priests and the scribes follow Jesus from Pilate to Herod and keep pressing their attack against him.[32] Subsequently, they hear Pilate announce his decision to chastise Jesus and release him, but they will not agree to such an outcome. They cry out for Jesus' death and ask for Barabbas' release.[33] Pilate remonstrates with them, but they mount the chant, "Crucify, crucify him."[34] Pilate again indicates his unwillingness to do this, but they intensify their outburst until Pilate finally relents.[35]

In Luke's account no other person or group plays a role comparable to that of the chief priests and their allies in bringing about Jesus' death. The Pharisees receive no mention.[36] Judas does little more than provide the priests with an opportunity.[37] Satan is present, but as a behind-the-scenes actor.[38] The crowds appear late in the proceedings, and only join in with what the priests have already begun.[39]

Herod Antipas mocks and reviles Jesus, but ultimately recommends that he be released. We shall see below that Pilate does have a degree of responsibility, but the role that Luke attributes to him is minor in comparison with that which he attributes to the chief priests, the scribes, and the elders. They are the ones who initially conspire to bring about Jesus' death and who strive to achieve this goal at every step of the proceedings.

In the light of these considerations, what interpretation should be given to Luke's report in the passage we have cited? Is its primary meaning that Pilate three times pronounced Jesus innocent? Or rather is it not that the chief priests pressured Pilate so aggressively that he eventually bowed to their demands? In our view, there is considerably more support for the latter interpretation.[40]

One additional observation needs to be made with respect to Luke's reports concerning the persons and groups who were responsible for Jesus' death. Luke shows quite precisely and specifically that it was the chief priests and their allies who brought about Jesus' death, but he does not in any way infer that the Jewish people as a whole were involved,[41] or even that the chief priests were the representatives of the Jewish populace.[42] Unfortunately, too many of Luke's commentators still frequently overlook this nuance in Luke's account. They try to determine the degree to which Luke emphasizes "Jewish responsibility" (as opposed to Roman responsibility) for Jesus' death;[43] but, as we have seen, Luke does not attribute significant responsibility to any Jewish group other than the chief priests and their allies.

5. JESUS' CRUCIFIXION

Luke's description of Jesus' execution does not diminish the responsibility of the chief priests and their allies for Jesus' death. Luke indicates that Roman soldiers, acting on Pilate's orders, took Jesus outside the city and crucified him but he does so in a way that does not de-emphasize the leading role that the chief priests have played.

In the four passages below Luke does not explicitly state that the Romans executed Jesus. Instead, he gives indirect signs that point to their involvement. Considered together, these signs clearly establish a degree of Roman responsibility; however, everything still takes place under the impetus of the chief priests.

So Pilate gave sentence that their demand should be granted. He released the man who had been thrown into prison for insurrection and murder, whom they asked for; but Jesus he delivered up to their will. And as they led him away, they seized one Simon of Cyrene, who was coming in from the country, and laid on him the cross, to carry it behind Jesus [23:24–26].

And when they came to the place which is called The Skull, there they crucified him, and the criminals, one on the right and one on the left. And Jesus said, "Father, forgive them; for they know not what they do." And they cast lots to divide his garments. And the people stood by, watching; but the rulers scoffed at him, saying, "He saved others; let him save himself, if he is the Christ of God, his Chosen One!" The soldiers also mocked him, coming up and offering him vinegar, and saying, "If you are the King of the Jews, save yourself!" There was also an inscription over him, "This is the King of the Jews" [23:33–38].

Now, when the centurion saw what had taken place, he praised God, and said, "Certainly, this man was innocent!" [23:47].

This man went to Pilate and asked for the body of Jesus [23:52].

In the first passage it is not initially clear who is leading Jesus away. Either Pilate's soldiers or the chief priests and the temple police might be referred to by the pronoun "they" in the third verse.[44] However, when Luke subsequently indicates that Simon of Cyrene was constrained to carry the cross, we realize that Jesus is to die by crucifixion, the form of execution that the Romans usually employed.[45] That Roman soldiers actually put Jesus to death is confirmed by information that Luke subsequently gives us.

The second passage states that Jesus was crucified under an inscription which read, "This is the King of the Jews." The use of such an inscription and the description of Jesus' offense as an offense against Roman rule both indicate that it was the Romans who actually carried out his execution.[46] (The inscription's meaning is that Jesus had opposed Roman rule by trying to establish himself as a king over the Jews.) Further confirmation comes from the Roman centurion's presence, indicated in the third passage above.[47] After witnessing Jesus' death and the subsequent miraculous events, the centurion testifies to Jesus' innocence. His exclamation is rendered even more dramatic given the likelihood that he had been in charge of Jesus' crucifixion.

The fourth passage cited above is excerpted from a longer description concerning Joseph of Arimathea.[48] To gain possession of Jesus' body, Joseph had to secure Pilate's permission. The fact that Pilate had retained jurisdiction over Jesus' body is a further indication that the crucifixion had been carried out by Roman soldiers acting under Pilate's directions.

Luke's passion account does therefore indicate that the Romans carried out Jesus' execution. However, Luke gives us this information in the context of other reports that indicate that the chief priests and their allies played the leading role in bringing about Jesus' death. The chief priests pressure and persuade Pilate to serve their purposes, and Pilate eventually bends to their will.[49]

6. JESUS' RESPONSES TO HIS JUDGES

We have already referred to Jesus' response to the questions of the chief priests and other sanhedrin members, his response to

Pilate's single question, and his refusal to answer any of Herod's questions. We will now analyze the general pattern that these responses form and view them against the background of what Luke has already told us about Jesus' social and political stance.

Jesus did not cooperate with or defer to the authorities who judged him: This conclusion emerges from a consideration of Luke's report of Jesus' four responses at his trial. Luke has already indicated that Jesus had little regard for the chief priests. He would have been even less likely to cooperate with them now that they were openly seeking his death. It therefore is not surprising that Jesus answers their first question by telling them that it is useless for him to try to respond to them.[50] Nor is it surprising that he gives a terse and noncommittal reply to their second question.[51]

Since Luke does not show Pilate and Herod actively seeking Jesus' death, their case is somewhat different. Seemingly it would be in Jesus' interest to cooperate with them, yet Luke indicates that he did not do so.

When Jesus is brought before Pilate, he has already been beaten by the chief priests or their subordinates, and the hearing before the sanhedrin has confirmed that the chief priests have every intention of seeing him put to death. It seems that Pilate holds Jesus' only hope of remaining alive. In this context Jesus' reply to Pilate's question, "Are you the king of the Jews?" is all the more remarkable. It is the same kind of terse, noncommittal answer that he gave to the second question of the sanhedrin members: "You have said so."[52]

Before a sanhedrin dominated by the chief priests,[53] Jesus was in extremely hostile surroundings, and in such circumstances such a reply would be highly appropriate. Before Pilate, the situation was more favorable to Jesus; yet Jesus gave virtually the same reply as he had previously given to the council members. Conceivably Jesus could have repudiated the chief priests' charges and indicated their treacherousness. Or he might have tried to give Pilate an accurate description of his own position. But he does neither. Instead he runs the risk of antagonizing Pilate by turning the question back to him.

Nearly the same pattern is repeated when Jesus is interrogated by Herod. Luke indicates that Pilate was inclined to release Jesus, but, feeling himself under pressure from the chief priests, he decided to pass the matter on to Herod. Thus, by implication, what Herod decides will have a considerable influence upon whether Jesus lives or dies, and it will be to Jesus' benefit to have Herod return a favorable verdict.

Since he was present when Pilate announced his own favorable view, and since he would easily appreciate Pilate's purpose in sending him to Herod, Jesus presumably recognizes how important it is to create a favorable impression with Herod. Yet he does not take pains to do so; in fact, he refused to answer any of the questions Herod put to him.

What are we to make of Jesus' positions in each of the above instances? Why does Jesus reply to Pilate as he does, and why does he refuse to answer any of Herod's questions when it would have been in his interests to be cooperative and deferential.

We have said that Luke frequently describes people's actions without giving much information about why they take them. We noted that Jesus' response to Pilate and Herod were leading examples of this. Indeed, if the body of Luke's gospel had somehow become separated from his trial narrative, and only the latter chapters had reached us, further understanding of Jesus' responses to Pilate and Herod would be virtually impossible.

Fortunately, however, we can use the rest of Luke's account to throw additional light on Jesus' responses. An important insight from our earlier chapters now needs to be recalled: In Luke's gospel Jesus shows virtually no deference to any of the political authorities to whom he theoretically owes allegiance.[54]

When we recall Jesus' earlier refusal to alter his ministry as a consequence of Herod's threat and his refusal to accord any privileged position to the Roman empire in responding to the tribute question, the lack of cooperation that Luke attributes to him at his trial becomes considerably more understandable. Indeed, seen against the backdrop of Jesus' earlier sarcastic references to "benefactors" who dominate their subjects and his deprecating reference to Herod as "that fox," Jesus' lack of deference to both Pilate and Herod is surprisingly consistent with his earlier response to them or their counterparts.

We should also recall here the great differences between the patterns that Jesus advocated and those in effect around him. Jesus' approach to material possessions and that followed by Herod and the top Roman officials could hardly have been greater. Similarly, Jesus' advocacy of an enhanced status and new roles for women put him at variance with the social patterns that these authorities supported. Again, Jesus' rejection of the use of violence contrasted startlingly with the violence and domination upon which Roman rule was premised. In general, Luke shows Jesus as deeply committed to establishing social relationships based upon service and humility; since such qualities were little valued in the society around him, there was a constant tension between his positions and those sanctioned by the existing order.

On one occasion Jesus specifically contrasted his own service-oriented practices with those based on domination, and criticized the kings of the Gentiles for adopting the latter. He also indicates that "the things of Caesar" should be evaluated on a similar basis. Just as Jesus withheld his approval from rulers whose practices were not based on service and humility during his ministry, he continued to do so during his trial. Just as he refused to acknowledge their eminence during the period of his teaching, he refused to do so at his arraignment. To be sure, the atmosphere prevailing at the trial is considerably different from that which prevailed earlier in his ministry;[55] nevertheless, the stance which Luke shows Jesus adopting toward Pilate and Herod at his trial is substantially the same as that which he had previously adopted. It is not a stance of either cooperation or deference.

7. THE VERDICTS OF PILATE AND HEROD

Just as Luke does not tell us much about why Jesus responded to Pilate and Herod as he did, he tells us almost nothing about why Pilate and Herod both found Jesus innocent of the chief priests' charges. Luke describes Pilate's initial conclusion as follows:

And Pilate asked him, "Are you the King of the Jews?" And he answered him, "You have said so." And Pilate said to the chief priests and the multitudes, "I find no crime in this man" [23:3–4].

Since the sanhedrin had held a formal hearing, since the council members' charges against Jesus were grave, and since Jesus responded tersely and noncommittally to Pilate's single question, Pilate seemingly had good reason for finding Jesus guilty. Yet immediately after questioning him, Pilate declares: "I find no crime in this man." A short while later, he states that Herod too has found Jesus innocent.

We might hope to find in Luke's previous reports about Pilate and Herod some clue that would help to explain the verdicts they later reached, but Luke gives us very little information regarding either Pilate or Herod.[56] In a general way Luke's account indicates that (as we might expect) they were interested in maintaining Roman rule;[57] but he tells us very little about how they made judgments about persons and events. This contrasts with Luke's relatively ample information about the way in which Jesus evaluated various persons and practices.

Luke's earlier chapters do, however, indicate something about Jesus that helps us gain a perspective on the response that Pilate and Herod made to him at his trial: As we have seen, Luke's various descriptions clearly establish that Jesus was not a Zealot.[58]

The basic thrust of the chief priests' accusations against Jesus was that he had taken a position similar to that of the Zealots. They alleged that he wished to overturn Roman rule and install himself as a king over the Jews. Our interpretation is that even though Jesus would not cooperate with them, both Pilate and Herod still discerned almost immediately that Jesus was not a Zealot or comparable to the Zealots and that the chief priests' charges were therefore false.

From Luke's trial account we only know that Pilate and Herod found Jesus innocent, and, on the limited information that Luke has given us elsewhere, we cannot say a great deal about their reasons for doing so. There are other explanations for their decision which would not contradict Luke's narrative;[59] but in our view this explanation best correlates with Luke's overall account. They could see that Jesus had done something to earn him the chief priests' enmity, but this was not an affair in which they should become entangled. Their main objective was to safeguard the Roman sway over Palestine, and it was clear that Jesus did not pose the kind of threat to Roman rule that the Zealots did.

CHAPTER SIX

Was Jesus Dangerous to the Roman Empire?

To summarize our findings and place them in perspective, we pose the question: Was Jesus as Luke has portrayed him dangerous to the Roman empire? We have seen that according to Luke, Pilate and Herod found Jesus innocent, judging that he did not constitute a serious threat to Roman rule. But were they correct? Based upon Luke's extensive information concerning Jesus' social and political stance, our conclusion is that they were not. Although he consistently rejected the use of violence against persons and was not a Zealot, Jesus still posed a threat to Roman rule.

1. LUKE'S DESCRIPTION OF JESUS' STANCE

In his teaching and ministry, Jesus in Luke espouses a concern for persons and groups from all social levels and backgrounds, but especially for the poor and the sick, for women and Gentiles.[1] In some instances Jesus expressed this concern in ways not particularly disruptive of the existing social patterns, and not particularly challenging to those who benefited from them; but more often than not he taught and acted in such a way as to explicitly or implicitly call for radical modifications in these patterns.

This is especially evident with respect to the use of material possessions. Luke includes many passages that pertain to this theme of Jesus' ministry; considered together, they form a truly striking picture. As we have seen, Luke indicates that Jesus adopted an extremely strong position against surplus possessions.[2] Jesus himself lived simply and sparingly and he praised others like Zaccheus when they took steps to do likewise. However, even more important (in terms of its disruptive effect) Jesus stringently criticized the rich for accumulating possessions that they did not need instead of sharing their goods with the poor and the hungry.

While Luke does not give as much information about Jesus' stance toward women as he does about his stance toward the poor, the rich, and the use of material possessions, it is clear that this too was an area in which Jesus' teaching and practice were potentially disruptive.[3] In particular, Jesus' practice of travelling with women not related to him or the apostles through marital or family bonds was greatly at variance with the prevailing social patterns.[4]

Jesus' insistence that social relationships be governed by the themes of service and humility constituted a third serious challenge to the existing social order.[5] We have seen that this order was premised upon domination and exploitation and that violence (or the threat of violence) was central to its effective operation.[6] Jesus, in contrast, rejected the use of violence and criticized the Gentile kings for their practice of dominating over their subjects.[7] He also emphasized that the spirit of humility and service was to be carried through in everyday living. Those who would be his disciples should not allow themselves to seek prominent places at banquets or compete with one another in seeking other forms of honors.[8]

Moreover, Jesus constituted, at least potentially, a serious threat to the Roman empire because he refused to defer to or cooperate with the various political officials who were responsible for maintaining those patterns.

Responding to the question concerning the payment of tribute, Jesus took the position that the Roman emperor and empire were not to be accorded an autonomous or privileged position within the order of creation; they were rather to be evaluated on the basis of how closely they corresponded to the patterns desired by God.[9] Luke also shows Jesus maintaining this same critical stance with respect to Caesar's local officials: Pontius Pilate and Herod Antipas. The points of contact between them and Jesus are relatively few (Jesus' only real contact with Pilate is at the time of his trial); but in Luke's description Jesus never defers to either Pilate or Herod and is outspokenly critical of Herod, "that fox."[10]

Jesus' response to the chief priests and the other sanhedrin members is similar except that Jesus is far more explicitly critical of them and their practices. To some extent, they too had official positions within the existing social order, yet Jesus never shows deference to them either as religious or political leaders. Indeed, Luke tells us that it was Jesus' aggressive action in protesting their administration of the temple that eventually led to his death. Jesus refused to justify his conduct when they questioned him about it; then in the parable of the wicked tenants, he vigorously attacked them as irresponsible and murderous stewards. At his hearing before the sanhedrin, Jesus maintained this defiant stance, telling them that he would not answer their questions because they would not take his answers seriously.[11]

Was Jesus dangerous to the Roman empire? The two factors that we have just elaborated make it clear that he was, at least potentially, a serious threat to the continuance of Roman rule in Palestine and to the empire itself. If large numbers of people ever came to support the new social patterns that Luke portrays Jesus advocating, and if large numbers came to adopt his stance toward the ruling political authorities, the Roman empire (or indeed, any other similarly-based social order) could not have continued.

Although Jesus did not constitute the same type of threat to Roman rule as the Zealots and the Parthians, the threat that he posed was, ultimately, not less dangerous. Unlike the Zealots, the Jesus of Luke's gospel does not make the overthrow of Roman rule the central focus of his activity, nor does he support any of the other forms of government (including that probably advocated by the Zealots) that might have been considered as replacements for Roman rule. Nevertheless, by espousing radically new social patterns and by refusing to defer to the existing political authorities, Jesus pointed the way to a social order in which neither the Romans nor any other oppressing group would be able to hold sway.[12]

2. LUKE'S JESUS AND MOHANDAS GANDHI

Any effort to make a thorough-going analysis of the similarities and differences between the social and political stance of Luke's Jesus and that of Mohandas Gandhi would carry us far beyond the limits of our present study; but, by making a few comparisons, we can more graphically illustrate the principal conclusions that we have reached.[13] We have argued that Luke's Jesus was potentially a danger to the Roman empire. We would now suggest that he was so in approximately the same way that Gandhi was dangerous to British rule in India.

Gandhi, it will be recalled, came to envision a society profoundly different from that which he saw around him in India. He had a utopian vision of a transformed society in which poverty, disease, and hunger would be eradicated, and in which India's opprobrious caste system would no longer operate. He also foresaw a favorable resolution of the traditional hostilities between Hindus and Moslems.

Nonviolence, *ahimsa*, occupied a prominent position in Gandhi's overall stance. He described his basic approach as *satyagraha* (literally, "truth-force") and he regarded ahimsa as the crucial test for satyagraha. He believed that significant and lasting social change could take place only if the oppressor and the enemy could be converted, and he held that nonviolent struggle was the only efffective way for bringing about such conversion. Gandhi's convictions regarding nonviolence were closely tied to his concept of God. He saw God primarily in terms of truth and held that each person, including enemies, embodied something of the truth that pertained to God. The beauty of nonviolent struggle, he maintained, was that it allowed this truth to emerge.

At different periods in Gandhi's public career, the social dimension of his stance had greater or lesser importance in comparison with his more explicitly political activities. Early in his career, he combined an emphasis on social reform with opposition to specific British policies and headed the Congress movement, whose purpose was to prepare India for self-rule. Then, from 1932 to 1942, he turned away from explicitly political activity in order to concentrate on promoting the grassroots renewal of Indian village life through such measures as village spinning industries and village sanitation projects. In 1942 he returned to the political arena to campaign vigorously for the end of British rule under the slogan "Quit India."

We should also note how the British themselves regarded Gandhi. Clearly, if large numbers of Indians were to adopt Gandhi's general stance, then continued British rule in India would eventually become impossible; similarly, if other subject peoples throughout the British empire began to espouse a similar approach, the empire itself would be placed in jeopardy. What was the British response? At various times the British authorities imprisoned him; yet in general they did not seem to regard him as a serious threat to their position. Even after Gandhi had gained substantial support, Churchill and other English officials were not nearly as concerned about him as they were about the more avowedly militant members of the Congress party and their Moslem counterparts.

There are remarkable similarities between what Luke tells us about Jesus and what we know about Gandhi. Both advocated social patterns that were considerably in advance of those that prevailed in the society around them. To varying degrees, both refused to defer to the political authorities who were responsible for maintaining the existing social order. Both possessed strong religious faith. Both emphasized nonviolence. Both were judged not to constitute a serious threat to the ruling colonial power (this was true for Gandhi at least initially).

These parallels are not exact; moreover, there were important differences in Jesus' and Gandhi's respective situations. Although both lived under colonial powers, there were significant differences between Palestine's situation under Roman rule and India's situation under British rule. Although Gandhi was assassinated by a member of the dominant religious group (he was killed by N.V. Godse, a member of one branch of the militant Hindu nationalist organization Mahasabha), no group of Hindu leaders operated against him in the way that Luke describes the chief priests systematically operating against Jesus. Nevertheless, the similarities in their respective approaches are close enough to be highly instructive. And, by reflecting about the stance that Gandhi adopted in the twentieth century, we are better able to appreciate Luke's description of the stance that Jesus adopted in the first.

3. OTHER INTERPRETATIONS OF JESUS' STANCE

In Appendix IV we respond to Conzelmann's interpretation of Jesus' social and political stance in Luke. Here we also want briefly to take account of several influential studies that have drawn upon material from all the gospels (as opposed to working within the confines of a single gospel) in making their interpretations of Jesus' stance. Criticizing their results will enable us to further develop our own argument and will also demonstrate the contrast between our conclusions and the views that currently prevail in New Testament studies.

Since the conclusions that we have reached apply only to Luke's gospel, we cannot use them to make a definitive criticism of the positions taken by scholars who have drawn upon all four gospels. While our criticisms cannot be definitive, they can nevertheless be *substantial*, because in making their judgments about Jesus' social and political stance, these scholars have a responsibility to take account of the material in Luke's gospel. If there are important discrepancies between their conclusions and the findings that we have made, we can criticize them for failing to reflect adequately the information contained in Luke's account. This in itself would be serious, and it would also raise questions about how adequately they had interpreted the other gospels.

The following citation from Alan Richardson's recent work, *The Political Christ*, contains conclusions representative of his study:

The only directly political utterance of Jesus is the pronouncement "Render unto Caesar" at the conclusion of the story of the tribute money in Mark 12:13–17 (the parallel versions in Matt. 22:15–22 and Luke 20:22–26 may be regarded as the earliest commentaries upon it). . . . Unmoved by nationalist prejudice, Jesus asserts the duty of paying one's dues to the *de facto* authority responsible for law and order, but without in any way reducing the claims of God. Judas of Galilee had raised an insurrection after the original imposition of the census: Jesus of Galilee was no upholder of the so-called "fourth philosophy."[14]

Our conclusions concerning Jesus' criticism of various political leaders demonstrate the deficiencies in Richardson's position. Moreover, Luke ascribes several "directly political" statements to Jesus; he does not show Jesus approving the payment of tribute; and to describe Jesus' social and political stance by stating, as Richardson does, that he was not a Zealot, is an extremely limited description.[15]

The deficiencies in the assessments of Rudolf Schnackenburg in his *The Moral Teaching of the New Testament* are less glaring than Richardson's, but almost equally serious. In the representative passage cited below, Schnackenburg indicates that Jesus' purposes were "religious" and "moral" and that he was not interested in "worldly affairs."

It is a grotesque misinterpretation to characterize him as a social revolutionary because of what he said against the rich, or as the planner of a new social order (cf. Tolstoi) on the basis of his precept to renounce revenge, or as a communist on account of his commandment to love one's neighbor, or as a pacifist in the political sense because of his commandment to love one's enemies, or as an opponent of learning and civilization because of his attacks on the Scribes. All these forms of radicalism are orientated towards this world: none of them can appeal to him for support, for they misconstrue his basic purposes in these pronouncements, purposes which are wholly religious and moral. For his own part, he did not allow himself to become involved in "worldly affairs."[16]

But we have seen that Luke does not show Jesus positioning any dichotomy between the so-called religious sphere and the so-called worldly sphere.[17] Further, Luke's descriptions of Jesus as critical of various political rulers clearly runs counter to Schnackenburg's assertion that Jesus was not involved in "worldly affairs."

These references from two fairly recent and (particularly in Schnackenburg's case) influential works should provide some indication of the context for our own work. We will also briefly note two short works by Martin Hengel and two works by Oscar Cullmann.

Hengel's two works, *Victory Over Violence* and *Was Jesus a Revolutionist?*, both address the subject of Jesus' responses to violence and to the Zealot movement. Hengel's main point is that Jesus rejected the use of violence and that this differentiated him from the Zealots. With these two conclusions we concur, and our own analysis of Luke's account provides additional support for Hengel's argument. However, because Hengel does not contrast Jesus' nonviolence with the violence of the Romans and because he does not situate Jesus' nonviolence within the context of his overall social and political stance, he portrays Jesus as more complacent about the existing social and political conditions than Luke's account allows.[18]

While Luke indicates that Jesus rejected the use of violence against persons, he also indicates that Jesus frequently challenged and contravened the social patterns that the Romans and their allies maintained. Hengel fails to recognize adequately this latter aspect of Jesus' stance, and as a consequence his almost exclusive emphasis upon Jesus' rejection of the Zealot position results in a serious distortion. Indeed, Hengel's interpretation implies that Jesus indirectly aided the Romans by counselling his disciples not to follow the example of the Zealots; but, as we have seen, Jesus was far from being even an indirect supporter of the Romans.[19]

Cullmann's two works, *The State in the New Testament* and *Jesus and the Revolutionaries*, contain a number of helpful insights, but also serious weaknesses. In the former, Cullmann maintains that although Jesus did not regard the state as a "final" institution, he still accepted it and "radically renounces every attempt to overthrow it."[20] As we have argued above, this is not the stance that Luke shows Jesus adopting toward the Roman empire. In Luke's account, Jesus does not renounce *every* effort (nonviolent efforts are acceptable) to bring about widespread changes in the Roman social order.[21]

In Cullman's second work he assumes that a dichotomy exists between personal conversion and a "social reform program" and maintains that Jesus was interested only in the former.[22]

An analysis of Luke's account does not support such an interpretation. In Luke's description, an important element in Jesus' call is that he requires the disciples to commit themselves to new social patterns and practices.[23]

4. CONCLUDING THOUGHTS
ON LUKE'S ENTERPRISE

At the outset of this book we argued that one of Luke' primary concerns in writing his gospel was to provide the Christian communities of his day with important information regarding Jesus' life and ministry. Now at the conclusion of our study we pause to acknowledge the importance of his contribution and affirm his remarkable achievement.

Our study has focused upon only one dimension of Luke's description of Jesus, Jesus' social and political stance; but in this one area alone Luke has made a great amount of information and many important insights available to us. In a variety of ways he has sharpened and supplemented Mark's descriptions, and he has provided us with material that we would lack if we had only the gospels of Mark, Matthew, and John. In addition, Luke has preserved this material in a clear and well-organized manner. The nature of our own analysis has not allowed us to consider the movement of Luke's gospel as a whole, but, on the basis of what we have considered, we would still join with those who have acclaimed it "the most beautiful book in the world."

Is Luke's description of Jesus' social and political stance to be relied upon? Does his description really allow us to know Jesus of Nazareth and what he actually said and did? Our objective has been to understand the description that Luke has given us, and we have not treated most questions about the reliability of Luke's account.

Certainly in the years between Jesus' death and the time of Luke's writing, there were ample opportunities for errors to be made and for those who handed on the traditions about Jesus (including Luke himself) to alter them in such a way that Luke's final account could contain as much distortion as accuracy. On the other hand, we know that Luke wanted to write "an orderly account," and we also know that Luke's descriptions relative to empire history are, in fact, amazingly accurate.

We find these latter two considerations persuasive and are thus inclined to hold that the stance Luke attributes to Jesus corresponds to the stance that Jesus actually had. It can be argued, however, that such a position is as much a matter of perspective as it is of reasoned analysis and judgment, and this we are willing to admit. *Do Luke's descriptions give an accurate portrayal of Jesus' stance?* In the end, given the lack of conclusive evidence, it is likely that any reply will hinge on one's personal perspective. *What kind of social and political stance does Luke attribute to Jesus?* This is a question more susceptible to resolution through analysis and argument, and it is to this question that our study has been addressed.

The Romans and the Herods

The writings of the ancient historians Josephus and Tacitus, the works of the ancient Jewish philosopher Philo, the Old Testament, inter-testamental and rabbinic writings, and the findings of modern archeologists, numismatists, and epigraphers provide us with an abundance of material.[1] It is important, however, to recognize that none of the sources available to us can be used uncritically. Josephus, on whom we shall be relying extensively, has his own particular biases as well as his own particular interests and concerns; the same is also true of Philo and Tacitus.[2] With respect to the Old Testament, inter-testamental, and rabbinic literature, we are on ground that is more sound if we recognize that the processes by which they finally came to written form may well be comparable in complexity to those by which the gospels were produced. With respect to coins, inscriptions, and archeological reconstructions, it is important to recognize that the information gained from these sources always needs to be integrated with and clarified by the information gained from literary sources.

Here we will summarize the *political* (in the sense of *governmental*) arrangements that were in effect for Judea and Galilee at the time of Jesus. During most of Jesus' lifetime, that is from A.D. 6 onward, Judea was ruled directly by Roman governors. In contrast, Galilee constituted the main portion of a small neighboring tetrarchy administered by a local, Roman-approved ruler, Herod Antipas. These arrangements had not been in effect very long, however, and had come about as a result of the interaction of a number of persons and groups. These conditions were far from stable.

1. FROM INDEPENDENCE TO ROMAN CONTROL

From approximately 200 to 175 B.C., the Seleucids, descendants of one of Alexander the Great's generals, ruled over much of Palestine. However, in 175 a Jewish group consisting of members of the Maccabean family and their followers entered into armed resistance against the Seleucids and eventually wrested Judea and other territories of Palestine from Seleucid control. The rise to power of the Maccabees (or Hasmoneans as their descendants were called) meant considerable political freedom for the Jewish inhabitants of Judea, Galilee, and the neighboring territories. For the first time in hundreds of years, they were governed by rulers of their own religious faith.[3]

The Hasmoneans initially enjoyed widespread popular support as a consequence of the victories they had won. This enabled them to establish themselves as princes, although they had not originally been one of the families to whom the Jews were accustomed to look for religious (or political) leadership. In time, the Hasmoneans attempted to consolidate their position as princes by proclaiming themselves hereditary high priests. Because the high priest's office had traditionally been restricted to priests of Zadokite descent, there was popular opposition to this move, but the Hasmoneans maneuvered the change in such a way as to win approval for it in a plebiscite.[4]

With the secular office of prince and the religious office of high priest under their control,[5] the Hasmoneans seemed to be secure in their control of Palestine, particularly of its heavily Jewish areas (especially since the Seleucid kingdom continued to decline). However, not long after these arrangements had come into effect, a bitter quarrel developed within the family itself, and both factions took the fateful step of appealing to the Roman general Pompey for help.[6] In the end, the Romans sided with the Hasmonean leader Hyrcanus II, and his Idumean ally, Antipater; but a more important consequence than the "victory" of Hyrcanus was that the Romans were now established in the area of Palestine.

2. THE RULE OF HEROD THE GREAT

Because he had displayed considerable military ability and political acumen throughout a period of extreme turbulence, the Romans eventually chose one of Antipater's sons, Herod, to administer their interests in Palestine. In addition to his other abilities, Herod had proved himself adroit in shifting his allegiance to whichever Roman leader emerged victorious in a particular power struggle. Josephus reports that when Herod had first gone to Rome to petition support from Antony and Octavian (who later took the name Caesar Augustus), he had not expected to obtain the title and power of king. Because of his father's Idumean background, Herod's relationship with the Jewish population of Palestine was not strong.[7] Because of this and because there were members of the Hasmonean family capable of serving as kings, he may have supposed that the Romans would prefer to install a Hasmonean in that office.[8] Nevertheless, presented with the chance to rule, Herod did not let the opportunity slip through his fingers, and he immediately began to deal with the obstacles that still remained.

Herod's first hurdle was to defeat the rival Hasmonean faction and secure the death of its leader. This he accomplished through the military support Antony arranged for him.[9] He was, however, still faced with the problem of gaining the allegiance of his Jewish subjects, who were accustomed to look upon him as an ally of the Hasmonean faction led by Hyrcanus and not qualified to rule them in his own right.

Herod's first concern was to remove any Jewish leaders or groups who constituted a threat to his position.[10] To this end he arranged to have his brother-in-law, Aristobulus, drowned.[11] This had the added benefit of removing the last person with hereditary claim to the office of high priest and paved the way for Herod to make his own appointment. Next he had his former ally, Hyrcanus, put to death,[12] and he repressed the Jerusalem sanhedrin, putting to death the majority of its members.[13]

In order to foster popular tolerance for his rule, Herod, particularly at the beginning of his reign, took care to respect the sensitivities of his Jewish subjects with regard to the observances of the Jewish law. He used his influence with Augustus to secure better treatment for Jews in other parts of the empire.[14] In certain instances, too, he took specific steps to relieve the economic distress of those over whom he ruled.[15] Perhaps his most widely recognized and successful public relations endeavor was his brilliant enlargement and reconstruction of the temple in Jerusalem.[16]

Herod's efforts to establish himself with his Jewish subjects were aided by a number of Roman policy decisions regarding the Jewish religion. Several of these were made before Herod took office, but their continuance during his reign assured that conflicts did not develop in a number of situations in which they well might have. Recognizing that the Jews' commitment to the observance of the Sabbath would prevent them from fighting on that day,[17] the Romans exempted Jews from conscription.[18] The Romans also refrained from instituting (or encouraging) among the Jews any of the forms of emperor worship that were developing elsewhere in the empire.[19] One example of Roman tolerance in this regard was that sacrifices were offered in the temple *for* the emperor, but not *to* him.[20] Over the objections of the Roman officials and local rulers in other parts of the empire, Augustus and Tiberius permitted Jews throughout the diaspora to pay the temple tax that Jewish law required and directed that the transportation to Jerusalem of the money so collected should not be impeded.[21]

As a result of the measures that he himself initiated and aided by the concessions that the Romans granted, Herod's rule, from his own standpoint and that of the Romans, proved to be successful. From 37 to 4 B.C. he ruled in relative prosperity, and Augustus was so pleased with his stewardship that he twice made him gifts of additional territory, significantly augmenting the extent of Herod's kingdom.[22]

Even though it may not bear directly upon Herod's political achievements, we should note that Herod's personal and familial relationships evidenced the highest levels of chaos and disruption imaginable. In the course of his reign Herod put to death three of his sons, one of his wives, and several of his advisors. The web of intrigues and rivalries that developed around him was truly incredible, and Herod's own jealousies and suspicions further inflamed the various situations.[23]

These familial aberrations of Herod almost caused Augustus to become disillusioned with him. Indeed, Augustus is reported to have said that he would rather be one of Herod's pigs than one of his sons.[24] And it is largely because of the cruelty and instability that Herod showed to those who were closest to him that one writer has described his as a "malevolent maniac."[25]

3. THE ARRANGEMENTS FOLLOWING HEROD'S DEATH

Herod's death presented Augustus and his advisors with the task of making new arrangements that would continue to serve Roman interests in the area that Herod had governed. On the whole, Augustus had been satisfied with the type of rule that Herod had provided, and he now wished to find a formula for providing Rome with a continuation of these benefits. Herod had managed to attain a degree of order and stability previously lacking in this area. Such conditions, whether in Palestine or elsewhere in the empire, were always foremost among Rome's objectives since they enabled the trade and commerce of the empire to go forward unhampered. By this time the Mediterranean had become a Roman lake, and the territories under Herod's rule constituted an important link between the Roman province of Syria on the northeast shore of the Mediterranean and the province of Egypt to the south. Not only did stability in

Palestine facilitate commerce between these two important provinces, but political stability and order there tended to support and encourage the same conditions in the territories that made up the Syrian and Egyptian areas. Conversely, there was always the danger that turbulence and unrest in Palestine might prove contagious.

Herod had also provided the Romans with significant military support. When Antony and Augustus had originally recommended to the Roman senate that Herod be named king, one of the reasons they gave was that Herod's military abilities would give the Romans an important bulwark against the Parthians, Rome's enemies to the east.[26] Since the Parthians continued to be a threat throughout Herod's reign, to have Herod's troops[27] and Herod's personal military abilities at their disposal was a significant asset for the Romans. Herod could further be relied upon to furnish smaller contingents of troops for any police actions that might occasionally prove necessary. Thus, as long as Herod ruled, all of Palestine's military needs could be attended to without the deployment (and the expense of deployment) of regular Roman forces. Roman troops were thus available for assignment elsewhere.

It also seems likely that Herod contributed to the empire's financial needs through the regular payment of tribute. Some scholars have argued, on the basis of Roman practice in other comparable situations, that it is not likely that Augustus required tribute payments from Herod. However, as we shall see below, one of Josephus' reports suggests that Herod did collect tribute from the people under his jurisdiction.

Shortly after Herod's death, three of his sons hastened to Rome to present their respective cases to Augustus. Herod's fifth will had named Antipas as his principal heir. Subsequently, though, Herod had amended this will, dividing his territories among Archelaus, Antipas, and Philip, with Archelaus receiving the largest share. In addition to the delegation of Herod's sons and their entourages, the Roman governor of Syria allowed a delegation of Jews from Judea to travel to Rome. Their purpose was to oppose rule by any of Herod's sons, and they petitioned Augustus to bring Judea under direct Roman rule.[28] After taking several weeks to consider his options, Augustus eventually decided to continue the rule of the Herod family with Archelaus as principal heir.

Under the terms of Augustus' decision, Archelaus received jurisdiction over the bulk of his father's kingdom including Judea, Idumea, and Samaria.[29] He was given the title of ethnarch, indicating that his rank was somewhat higher than that of tetrarch, but considerably lower than that of king.[30] The income that Archelaus was to receive from the territories entrusted to him was set at six hundred talents.[31]

Antipas received jurisdiction over Galilee and Perea, which constituted

about one-fourth of Herod's original kingdom. His official title was tetrarch, and the revenue to come from his dominions was set at two
hundred talents. Herod's third son, Philip, was given Batanea,
Trachonitis, Auranitis, and a part of Zenodorus. He was to receive a
revenue of one hundred talents. He also was given the title of tetrarch.
Since he had withheld the title of king from him, Augustus may have
had reservations regarding Archelaus' ability to rule effectively. At any
rate, after nine years Archelaus had to be replaced. He was banished to
Vienna in Gaul, and Augustus made arrangements to have his territories
brought under direct Roman rule.[32] For this purpose he delegated
Quirinius, governor of the Syrian province, to oversee the actual organization of the new province of Judea, and ordered him to conduct an assessment to regularize taxation.[33] It is not clear from Josephus' account
whether Judea was to be an independent province or whether it was to be a
semiautonomous part of the province of Syria. We do know that the
governors of Syria had authority to intervene in Judean affairs if the
occasion warranted it.[34]

4. THE JERUSALEM SANHEDRIN

It was a general feature of Roman policy in their provinces to utilize
local leaders and existing institutions whenever possible.[35] Since Archelaus had failed to fulfill his role adequately, Rome's inclination was to
search for a local entity to whom Archelaus' responsibilities could be
entrusted. In Judea a local institution that was eminently fitted for such a
role was already in existence. It was the Jerusalem sanhedrin.

There is a rabbinic tradition that the *sanhedrin* (the term means supreme
council) had its origin in a council of seventy elders that assisted Moses in
the task of governing Israel; however, it is more likely that the sanhedrin
originated when the Jewish exiles returned from Babylon and re-
established national life in Jerusalem.[36] Our information on the sanhedrin's development is, however, not extensive, and the situation is further
complicated by the possibility that a second, more deliberative sanhedrin
existed alongside the executive and judicially oriented sanhedrin with
which we are primarily concerned.[37]

Shortly after their arrival in Judea, the Roman governors began to
delegate to this body responsibility for almost all aspects of ordinary,
day-to-day living.[38] Since the Jews of Judea, as well as those of other
Palestinian territories, recognized the sanhedrin as having the highest
legislative, executive, and judicial authority,[39] the Romans very likely
found it an effective vehicle for translating their own general objectives

into the specifics of daily living. In time they entrusted the sanhedrin even with jurisdiction over legal and judicial matters (except for "political offenses"),[40] and there is a possibility that the sanhedrin possessed authority for enacting capital punishment.[41]

Under the Roman governors the sanhedrin had seventy-one members, and the majority of these came from the wealthier classes. The chief priests and their Sadducean lay allies exercised considerable influence. The reigning high priest was ex officio president and convenor of the council, and the priest who had previously held the high-priestly office, as well as priests who held positions of importance at the temple, were also council members. In addition to the priestly and Sadducean groups, there were a number of scribes who held seats by virtue of their scholarship and professional abilities. These scribes frequently came from humbler socioeconomic circumstances, and in their interpretation of the Jewish law were generally Pharisees.[42]

5. DIRECT RULE

In retrospect it is clear that Augustus' decision to place Judea under direct Roman rule did not promote Rome's own objectives and ultimately resulted in disaster for the Jews of Judea and Galilee. Instead of fostering the order and stability they had desired to achieve, the Romans saw their efforts result in turbulence and disorder. On the other hand the Jews of Palestine suffered the destruction and devastation of a tragic war. A considerable part of this turbulence and upheaval was the result of the failure of many of the Roman governors who served in Judea to understand and respect the religious commitments of their Jewish subjects. While Herod the Great had not always followed the specific dictates of Jewish law, he had possessed a basic understanding of its place in Jewish life.[43] In general, the same could be said for Antipas and Philip, and even for Archelaus.[44]

In contrast, the Roman governors seem to have lacked this understanding.[45] Their failure to appreciate and respect the nature of the Jewish religious commitment can be explained partially by the fact that the men who served as governors of Judea did not have a strong background in the art of diplomacy.[46] Against the background of the concessions established by Augustus and Tiberius, their failures in administration were particularly glaring.[47]

One of the Jewish laws that gave rise to considerable controversy during the period that we are considering was that which prohibited all forms of idolatry. Oaths, images, or inscriptions which conveyed or seemed to convey to a living creature the honor due to God alone were strictly forbidden, and dedicated Jews were committed to oppose any practices that brought "idols" into the life of the community.[48] In the two instances in which Herod chose to disregard the implications of this law, a considerable public outcry resulted.[49] There were also two cases in which large numbers of Jews opposed Pilate's own infractions of it. The Jewish commitment on this point was so strong that they placed their lives in peril to make these protests.

It should not be thought, however, that the Roman governors, Pilate included, were completely devoid of sensitivity for Jewish religious customs. Both the bronze and the copper coins that were minted while Judea was under direct Roman rule give testimony on this point. All of these coins are free from any images or inscriptions that would have offended the Jews.[50] Had the Roman prefects displayed a comparable sensitivity in the rest of their dealings with their Jewish subjects, much destruction and tragedy might have been avoided.

6. PONTIUS PILATE: GOVERNOR OF JUDEA

Observations concerning the sensitivity lacking in the Roman governors of Judea have particular application to the rule of the fifth governor, Pontius Pilate, who served from A.D. 26 to 36. Reports available indicate that, largely because of his own blunders, his term of office was particularly stormy.

Soon after he took office Pilate apparently decided to show the Jews that he did not feel obligated to respect their laws; and, under cover of darkness, he sent his soldiers to set up standards bearing the likeness of Tiberius within the city of Jerusalem.[51] When these were discovered, there was a great popular outcry, and a large number of the city's inhabitants went immediately to Caesarea to protest to Pilate.[52] When Pilate threatened to massacre them, the people proclaimed their willingness to suffer death. Recognizing, then, how seriously committed they were, Pilate had the standards removed.

In addition, we have other reports of Pilate embroiled in controversy with his subjects; such controversy finally led to his dismissal from office. Vitellius, the Roman governor of Syria, relieved Pilate of his command and sent him to Rome to report to Tiberius. Pilate never returned to his post.[53]

Finally we cite the condemnation of the reign of Pontius Pilate that appears in Philo's *Embassy to Gaius*.[54] Philo (quoting Agrippa) tells us that

Pilate was fearful of having a Jewish embassy sent to Rome because he feared that they would "also expose the rest of his conduct as governor by stating in full the briberies, the insults, the robberies, the outrages and wanton injuries, the executions without trial constantly repeated, the ceaseless and supremely grievous cruelty."[55]

7. HEROD ANTIPAS: TETRARCH OF GALILEE

Herod the Great's other two heirs, Antipas and Philip, were more capable administrators than Archelaus and continued to rule over the territories assigned to them until the death of Augustus, at which time they were reconfirmed in their positions by the new emperor, Tiberius. Philip ruled in relative peace for thirty-seven years, and, judging from the compliments that Josephus accords him, he must have been the most humane of all the Herods that ruled.[56]

For most of Antipas' reign, Galilee and Perea were located between the two Roman provinces of Syria and Judea, and Antipas must have been conscious of the need to stay in the good graces of Rome. For this reason, when he constructed a splendid new capital city, he named it Tiberias in honor of the emperor.[57] Similarly, when he rebuilt the city of Betharamphta, he named it Livias, in honor of Tiberius' wife.[58]

While we do not have reports of any conflicts or friction between Antipas and the Roman officials in the neighboring provinces during the first thirty years of Antipas' reign, both Philo and Josephus indicate that Antipas had at least minor disagreements with the neighboring governors during the last years of his rule. These tensions seem to have been generated because Antipas succeeded in having a report of a treaty conference reach Tiberius before Vitellius' report arrived. Tiberius subsequently let Vitellius know that Antipas' report had arrived first, and Vitellius is said to have flown into a rage.

Although Vitellius did not give vent to his resentment toward Antipas at that time, he was only too happy, on receiving news of Tiberius' death, to call off a military campaign that Tiberius had ordered him to undertake, a campaign to avenge a defeat that the Nabateans had inflicted on Antipas.[59] The defeat had been administered by Aretas, king of the Nabateans, after Antipas had divorced Aretas' daughter to marry Herodias, his half-brother's wife.[60]

This marriage had repercussions for Antipas that were ultimately even more serious. As Josephus recounts, the ambitious Herodias urged Antipas to petition the new emperor, Caligula, for the title of king. Antipas finally consented to make the journey to Rome to present his case, only to find that his brother-in-law had already given Caligula information damaging to Antipas. As a result, Antipas was deposed and sent into Gaul.[61]

8. TAXATION

According to the system developed under the emperors, it was the custom for Rome to collect tribute from the provinces by levying both direct and indirect taxes. Direct taxes included the *tributum agri*, levied on agricultural products, and the *tributum capitis*, a tax on each person living within a province or territory. Indirect taxes were not so comprehensive as direct taxes; they included payments such as road tolls, customs dues, market taxes, and the like.[62] Given Rome's usual methods of operation, it is likely that a more efficient manner of collecting the taxes was one of the objectives of Gabinus, Roman governor of Syria, when he reorganized the new territories.[63]

This redistricting may have facilitated the use of the tax collecting technique known as "farming."[64] Under this method private corporations bid for the tax concession in a particular territory and then supervised the actual collecting at a profit to themselves. We know that the Romans made use of this technique in Palestine because Julius Caesar prohibited the farming out of taxes on agricultural output or on the total population.[65] However, it is likely that the Herods and the Roman governors continued to contract with local tax farmers for the collection of indirect taxes such as customs dues.[66]

In trying to dissuade Augustus from allowing Herod's three sons to continue their father's rule, the Jewish delegation argued that they had already suffered enough at the hands of the Herods. One of the specific charges they made was that Herod the Great had extorted extra payments over and above the tribute normally required each year.[67] The phrasing of this charge suggests (but does not establish) that even though Herod had the rank of king, and even though he maintained good personal relations with Augustus throughout most of his reign, he still was responsible for tribute payments to Rome.[68] However, regardless of whether Herod had to pay a portion of what he collected in tribute, the Jews found the taxation that he did impose very oppressive.[69]

Implicit in the petition that the Jewish delegation made for direct Roman rule was the hope that once the Herods were removed the tax rate would be reduced. This hope did not materialize, a sharp disappointment for the Jews. Tacitus tells us that ten years after Archelaus had been banished, yet another delegation, along with a delegation from Syria, made the long trip to Rome to protest the excessive taxes that were being levied by the Roman governors of Syria and Judea.[70]

Whether this delegation succeeded in gaining any reductions Tacitus does not tell us. However, it would seem that no lasting changes in Rome's tax practices were obtained, for in A.D. 37 the tax rates in Judea were again so high that the Roman governor of Syria made a special intervention to abolish the market taxes for Jerusalem.[71]

Social and Economic Factors

Having examined in Appendix I the political arrangements in effect for Judea and Galilee during Jesus' time, we now turn to the various economic and social patterns that characterized Palestinian society in that period. In the analysis that follows, we will continue to draw upon the sources that we made reference to at the beginning of Appendix I, and the observations that we made at the time regarding methodology should also be kept in mind here.

One additional consideration is that in this Appendix we will frequently orient our analysis to factors that pertained to Palestine as a whole and not attempt to differentiate the socio-economic conditions in Judea and Galilee from those prevailing in the surrounding territories. Similarly we will frequently speak of Judea and Galilee as though they were a single socio-economic entity and not always pause to underline the differences between them. There are two reasons for following this approach. On the one hand the Judaism professed by the Jewish populations of Idumea, Perea, etc., was a strong force tending to orient them toward the social practices maintained by the Jews of Judea and Galilee. Second, as a result of their similarities in such things as climate and land formation, the various Palestinian territories often showed considerable similarities with respect to the type of economic activity carried on and the general character of daily life.

1. POPULATION

Our information on the populations of the various territories in Palestine is so meager that it is possible only to make general approximations.

Based upon information gleaned from Josephus and from rabbinical sources, Joachim Jeremias takes a figure of 20,000 male clergy as his starting point and triples that figure to allow for women and children. Then, on the assumption that the levite (clergy) segment would have constituted one-tenth of the total population, he concludes that at the time of Jesus the Jewish population in Palestine must have been in the neighborhood of 500,000 to 600,000.[1]

This figure does not take into account the non-Jewish inhabitants of Idumea, Samaria, and parts of Galilee, and further calculations would be required if we were to arrive at a separate figure for any one of those territories or for Judea itself. Stephen Hoehner is of the opinion that the total population of Galilee was in the neighborhood of 200,000. However, beyond stating that the territory was thoroughly Judaized by New Testament times, he does not indicate just what the Jewish and non-Jewish populations were. Thus, it is not possible to use his figure to try to make further determinations regarding the total population of Judea or the Jewish populations in other territories.[2]

2. ECONOMY

The information available enables us to have only a general understanding of the economic patterns in the Palestine of Jesus' day. It is clear that the economies of all of the Palestinian territories were based on agriculture,[3] and we possess information about most of the products produced as well as many of the agricultural methods in use. However, when we try to determine how adequate the total output in agriculture was with respect to the needs of the total population, we find ourselves in the realm of conjecture.

Since deserts and mountainous terrain as well as fertile valley areas and plains are to be found within the territories of Palestine, it is well to keep in mind that the life in any given region might be considerably different from that in another. In general, though, the weather in the areas of greatest population concentration was such that the people could carry on agriculture and other economic activities throughout most of the year without having to face oppressive heat or cold.[4]

Although some grain crops could be grown there, the terrain and soil content throughout much of Judea was not well suited to the extensive cultivation of such crops as wheat. However, olives and grapes could be profitably cultivated and Judea seems to have produced goodly amounts of oil and wine each year. In addition, the shepherds in the hills of the Judean countryside also raised flocks of sheep and goats.[5]

Galilee produced a variety of grain crops and also produced olives, grapes, dates, figs, and walnuts in some quantity. Since Galilee's plains and valley areas were particularly suitable for cultivation, the primary emphasis may have been placed upon grains and other agricultural crops. However, we do know that cattle, sheep, and goats were raised in some of these areas. Galilee was also noted for its fishing industry, which was located at the Sea of Galilee and along the Jordan River. Fish taken by Galilee's fishermen were dried and packaged for export throughout the Roman empire.[6]

At the time of Jesus, the copper and iron mines of Judea were yielding only minimum amounts of these ores, and Palestine as a whole seems to have been lacking in mineral resources. Limestone was the only mineral product that it had in abundance although enough good clay to support a small pottery industry was also available.[7] In addition to the general importance of agriculture and the importance of regional industries such as fishing and pottery-making, trade and commerce also played a role in the economic life of Palestine.[8] One of the main trade routes passed through Galilee, and as we shall see below, the Jerusalem temple brought thousands of pilgrims there each year.

As we noted above, it is difficult to judge whether the economic resources that Palestine possessed were adequate to provide for the needs of its population. Besides lacking reliable population figures, we also face considerable difficulty in integrating the data we have about land, climate, crops, and methods of cultivation in such a way as to make possible a reasonably accurate estimate regarding the total agricultural output. From Josephus and other sources we know that famines occurred from time to time, but this information does not tell us how plentiful food was in nonfamine years.

Given the difficulties that are involved in making such a calculation, many scholars who have written analyses of the socio-economic situation of Palestine at the time of Jesus have refrained from taking a position regarding the general level of economic prosperity. In fact, C. C. McCown is one of the few scholars who has expressed himself on this issue. We cite his conclusions not so much because of the specific documentation that he has advanced in support of them, but more because they represent a competent scholar's intuited sense of what the rural situation actually was.

McCown's first judgment is that Palestine's nonagricultural resources and industries were far too limited to make a substantial contribution to general economic output, and he therefore believes that the general level of economic prosperity was determined by the productivity of the agricultural sector. His second judgment is that, when everything is taken into account, the annual output in agriculture would not have been sufficient to meet the needs of Palestine's populations. He is thus inclined to believe that there were fairly large segments of the population who lived in or on the edge of poverty.[9]

3. RELIGIOUS INSTITUTIONS: THE LAW

While there were differences among the various Jewish parties over how the law was to be interpreted and how strictly it was to be observed, the Mosaic law enjoyed a pre-eminent position within the Judaism of Jesus' day. This reverence for the law was all the more remarkable since the law's prescriptions were so comprehensive and all-embracing.[10] The law gradually developed general principles on which the ongoing life of the Jewish community was to be based, but it also indicated specific applications in concrete situations. Thus extensive legislation came into being, a corpus of legal directives relating to virtually all aspects of Jewish personal, familial, and societal life.[11]

The theology of the law, the understanding of it as the expression of God's purposes, is an important subject in its own right; but in the present context, we can only mention it in passing. The same thing is true with respect to the subject of the law's development up to the point where it came to final expression in the books of the Pentateuch. In the interest of concentrating our attention upon the parts of the law that particularly relate to the subject of social responsibility, we will also have to forego any treatment of those parts of the law that pertain to sacrifices and ritual purity.

The point in giving our attention to several of the passages of the law that make provision for the poor and the weak is that it is important for us to appreciate several of the chief characteristics of the Jewish traditions with respect to social responsibility. The nature of Jewish social concern could also be illustrated by references to the prophetic writings and by references to certain sections of the wisdom literature, but for our purposes it is more effective to show the ways in which the law itself called for social responsibility.[12]

Throughout the Old Testament period, the social situation in Palestine was such that widows, orphans, and strangers were the principal groups in need of societal protection. Under the existing socio-economic patterns, they were particularly vulnerable to poverty and injustice even though others also suffered from these two evils.[13]

Thus, in addition to requiring responsible conduct toward all who were poor, the Mosaic law frequently specifies these three groups as those to whom concern must especially be shown. This pattern is evident in two of the passages that follow.

The following passages are taken from chapters twenty-two and twenty-three of the book of Exodus and represent some of the chief provisions of the part of the Mosaic law that is frequently referred to as "the code of the Covenant."

> You shall not wrong a stranger or oppress him for you were strangers in the land of Egypt. You shall not afflict any widow or orphan. If you do afflict them and they cry out to me, I will surely hear their cry [Exod. 22:21–23].

> If you lend money to any of my people with you who is poor, you shall not be to him as a creditor, and you shall not exact interest from him. If you ever take your neighbor's garment in pledge, you shall restore it to him before the sun goes down; for that is his only covering, it is his mantle for his body; in what else shall he sleep? And if he cries to me, I will hear, for I am compassionate [Exod. 22:25–27].

> You shall not pervert the justice due to your poor in his suit [Exod. 23:6].

> You shall not oppress a stranger; you know the heart of a stranger, for you were strangers in the land of Egypt [Exod. 23:9].

In addition to establishing the general principle that the Israelites were to be mindful of the poor among them (Deut. 15:7–9 also requires that the Jews should maintain a general attitude of concern), these passages also indicate specific practices that are incompatible with this principle. Demanding interest on loans made to the poor or holding the poor person's garment overnight are thus both specifically prohibited. In addition, the legal code contained in the book of Leviticus itemized one further type of conduct as being incompatible with a responsible stance toward the poor. As we see from the following passage, it was also forbidden to make a profit from selling food to the poor:

> And if your brother becomes poor, and cannot maintain himself with you, you shall maintain him; as a stranger and a sojourner he shall live with you. Take no interest from him or increase, but fear your God; that your brother may live beside you. You shall not lend him your money at interest, nor give him your food for profit [Lev. 25: 35–37].

Over and above the prescriptions that governed the affairs of everyday life, the Mosaic law stipulated that every seventh year was to be kept as a "sabbatical year" and set down specific ordinances relating to the way in which this period was to be observed.[14] This legislation contained prescriptions dealing with several aspects of Jewish life and included three laws concerning the treatment of the poor and those otherwise in unfavorable circumstances.

One of these laws established that, in the seventh year, all those in servitude were to be given the option of regaining their freedom (Exod. 21:2; Deut. 15:12–14). (We shall have more to say regarding the conditions of this servitude in the concluding section of this Appendix.) A second established that the poor were to have a special claim upon whatever products grew in the fields and vineyards during this year (Exod. 23:11). Third, and this is the feature that is of particular interest to us, the code of laws in the book of Deuteronomy decreed that all loans outstanding at the beginning of the seventh year were to be cancelled. This law was enacted as follows:

> At the end of every seven years you shall grant a release. And this is the manner of the release: every creditor shall release what he has lent to his neighbor; he shall not exact it of his neighbor, his brother, because the Lord's release has been proclaimed [Deut. 15:1–2].

The original purpose of this law seems to have been to set up a legal bulwark against lifelong indebtedness. Those who fell into debt might remain in debt for up to six years, but if they had not been able to repay their debts by the time the seventh year arrived, they were still to have the opportunity to make a new beginning. Since the poor were particularly vulnerable to unexpected emergencies, it is likely that they were the ones most frequently in debt and it is thus likely that this law represented yet another effort to develop practices that provided some measure of relief to the poor of the society.

However, despite the lofty ideals that such a law embodied, there are reasons to believe that the risks it required lenders to bear may have resulted in their unwillingness to lend to the poor at all. This seems to have been the case even though the same chapter of Deuteronomy goes on to caution lenders against calculating the nearness of the seventh year and using its nearness as a basis for hardening their hearts against those petitioning loans (Deut. 15:9–10).

Since this particular regulation was not included in the subsequent compilation of sabbatical year legislation in the book of Leviticus (25:2–7,

13–24), some commentators believe that in practice the law was not benefiting the poor. This argument receives additional support from the *probosol* (literally, a certificate) that the later rabbinic tradition developed.[15] Under certain specified conditions, this probosol made it possible for the obligation of repaying loans to continue even though a sabbatical year might occur before the loan was repaid.

When the probosol was to be used, the petitioner for the loan went before the court and witnesses and declared that during the time of the sabbatical year the title to the loan would become the court's property. Before the seventh year, the creditor issuing the loan retained the title for repayment; when the seventh year had passed, the court returned the title to him. However, during the sabbatical year itself, the title to the loan was technically the property of the court and thus not subject to cancellation.

From one standpoint it can be argued that the probosol actually furthered the underlying concern of the original law by making it possible for poor people to obtain loans that otherwise would have been denied them. On the other hand, there are also grounds for holding that this arrangement actually frustrated the law's original intent because it removed the protection against long-term indebtedness that the law had accorded. However, in terms of our own study, we are concerned not so much with evaluating this probosol as we are with the very fact of its enactment.

The rabbinic literature attributes the authorship of this probosol to Hillel, an eminent rabbi who was a near contemporary of Jesus. Jacob Neusner points out that although rabbinic tradition ascribes this provision to Hillel, this does not necessarily establish that Hillel was actually its author.[16] But even if we heed Neusner's warning, it still seems likely that the probosol was developed somewhere around the time of Jesus.[17] This point is of particular interest to us, for it indicates that the precepts regarding social responsibility, precepts that the Jewish law had developed hundreds of years earlier, were still very much live issues at the time of Jesus.

4. RELIGIOUS INSTITUTIONS: THE TEMPLE

From the first Jewish settlements in Palestine until the time of David, sacrifices could be offered to God at any number of sanctuaries located throughout the territory held by the Jews. Gradually, though, beginning with David's transfer of the Ark of the Covenant to Jerusalem and Solomon's construction of a temple to house it, the Jerusalem temple came to have pre-eminence as a place of worship. Finally, largely due to the steps taken by two later kings and the writers of Deuteronomy, the temple at Jerusalem passed from being the leading place at which sacrifices could be offered to being the *only* place where sacrifices could legally take place.[18]

The temple that Solomon built was destroyed by Nebuchadnezzar in 587 B.C.; but after the Jews returned from exile, construction on a new temple soon began. This second temple was eventually completed around 515 B.C.; it was still functioning five hundred years later when Herod the Great decided to greatly expand and enhance it. He began this project in 20 B.C. and completed the essential part of the enlargement within one and one-half years, even though the process of completing the secondary work dragged on into the middle of the first century A.D.[19]

By all accounts, the Herodian temple was a stunning work of architecture. It featured a beautifully designed sanctuary that was rendered even more impressive by the spacious porches, courts, and colonnades that surrounded it. The total temple area was enclosed with an imposing wall, the thickness and height of which rendered the interior virtually impregnable. The white stone and the gold appointments used for the sanctuary and the gates gave the temple a dazzling appearance in the sunlight; the temple's position in an elevated section of the city further magnified the impact of its beauty. Pilgrims coming to the city from outlying areas might see the temple white and gold in the sunlight long before they reached the gates of the city itself.

Because the Jerusalem temple was regarded as the house of God and because it was the only place where sacrifice could legally be offered, Jews from all the districts of Palestine and from all over the world made pilgrimages to Jerusalem for the principal Jewish feasts. Jeremias has estimated that for the Passover festival from 60,000 to 125,000 pilgrims might travel to Jerusalem. This is a particularly striking figure, since the normal population of the city was probably somewhere between 25,000 and 30,000.[20]

Since the prescribed temple rites necessitated the purchase of sacrificial animals such as sheep or cattle or products such as wheat flour and fruits, the regular influx of pilgrims had a significant positive impact upon the city's economic life. Each year approximately 18,000 lambs were required for the celebration of the feast of Passover, and comparable demands were placed upon other sectors of the Jerusalem and Judean economies. Thus a significant number of merchants, tradespeople, and livestock owners earned their living from the economic activity generated in connection with the temple.[21]

At the same time the temple contributed to the economic prosperity of Jerusalem and the surrounding countryside, the temple itself required extensive financial support from the Jews of Palestine and the diaspora. In the period preceding the Babylonian exile, the Jewish kings had assumed much of the responsibility for the maintenance of the temple and the temple's related activities.[22] However, this means of support was no longer available after the exile, and so steps had to be taken to ensure a more broadly based support. Not only did the temple itself have to be reconstructed and then maintained; the support of the clergy, particularly those permanently attached to the temple, also had to be put on a firm basis.

As the arrangements were subsequently worked out, the livelihood of the priests was provided for in three ways. First, the priests were to receive the choicest portion, often including the hides, of most of the animals sacrificed.[23] Second, the priests received the "first fruits" that farmers and shepherds were required to offer at the time of the harvest each year and that parents were required to present at the birth of the first son. Since the law stipulated that only the best flour, the choicest fruits, and the purest first-born animals could be used to fulfill this "first fruits" obligation, the gifts presented to the priests on these occasions were of the highest quality.[24] Third, the portion that the priests themselves received from the tithes paid to the levites (the lesser ranked clergy) also provided them with a means of support. The Jewish law required that one-tenth of the total harvest of the most important agricultural products was to be turned over to the levites and that the levites were then to turn one-tenth of what they had received over to the priests.[25]

It is difficult to know for certain exactly how well this tithing mechanism worked in practice, but there are at least two indications that those responsible for paying tithes did not always do so voluntarily. In the book of Nehemiah the levites and the priests are allowed to collect the tithes themselves, suggesting that the payments were not being brought to them regularly (Neh. 10:38b–39). Josephus indicates that in New Testament times occasionally the chief priests actually sent bands of ruffians to ensure that the tithes were collected.[26]

The foregoing provisions were developed to provide the personnel of the temple with a means of support, but what of the considerable monies that were needed for the maintenance of the temple itself? In addition to the normal expenses connected with the upkeep, it seems likely that at least part of the expansion and renovation that Herod the Great initiated would have had to be paid for from the temple's own treasury.[27]

In Appendix I we indicated that one of the important concessions the Roman emperors accorded to the Jews of the empire was the freedom to take up an annual collection for the temple in Jerusalem.[28] This was the source of revenues necessary for the ongoing operations of the temple. The basis of this collection was the requirement that all Jewish men pay a half-shekel "temple" tax each year.[29] Since a half-shekel was the equivalent of two day's pay for an average laborer,[30] a considerable amount of money must have been collected each year. One of the reproaches that Titus addressed to the inhabitants of Jerusalem during his final siege was that they had accumulated a surplus of funds from the collection of the temple tax and then used these funds to attack the very ones (the Romans) who had originally permitted them to make the collection.[31] In addition, from Pompey's time onward various Roman leaders had plundered the temple treasury or used temple funds for their own purposes; this also suggests that the treasury contained substantial amounts of money.[32]

The central role of the temple in the life of the Jewish community of Jesus' day is clearly evident. And yet, barely forty years later, this magnificent architectural work, this highly influential religious institution, lay in ruins. Titus' final siege proved successful, and the temple of Jerusalem was destroyed never to be rebuilt. Out of necessity the Judaism that survived this destructive event began to move in new directions. That it was able to do so was due to the existence of a third important Jewish religious institution: the synagogue.

5. RELIGIOUS INSTITUTIONS: THE SYNAGOGUE

We cannot be certain about the exact time and circumstances of the synagogue's origins, but it was a well-established institution long before the time of Jesus. Whether its roots are to be found in the efforts of the Jewish community to remain faithful to the law during the period of the exile, or whether it was developed by the Jewish groups who remained behind in Palestine, the synagogue's emergence and growth was definitely intertwined with the increasing influence of the Mosaic law upon the life of the Jewish community.[33]

The synagogue came to be a council house and a place of assembly as well as a place of prayer and a hospice. Nevertheless, its central enduring purpose was the proclamation and exposition of the law. Every synagogue possessed a Torah scroll from which the law was proclaimed, and it was this proclamation that gave the synagogue its reason for being.[34]

In contrast to the centralization of worship that the Jerusalem temple represented, the numerous synagogues established throughout Palestine and in other parts of the empire represented a decentralization in the teaching of the law. Wherever sizeable numbers of Jews were settled, synagogues were to be found, and larger communities might possess more than one. Knowledge of the law was thus easily accessible to all Jews, even if great distances separated them from Jerusalem.

Although as an institution the synagogue was oriented to the laity and dominated by the Pharisees, it should not be thought that it was in rivalry or competition with the temple. Rather, the relationship was complementary. The laws concerning sacrifice and temple worship as well as those concerning tithing were read in the synagogue. The Pharisees themselves were supporters of the temple worship, even though they might disagree with the approach that the largely Sadducean priests followed with respect to the interpretation of the law.[35]

As we have already noted, more than anything else it was the existence of the synagogue that enabled Judaism to withstand the disaster of A.D. 70 when Jerusalem fell and the temple was destroyed. Because of the synagogue, devotion to the law continued to be firmly established within Jewish life, and out of this devotion came the strength to go forward.[36]

6. SOCIO-ECONOMIC GROUPS

The Wealthy. The data available do not enable us to make a precise analysis of the distribution of wealth in the Palestine of Jesus' day. Nevertheless, we do possess information about the principal means of acquiring wealth and the various groups of rich and poor.

In the agriculturally based economy of Palestine in Jesus' time, the ownership of land and of properties such as buildings or livestock was an important source of wealth. Wealth was also derived from trade and commerce. Finally, persons who held high political or religious office were also likely to acquire wealth as a consequence of the opportunities for enrichment that their offices afforded them.

There were two groups of persons who had gained their wealth from all three of these sources. The first was the Herods, their families, and their retinue. The second consisted of many of the chief priests and their families.

The Herods and their families not only received revenues from taxes and profits from the trade and commerce within their territories; they also owned an extremely large proportion of the land within their respective kingdoms. Besides criticizing Herod's high taxes, the Jewish delegation that went to Rome to oppose Herod's sons also charged that Herod had made a practice of illegally confiscating the property of the "nobility."[37] We also know that on at least one occasion Augustus gave land as an outright gift to a member of Herod's family.[38] Taking these and other factors into account, one commentator has conjectured that Herod owned privately somewhere between one-half and two-thirds of his kingdom.[39]

It is likely that a considerable part of this privately-owned land passed to

Herod's sons at the time of his death. We do know that after he banished Archelaus to Gaul, Augustus then asked Quirinius to oversee the liquidation of Archelaus' estates.[40] Similarly, the fact that Antipas gave land at his own expense to those who consented to settle in his new capital city, Tiberias, indicates that he had privately owned land.[41]

In Appendix III we indicate the specific positions the chief priests held at the temple and on the sanhedrin, and we also sketch the historical circumstances in which the reigning high priests held office; here our concern is that the chief priests had access to the principal sources of wealth. Since they shared substantially in the income that the various sacrifices produced (as we noted earlier, the hides of the animals were particularly valuable), and since there are grounds for believing that they also received salaries from the temple treasury,[42] their positions as religious leaders automatically provided the chief priests with a considerable livelihood.

Second, because there was so much trade and commerce connected with the temple, the chief priests had opportunities to profit from their contacts, or even partnerships, with the merchants and traders who ran the various temple-related concessions. Commercial space in the temple's outer courtyards was a particularly valuable commodity and, since the chief priests had jurisdiction over this area,[43] it is reasonable to suppose they would have frequently allocated the best places to members of their own families involved in commerce or to merchants who were members of the Sadducean party. Third, since Josephus (who came from a leading priestly family) had extensive estates[44] and since the rabbinic literature refers to the landholdings of priests, it is probable that some of the chief priests had personal lands.[45]

There is a difference, of course, between having access to the means of wealth and amassing it, and the fact that some of the chief priests did acquire wealth does not mean that all of them did. On the other hand, some of the stories reported in rabbinic literature do convey the impression that the leading priestly families in Jesus' time had amassed considerable wealth and sometimes used it wantonly. According to one of these accounts, the wife of one of the high priests in the Boethus family wanted to see her husband officiate at the temple on the Day of Atonement. Since this was a day on which everyone was required to go barefoot, she arranged to have the distance between her house and the temple carpeted![46]

We would need to have a number of reports such as this to establish conclusively that all the chief priests of Jesus' day had such resources at their disposal. Nevertheless, given the general conditions in the Palestine of Jesus' time, it is extremely likely that the chief priests were among the wealthiest groups of society. Even apart from any income they received from landholdings or commercial interests, the income from their official temple functions would have been sufficient to establish them in positions of relative wealth.

Along with the leading priestly families and the various members of the Herodian courts, successful merchants and large landowners constituted the bulk of the wealthy class of Jesus' day. John of Gischala, who figures prominently in Josephus' narrative, is an example of one who became rich through commerce. Josephus tells us that John gained large profits from selling corn and oil.[47] Many of the wealthier laity joined with a majority of the chief priests to constitute the membership of the Sadducean party. We shall have more to say about the theological positions of this party when we discuss the leading Jewish groups in Appendix III. However, regarding their socio-economic orientation, Josephus writes that they had "the confidence of the wealthy alone but no following among the populace. . . ."[48]

Artisans, Small Landholders, Merchants. We possess relatively little information regarding the situation of those who fell somewhere between the rich and the poor in the Palestinian society of Jesus' day. We may suppose that those who owned small plots of land, a number of merchants and handicrafters, and the lower echelons of the priests fell within this category. However, our ability to describe the specific features of their living situation is limited largely to the realm of conjecture.

We are similarly limited in our efforts to estimate the percentage of the total population that this middle group would have constituted. Perhaps the most that can be said is that, since agriculture was the mainstay of the economy and land ownership the main source of wealth, the percentage of those who possessed some degree of economic security is likely to have been relatively small. As we have seen, a large proportion of the land was owned by a small number of families, and thus there was only a limited number of small parcels that could have been in the hands of individual owners.

The Poor. We have seen that the law accorded special attention to widows, orphans, and strangers, and we may therefore suppose that many members of these groups were numbered among the ranks of the poor. In addition to these groups, it is probable that a substantial number of the "day laborers" lived in or on the brink of poverty.[49] Poverty may also have been the lot of some of those owning land if their holdings were extremely small or unprofitable. If the owners of small parcels of land paid their temple taxes as well as the taxes levied by the Romans and the Herods, it is all the more likely that they lived on the edge of poverty.[50]

Women. The Jewish society of Jesus' day was strongly patriarchal in character, and as a consequence women were in a subordinate position with regard to both family life and public life.[51] Until the time of her marriage, a woman was considered to be the property of her father, and it was his responsibility to reject or accept the marriage proposals his daughter received. At her marriage the woman became subject to the jurisdiction of her husband, and, in addition to being his companion, she was expected to take a leading role in the work of the house. It was also hoped that she would give birth to a son (and heir) within a short time.[52]

Although monogamy was the usual form of marriage, polygamy was also possible,[53] and the first wife's position might be worsened by the presence of additional wives or concubines. Even more detrimental to the woman's position were the conditions governing divorce; her husband could enact a divorce relatively easily, but she did not have the right of divorce at all. If her husband presented her with a formal "bill of divorcement," the woman was free to marry again; but if he did not choose to do so, she had no recourse but to return to her father's household.[54] The death of her husband could also undermine a woman's position. If there were male heirs, neither she nor her daughters were legally entitled to any of the inheritance.[55]

The Jewish woman's inferior position was also evident in the restrictions placed upon her participation in the public life of the community. Although there were exceptions, women were generally not expected to assume any public role or have any public identity apart from being the wives of their husbands or daughters of their fathers. Women were able to circulate relatively freely in the cities, but it was not usual for a woman to converse in public with a man to whom she was not related.[56] At the temple women were limited to the Court of the Gentiles and the Court of Women,[57] and at the synagogue they were assigned seats in a screened-off section.[58]

At the conclusion of his chapter on the social position of Jewish women in Jesus' time, Joachim Jeremias presents a brief summary of the situation that women faced: "We have therefore the impression that Judaism in Jesus' time also had a very low opinion of women, which is usual in the Orient where she is chiefly valued for her fecundity, kept as far as possible shut away from the outer world, submissive to the power of her father or her husband, and where she is inferior to men from a religious point of view."[59]

Slaves. It is not possible to give a definitive answer to the question of whether slavery existed in Judea and Galilee during Jesus' time, but there are several indications that it did not.

The first and most important consideration arguing against the existence of slavery is that one of the provisions of the sabbatical year legislation called for the release of all "slaves" at the beginning of the seventh year (Exod. 21:2; Deut. 15:12–14). Since there is reason to believe that most of the laws governing the sabbatical year were observed,[60] we would thus have a situation in which the longest that any person could be kept in bondage was six years, and in which one of the most oppressive features of slavery (i.e., its lifelong duration) was absent.

Second, it is likely that a high percentage of Jews who were in bondage to other Jews (the law prohibited Jews from being sold as slaves to Gentiles)[61] had entered into such a relationship voluntarily.[62] Jews who had no means of paying off their debts frequently sold themselves to persons of wealth and worked off what they owed through labor in the fields, service in households, and so forth. That such an arrangement was frequently an attractive alternative to a life of destitution is seen from the fact that, even when given the option of release under sabbatical year legislation, numbers of those who were in this situation chose to renew their commitments to their owners and remain in servitude.[63] The voluntary dimension of this arrangement lends credence to Philo's statement that "even those who were called slaves were in fact workers."[64]

Third, it can also be argued that the number of those who were *not* voluntarily in servitude had declined significantly by New Testament times, for the period in which Herod and his sons ruled was one of relative peace with foreign powers. In earlier times, one of the main sources of forced labor had been prisoners of war;[65] but under the Herodian rule there would have been few, if any, prisoners brought to Judea and Galilee as a result of military victories.

Two other groups who did not enter servitude voluntarily were apprehended Jewish thieves who could not make restitution (Exod. 22:2) and Gentiles whom wealthy Jews purchased from slave traders.[66] It is possible that persons among these groups were in bondage in Jesus' time. However, even here (at least with respect to the second category) there were mitigating circumstances that must be taken into account. After a year's time Gentile "slaves" had to be given the opportunity to convert to Judaism. If they decided to do so, they remained in servitude only until the next sabbatical year. If they elected not to embrace Judaism, then they had to be sold to Gentile owners.[67]

It should also be noted that Jewish law required that good treatment be accorded to all who lived under conditions of servitude. Even though in servitude, Jewish men were to be considered the equals of the eldest sons in the owners' families. They had a right to good food, good clothing, and good shelter; and if they were married, their owners were further obligated to provide for their wives and children.[68]

Taken together, these considerations indicate that slavery in the strict sense of the term did not exist in Judea and the Jewish areas of Galilee at the time of Jesus. While a form of indentured servitude existed, most of those who were in such a situation viewed it as preferable to the alternatives available to them and thus embraced it voluntarily.[69] A small number of Jewish thieves probably served their time of bondage unwillingly (for them such servitude was akin to a prison sentence), but their maximum term of labor was seven years, and it might frequently involve a shorter period, depending upon how far away the next sabbatical year was. And ideally, they, like everyone else who was in servitude, could expect to receive relatively humane treatment from those whom they served.

Five Jewish Groups

Here we will give our attention to the responses that various Jewish groups made to the socio-political realities we have identified.

1. THE CHIEF PRIESTS

Offices and Family Backgrounds. The Jerusalem temple had by the time of Jesus developed into an extremely influential socio-economic institution. The various activities and enterprises associated with the temple assumed increased importance and brought increased influence to the priests responsible for administering them. Thus, in the time of Jesus, the priests who served as captains of the temple,[1] those who served as temple treasurers[2] and overseers,[3] and those who directed the weekly courses of priests[4] exercised considerable authority and constituted, along with the high priests, an influential body of "chief priests."[5]

By virtue of his preeminent position at the temple[6] and his position as president and convener of the sanhedrin,[7] the reigning high priest had greater authority and influence than any of the priests around him. There are, however, indications that during the period with which we are concerned the priests who served as high priests did not have the absolute authority or prestige that their predecessors had once enjoyed. Instead of functioning as rulers far separated from even the upper ranks of the priesthood, the high priests of Jesus' time were members of a small group of chief priests and ruled in collaboration with the other members of the group.

The single most important factor tending to limit the power and influence of the later high priests was that from the time of Herod the Great onward the high priesthood was no longer an office inherited and held for life. Such a pattern had previously been in effect, but as Herod wished to prevent the high priestly office from being used as a base of power against him, he assumed the prerogative of appointing and deposing the high priests. This practice was continued by the Roman governors, who, perhaps because bribery was involved,[8] sometimes changed high priests at extremely short intervals.[9]

A second restraint on the authority and power of the high priest was the considerable influence the priest who had previously held the office continued to have even after he had been officially deposed.[10] In addition to the moral influence that accrued to them through the relationships established during their terms of office, they continued to be voting members of the sanhedrin[11] and may also have retained "emeritus" positions at the temple.

Third, the reigning high priest knew that he held his office at the pleasure of the Romans, and that one of the other chief priests might be appointed in his stead.[12]

Finally, the fact that so many of the high priests and other chief priests were related to one another leads to the conclusion that the leading temple offices and the high priesthood were dominated by a group of chief priests rather than by the individual high priests. From the time of Herod until the outbreak of the Jewish war, the high priesthood and many of the most influential temple offices were dominated by the Boethus, Annas, Phiabi, and Kamith priestly families.[13]

Herod's third appointment to the high priestly office, Jesus son of Phiabi, held the office from 33 to 22 B.C., and two other members of the Phiabi family also served as high priests under the Roman governors. In 22 B.C. Herod appointed one of his fathers-in-law, Simon son of Boethus, as high priest; Simon served until 5 B.C., when the office passed in fairly rapid succession to Simon's son-in-law, to another relative, and then to one of Simon's sons. All in all, before the beginning of the Jewish war, eight members of the Boethus family served as high priests, and the family's general influence was so strong that they and their supporters came to constitute a group known as "the Boethusians."[14]

During the period of direct Roman rule, three members of the Kamith family as well as members of the Phiabi and Boethus families held the office of high priest. However, it was the house of Annas that above any of the others came to exercise a sustained influence. In A.D. 6, when he was reorganizing Archelaus' territories in preparation for direct rule, Quirinius appointed Annas as high priest. Annas held the office until A.D. 15 when Valerius Gratus replaced him with a priest of the Phiabi family. This priest served for one year and was replaced by Annas' son Eleazar, who served for one year. Eleazar's successor, a priest from the Kamith family, likewise served a one-year term.

When this priest was deposed, the new appointee was Joseph Caiaphas, Annas' son-in-law, who served a long term, from A.D. 18 to 37. From that point forward, five other members of the house of Annas (four of Annas' sons and one of his grandsons) held the office, bringing to eight the total number of priests of the Annas family who served in that capacity. Thus during Jesus' public ministry and for most of the period in which the Palestinian communities were developing, the leading priestly family was that of Annas.[15]

Lack of Legitimacy. Even though the office of high priest was greatly changed from what it had been in earlier times, and even though the high priests had become the appointees of Herod and the Roman governors, it was still of considerable importance that the families from which the high priests were chosen did not have a legitimate claim to hold the high priestly office. That they were in de facto possession of the office from 35 B.C. to A.D. 66 undoubtedly tended to convey the impression that they held their positions legitimately and appropriately; but in terms of Jewish law this was not the case, and there were groups within the Jewish populace that never forgot this.

With the exception of a high priest who served briefly during Herod's reign, priests of Zadokite descent did not hold the office after the Hasmoneans first came to power. Given such a long interval, it might have been expected that hope for a legitimate Zadokite succession would eventually die out. This did not happen, for when the Zealots gained power in A.D. 67 one of their first steps was to depose the then-reigning high priest and reestablish the Zadokite succession. Lots were drawn to determine who would serve as the new high priest, but only priests of Zadokite descent were eligible for the lottery.[16]

Sadducees and Sanhedrin Members. The original meaning of the term "Sadducee" is not clear, and it is difficult also to determine under what circumstances the Saducean party arose.[17] The approach they followed in the interpretation of the Jewish law was, however, one of their distinguishing characteristics during the period with which we are concerned. In contradistinction to the Pharisees, the Sadducees believed that the law was to be interpreted exactly as it was written without the benefit of any explanatory tradition. They rejected the oral tradition of the Pharisees and accused the Pharisees of constructing a "hedge about the Torah."[18]

Because their starting points with respect to the law were significantly different, the Sadducees frequently found themselves at odds with the Pharisees on specific doctrinal issues. For instance, the Sadducees believed that the soul perished with the body, while the Pharisees held that the soul was immortal. In addition, there appears to have been considerable difference between the relatively lax approach of the Sadducees toward the written law and the extreme dedication with which the Pharisees sought to observe the written law as interpreted by the oral law. Josephus leaves no doubt that he considered the Pharisees to have been more virtuous. He also states that the Jewish population in general rejected the Sadducean premise that the written law was sufficient in itself. He further indicates that although the Sadducees had the confidence of the wealthy, they did not have a real following among the people as a whole.[19]

The great majority of the chief priests were members of the Sadducean party and by reason of their high positions played a substantial role within the party even though they themselves did not comprise a majority of its members. The other principal group that constituted the Sadducean party was laity that Josephus designates by such terms as "the nobles and the most eminent citizens" and "the leading men."[20] The party's total membership was exceedingly small,[21] and but for their important positions at the temple and on the sanhedrin,[22] the Sadducees' positions on matters of law and doctrine would have been even less influential than they were.

Attitude Toward Roman Rule. The Roman governors entrusted the sanhedrin with considerable authority for the administration of everyday Jewish affairs, whereas Herod the Great (and presumably Archelaus), fearful of any Jewish individuals or groups who might constitute a threat to his position, had suppressed the sanhedrin and assumed responsibility for all administration himself. Thus, since their own position had never been more favorable, there was a clear rationale for the chief priests to give their support to Roman rule and to cooperate with the Roman governors.

The Romans had two objectives: general stability and order throughout the area and the regular payment of tribute. There are strong indications that, at least until the outbreak of the Jewish war, the chief priests cooperated with the Roman governors in both these objectives.

At the time Archelaus was deposed and Judea was brought under direct Roman rule, strong popular protest developed in opposition to the property assessment that Quirinius had instituted in connection with his assignment to reorganize Archelaus' territories. The leaders of this uprising may have felt that the proposed assessment would result in increased taxes, or they may have objected to the manner in which it was being carried out. Whatever the exact circumstances that surrounded the protest, the reigning high priest, Joazar, counselled cooperation with the assessment and tried to discourage those who were mounting the protest.

Josephus tells us that "although the Jews were at first shocked to hear of the registration of property, they gradually condescended, yielding to the arguments of the high priest Joazar, the son of Boethus, to go no further in opposition."[23] We are thus led to conclude that Joazar himself did not judge that the new assessment justified protest or rebellion. We said earlier that the chief priests and other sanhedrin members were probably influential in the Jewish delegations that travelled to Rome asking for direct rule; it would thus have been highly inconsistent for Joazar to have followed any other course of action. Now that the direct rule for which the sanhedrin members had asked had been granted, Joazar was obligated to cooperate with the specific steps required to implement it.

Neither Josephus nor Philo ever places any of the high priests and chief priests among those who took the initiative in opposing Pilate's violations of Jewish law. Even on the occasion when Pilate illegally appropriated temple monies to construct an aqueduct, Josephus' account mentions only that "the Jews" and "tens of thousands of men" opposed Pilate's actions. He does not report any response by the chief priests themselves.[24] While arguments from silence are not the strongest grounds on which to base an interpretation, Josephus' failure to mention any strong protest on the part of the chief priests does correspond well with our thesis that it was to their own best interests to support Roman rule.

Josephus further indicates that on several occasions prior to the outbreak of the war, the chief priests made impassioned appeals to the people not to break with Roman rule.[25] In fact, the collaborationist stance of the chief priests became so manifest during this period that when the radical elements finally gained control of Jerusalem, they killed the reigning high priest, Ananias, burned his residence, and put many of the other chief priests to flight.[26] It is true that once the war was under way, several of the chief priests gave their support to the war effort (some of them eventually serving as generals).[27] Even then, though, there were still instances in which some of these priests tried to work out compromise arrangements for a return to the pre-war situation.[28]

While we have stressed that the chief priests generally sought to cooperate and collaborate with the Roman rule, it should not be thought that they viewed their situation under the Roman governors as completely ideal. The fact that they had to strive continuously to achieve a *modus vivendi* with Roman officials who did not appreciate many of the features of the situation in Judea, who possessed considerable arrogance, and who sometimes sought to exploit the situation for their own private ends, must have been difficult for the chief priests to accept.

Although they were happy to use the sanhedrin for much of the daily administration, the governors who served in Judea did not have any particular reason to be solicitous for the welfare of the chief priests, and they probably treated them somewhat cavalierly. While it is true that of all the Jewish groups the chief priests were the staunchest supporters of Roman rule, it does not thereby follow that the Roman governors viewed them as friends or even as allies. In fact, it is more than likely that the Roman governors viewed the chief priests as *subjects* even though, as leading members of the sanhedrin, they might be useful for the fulfillment of Roman purposes.

In this same vein, we know also that the practice followed by the Roman governors in retaining possession of the ceremonial vestments of the high priest was a subject of controversy between the governors and the chief priests.[29] We further know that one of the deposed high priests once engaged in such outspoken criticism of the ruling governor that the governor subsequently had him assassinated.[30]

Such controversies caution us not to place such a heavy emphasis upon the chief priests' support of Roman rule that we fail to leave room for occasional antagonism between given priests and given governors. The general features of the situation were such that the chief priests could best maintain their own vested interests by supporting the main lines of Roman rule, but this did not mean that they were committed to follow slavishly the dictates of every governor. In addition, there is evidence that the chief priests in their own right were sometimes able to influence the assignment of a particular Roman as governor of Judea.[31]

Exploitative Practices. From a report of Josephus we learn that the chief priests sometimes violated the procedures according to which tithes were to be collected. The situation that Josephus here describes occurred around A.D. 59, but there is considerable likelihood that its roots went back many years earlier.

> There was now enkindled mutual enmity and class warfare between the high priests, on the one hand, and the priests and the leaders of the populace of Jerusalem, on the other. Each of the factions formed and collected for itself a band of the most reckless revolutionaries and acted as their leader. And when they clashed, they used abusive language and pelted each other with stones. And there was not even one person to rebuke them. No, it was as if there was no one in charge of the city, so that they acted as they did with full licence. Such was the shamelessness and effrontery which possessed the high priests that they actually were so brazen as to send slaves to the threshing floors to receive the tithes that were due to the priests, with the result that the poorer priests starved to death.[32]

We are also indebted to Josephus for information regarding the Zealots' policies when they came to power in A.D. 66. We have already mentioned that they killed the high priest and burned his residence. In addition, they burned the Archive building in which the money-lenders' bonds were kept.[33] Since the money-lending facility was one of the activities operated in connection with the temple, such a step suggests that there was a popular sentiment against the way in which loans made to the poor were handled and that there was resentment against the stewardship of the chief priests.

A further and more specific confirmation of such resentment is found in the "Pesachim" tract of the *Tosefta Menachoth*. Although the rabbinic traditions did not reach their written form until several hundred years later, they frequently supply us with extremely accurate information regarding first-century Jewish life. In this instance, the criticism against the four leading priestly families is consistent with the information we have from other sources. Though the passage does not detail the specific abuses that the rabbis believed the members of the four families to have been guilty of, it does clearly charge them with abuse of office:

> Woe to the Boethusim; woe to their spears! Woe to the family of Annas! Woe to their serpent hissing! Woe to the family of Kanthera; woe to their pens! Woe to the family of Ishmael ben Phiabi! Woe to their fists! They are High Priests; their sons are treasurers; their grandsons captains of the Temple, and their servants smite the people with their rods.[34]

Finally, *The Assumption of Moses*, a pseudepigraphic work written during the first century A.D., also contains a passage that harshly criticizes a group that many scholars have identified as the chief priests.[35] The conclusion of the passage seems to indicate that the rulers under criticism appeal to the sanctity of their offices to escape accountability. These charges could well have been appropriately addressed to the priests controlling the temple and to the sanhedrin during the period of Roman rule.

> And in the time of these, scornful and impious men will rule, saying they are just. And these will conceal the wrath of their minds, being treacherous men, self-pleasers, dissemblers in all their own affairs and lovers of banquets at every hour of the day, gluttons, gourmands, . . . devourers of the goods of the poor, saying that they do so on the grounds of their justice but (in reality) to destroy them, complainers, deceitful, concealing themselves lest they

should be recognized, impious, filled with lawlessness and iniquity
from sunrise to sunset: Saying: "We shall have feastings and luxury,
eating and drinking, yea we shall drink our fill, we shall be as
princes." And though their hands and their minds touch unclean
things, yet their mouth will speak great things, and yet they will say
furthermore: "Do not touch me lest thou shouldst pollute me in the
place where I stand. . . . "[36]

2. THE PHARISEES

Origins and Attitude Toward Mosaic Law. The Aramaic root from which
the word "Pharisee" probably comes has the meaning of "separated" or
"distinguished";[37] it is likely that the Pharisaic movement originally came
into existence when a rigorous observance of the Mosaic law by dedicated
Jews caused them to be differentiated or "separated" from those Jews who
followed a more traditional approach.[38]

We have already pointed out that the Pharisees supported the validity of
an oral tradition for interpreting the law, which put them at odds with the
Sadducees. A second feature of the Pharisees' approach distinguished
them from the great part of their Jewish contemporaries, namely, their
belief that the Mosaic laws regarding ritual purity were binding on all
Jews, not just priests.[39] Since the great majority of the Pharisees came
from the ranks of the laity,[40] their position can be seen as an effort to
strengthen the law's role in the life of the laity and to increase the average
lay person's dedication to it. Nevertheless, since the laws regarding purifications were intricate and difficult to observe, it seems likely that ordinary
unlettered Jews would have found this an excessively rigorous requirement, even if they admired the Pharisees' effort to take the law more
seriously.

Given their strong dedication to the law, it is not surprising that the
Pharisees were active supporters of the synagogues and leading participants in synagogue services. The Pharisees were also accustomed to join in
small communities called "societies,"[41] which enabled them to support
one another in their efforts to observe the law. By delegating various tasks
among its members, a society was able to oversee the payment of tithes,
the preparation of food, and so forth, in such a way that all of life's
ordinary activities could be carried out according to the law.[42]

The precise origins of Pharisaism as a movement remain obscure, but
we do know that a Pharisaic "party" had emerged by 135 B.C.[43] It is
reasonable to suppose that the movement itself began earlier with the
formation of a network of societies. Then during a period when there was

relatively little regard for the law by the Hasmoneans and their allies, the members of these societies may have joined together to form a political party that pressured for the observance of the law in public life.

The Leadership of the Scribes. Since the great majority of the chief priests were Sadducean and rejected the validity of oral tradition, the Pharisees could not be expected to look to them for moral leadership. For guidance in applying the law to everyday life, they turned to the scribes, scholars who had been formally trained in the study of the law.[44]

Although there were both priests and laity of Sadducean persuasion who served as scribes, by far the greatest number of scribes were Pharisees.[45] An extended period of study was a prerequisite to ordination as a scribe, and in most instances this began when the candidates were young. They began by attaching themselves to an ordained teacher and studied until they had mastered the main content of the law.[46] Having arrived at a high level of competence, they were ordained and were then authorized to pass judgments in civil cases and to give official interpretations on matters relating to everyday applications of the law.[47]

Ordination gave the scribe the right to be called "rabbi"[48] and to have a following of students. If a large group of students gathered around a rabbi and his interpretations came to be highly valued, they might be handed on to succeeding generations. In this way, various "schools" of interpretation developed within Pharisaism; indeed such a diversity ensued that we must be careful not to think of Pharisaism as a single position or line of interpretation that all Pharisees upheld.[49]

Attitude Toward Roman Rule. During Hasmonean rule, at least some of the Pharisees functioned as a political party, supporting particular Hasmonean leaders and attempting to exert influence through the sanhedrin. However, from the rise of Herod the Great till the end of the bitter Jewish war against Rome, the Pharisees seem to have moved away from direct political involvement and to have adopted an attitude of indifference regarding rulers and the forms under which they ruled.

The Pharisees' acquiescence in Herod's rise to power when many of the people sought to resist his rule[50] is one sign of this political "indifference." The fact that they did not align themselves with any of the factions that contended for power at the time of Herod's death is a second indication. Third, although they may have been involved in protests against Pilate's infringements of Jewish law, Josephus does not attribute to them an anti-Roman attitude (as he does to the Zealots) and does not indicate that they saw cooperation with Roman rule as contrary to their own commitment to observance of the law.[51]

It seems likely that the Pharisees cooperated with, or at least did not oppose, Roman rule in Judea. They would remain alert to, and aggressively counter, any transgressions of the Jewish law by the Roman governors; but they did not see any inherent conflict between Roman taxation and Roman-administered public order on the one hand and their own deep-rooted allegiance to the law on the other.

3. THE ZEALOTS

Origin and History. Josephus places the origin of what he calls "the fourth philosophy" in the uprising against Roman rule that Judas the Gaulanite led in protest over Quirinius' proposed assessment. He further states that the principles Judas enunciated proved to be the seeds from which great civil strife and warfare later developed.[52] It is not certain that all the Jewish partisans subsequently entering the movement against Rome embraced Judas' principles, but the best evidence available suggests that Judas' example and program exercised some influence over the Jews who later entered the anti-Roman struggle. Therefore, we apply the term "Zealot" here to anyone who participated in the revolutionary struggle from Judas' time onwards.[53]

Judas' call was based on the premise that the Jews could not tolerate Roman rule and maintain their allegiance to God.[54] The term "zealot" was traditionally used in Old Testament times and in the intertestamental period to describe those who were zealous for God's law.[55] It is therefore fittingly used to describe Judas' followers even though there were other Jews equally dedicated to God's law who did not concur with the Zealots' judgment that direct Roman rule was incompatible with God's law.[56]

We note three characteristics of the later stages of the Zealot movement. Perhaps the most important was the vicious factionalism that developed among the various leaders and groups who later took part in the struggle. The three rebel factions that were ensconced in the different sections of Jerusalem constantly pillaged and killed among themselves, and it was not until the very end that they were able to mount a unified effort against the forces of Titus.[57]

Second, as this dissension itself indicates and as the numerous atrocities reported by Josephus testify, a great dissolution took place with regard to the high ideals and lofty purposes that Judas had originally set forth as the basis of the revolutionary effort.

Third, it is to be remembered that when the Zealots gained control of Jerusalem, they set fire to the Archive building in order to destroy the money-lenders' bonds. Josephus tells us that they took this step in order to gain the sympathy of the poor against the rich;[58] this tends to indicate that the Zealots' program included social reform as well as the overthrow of Roman rule.

The Zealots and Violence. Since violence and force were commonly accepted within Judea, Palestine, and the rest of the Roman empire, the fact that Judas and his followers took up arms and attempted forcibly to throw off the Roman rule is not surprising. Nevertheless, while the approach initiated by the Zealots came to be the main one that the Jews of Judea and Galilee followed, there were at least two instances in which Jewish groups vigorously opposed Roman policies without taking up arms: the protest that a Jewish group made to Pilate when he affixed shields to one of the public buildings,[59] and the protest that occurred when his soldiers introduced offensive standards into Jerusalem.

Josephus' account of the latter Jewish protest is as follows:

> When the Jews again engaged in supplication, at a prearranged signal he surrounded them with his soldiers and threatened to punish them at once with death if they did not put an end to their tumult and return to their own places. But they, casting themselves prostrate and baring their throats, declared that they had gladly welcomed death rather than make bold to transgress the wise provisions of the laws. Pilate, astonished at the strength of their devotion to the laws, straightway removed the images from Jerusalem and brought them back to Caesarea.[60]

We said above that of the various Jewish groups the Pharisees, and possibly the Zealots, were the most likely to have been involved in such a demonstration. However, if we assume that the Zealots were consistent in their stance of armed opposition, it is not likely that they would have placed themselves in such a situation in the first place, and it is not likely that they would have been willing to sacrifice their lives without inflicting some toll upon Pilate's soldiers Since Josephus does not explicitly name the Pharisees or indicate that the Jewish group in question had an a priori commitment to a nonviolent approach, we are not arguing that the Pharisees, or any other group of that period, were committed to nonviolent resistance. However, at the time the Zealots were issuing their call to violent revolution against Rome, there was at least one instance in which a strong, but nonviolent, response was given to the Romans.

By the time of Jesus' public ministry the Zealot movement was well under way. As we have seen the uprising that Judas initially led occurred at the time of Quirinius' assessment in A.D. 6. The principles on which Judas based his appeal would have thus had ample time to diffuse throughout the territories of Judea and Galilee and reach the general Jewish populace, including Jesus and his disciples. While we do not have any specific references to Zealot campaigns during this period, it is likely that any of the controversies that developed between Pilate and the Jews would have been sufficient to keep alive the Zealots' argument that the Romans had to be expelled once and for all. Then, too, it was not very long after Jesus' death that the Zealot movement came to its full and tragic fruition.

4. THE ESSENES

History and Community Life. The descriptions of Josephus and Philo give us considerable information about the Essenes.[61] From 1947 onward, these sources have been greatly supplemented by the discovery of the "Dead Sea Scrolls" in the caves near the ruins of Qumran. These scrolls and the excavations at Qumran have revealed much about the mode of life of the Essenes and their outlook toward the surrounding world.

The Essenes seem to have originated as a distinctly Jewish sect during the early Hasmonean period, and they remained in existence until the outbreak of the Jewish war against Rome. For most of this period they seem to have been headquartered at Qumran, but some members were also to be found in segregated communities in the cities and towns of Palestine. Philo even indicates that an Essene-like community, the *Therapeutae*, had settled in Egypt.[62]

The Essenes may have originated when a group of priests and levites left the temple in Jerusalem to protest the abuses under the Hasmonean high priests.[63] But whatever the circumstances, this group eventually settled at Qumran, and, under the leadership of a "Teacher of Righteousness," came to see themselves as the faithful remnant of God's people.[64]

The community developed by the Essenes was highly structured. Each person admitted to the group was given a specific rank and assigned to a specific subcommunity. A priest and a "guardian" stood over each of these smaller groups, and a priest and a guardian were at the head of the whole community.[65] Despite this hierarchical ordering, those fully admitted into the community practiced a common ownership of property. Everything was placed in the hands of a steward who administered the common possessions.[66]

According to the Dead Sea Scrolls, the Qumran community also placed strong emphasis on monogamous marriage, holding that a man who took a second wife while his first was still alive committed adultery. However, Josephus and Philo also indicate that the Essenes were well known for their practice of celibacy. It would seem that some of the members were married, and some remained celibate.[67]

Attitude Toward Roman Rule. One of the Qumran documents, *The War Rule*, suggests that the Essenes expected to remain apart from the life of the general populace until the time of a messianic war. At that time, they would occupy Jerusalem and conquer all the surrounding territories, ultimately defeating the *Kittim*, the leading power of the Gentile world.[68] This reference to the *Kittim* may possibly be to the Romans and their forces under Pompey.[69]

When the ruins at Masada, the fortress from which the Zealots made their final defense, were recently excavated, a fragment of the *Angelic Liturgy* was uncovered.[70] Since this document had previously been found at Qumran and is known to have been part of the Essenes' literature, its presence at Masada may indicate that the Essenes had joined with the Zealots at the time of the final anti-Roman effort.

Since coins minted by the Zealots have been found at Qumran, and Roman arrowheads have appeared among the ruins, it is possible that the Essenes were attacked by the Romans in consequence of their support of the Zealots.[71] Josephus states that a number of the Essenes distinguished themselves in the war against the Romans and that one of the Jewish generals in this war was an Essene named John.[72]

5. THE JEWISH POPULACE AS A WHOLE

Josephus states that the Pharisees had approximately six thousand members and the Essenes four thousand.[73] It is extremely unlikely that the chief priests and their Sadducean lay allies together could have comprised a very large number. As for the Zealots, at least for the first decades of their existence, they too must have been very small in number. It is thus clear that in comparison with the population figures put forth by Jeremias and Hoehner, the total combined membership of the four groups that we have considered would constitute a small number.

We do not have a great deal of information about the outlook of the general populace with regard to the social and political questions we have been treating. We may surmise that the people as a whole resented the high taxes that prevailed under the Herods and under the Romans, but we do not know whether they saw much difference between Herod the Great's administration and that which the Roman governors subsequently instituted. We may suppose that the Jewish population of Judea initially preferred having the sanhedrin entrusted with the responsibility for the administration of daily life; but given a high degree of corruption among

the leading priestly families, this preference may not have endured very long. There are still significant gaps in our knowledge of the social and political setting at the time of Jesus, and this must be taken into consideration in any attempt to judge the situation of the Jewish populace as a whole.

Conzelmann's Interpretation: The "Political Apologetic" Argument

In our opening chapter, we analyzed Hans Conzelmann's view concerning the presence of a political apologetic in Luke's gospel, and we have referred to his interpretations several times since then. Since Conzelmann's work, *The Theology of St. Luke*, is widely influential, it is appropriate that we now underscore the great contrast between Conzelmann's findings and our own.

We have indicated that Conzelmann believes that Luke portrays Jesus in harmony with, and subservient to, the existing political order. Here we cite what is perhaps his most important statement on this subject:

> The existing wordly powers, Roman and Jews, come into the foreground of the story, particularly in the Passion. In both cases there is a combination of submission and sovereignty. Jesus submits to the Law—and thus provides a norm for his followers after his death—and accepts the political supremacy of the Emperor. On the other hand, he describes himself as King before the representative of the Empire, and over against Israel claims the supremacy as Christ—Son of man—Son of God. The explanation of this difference is to be found in the fact that his Kingship becomes manifest in

his supremacy over the Temple of which he takes possession; he exercises his supremacy by teaching, firstly about the Law, but also about his future position at the Parousia. Thus his Kingship does not stand opposed to the Empire on the political plane, yet it implies the claim to supremacy over the world, a claim which is made by the proclamation of the Kingdom of God.[1]

In our view, there are several unsatisfactory elements present in the above excerpt. First, Conzelmann seems to affirm that the Romans and the Jews have approximately the same standing. If this is the case, his position fails to appreciate the political circumstances under which Jesus' public ministry and trial took place. Although Luke shows the chief priests playing an extremely aggressive role, it was still Pilate, the Roman governor, who held the ultimate power. To designate the Jews as a worldly power is not consistent with what we know about the existing situation.[2]

Second, any interpretation that states that Jesus answered Pilate's question affirmatively needs to explain why Luke shows Pilate immediately responding with a declaration that Jesus is innocent; this Conzelmann does not do.[3]

Third, there are problems connected with Conzelmann's position that, although Jesus' kingship does not stand opposed to the empire on the political plane, it still implies a claim to supremacy over the world. As we have seen, Luke presents Jesus making concrete, "this-worldly" responses to social patterns and political authorities, yet Conzelmann here seems to suggest that Jesus' teaching and activity did not really place him in conflict with the existing social and political conditions and that Jesus was primarily concerned with a heavenly kingship. Since this kingship was on a different "plane" from that on which the Roman empire existed, Jesus could still be submissive to the Roman order on its own plane.[4] But once it is challenged, what evidence can Conzelmann adduce to support such an interpretation? What passages in Luke's gospel indicate that Jesus was concerned about heavenly kingship and submissive to the social order that the Romans were maintaining?

Since Conzelmann's statements in the above passage emerge from his general approach, a thorough criticism of his conclusions would require an extended analysis of his entire work as well as his theological presuppositions. This would take us beyond the boundaries of our present study. Here, however, two general observations may be germane. First, Conzelmann frequently does not treat the passages in which Luke shows Jesus refusing to cooperate with, or actually criticizing, his political rulers.[5] Second, he fails to appreciate Luke's portrayal of Jesus as one who consistently contravened the existing social patterns, patterns which the Romans were committed to maintain. Seemingly, these two tendencies allow Conzelmann to reach conclusions like those in the passage above.

The fact that Luke shows Jesus frequently contravening the existing social patterns and not deferring to the political authorities also undermines the position that Conzelmann and others have taken in stating that Luke desired to make a political apologetic for the early Christians. It is inconceivable that Luke would have described Jesus adopting such a challenging stance if his intention was to portray him as loyal to the Roman social order and submissive to Roman authority.

Among other things, Luke shows Jesus criticizing "the kings of the Gentiles" and "benefactors" for dominating their subjects, shows him referring to Herod Antipas (a Roman ally) as "that fox," and depicts him responding to Pilate tersely and noncommitally. It is particularly significant that Luke used his personal sources for many of these "controversial" descriptions of Jesus or else produced them himself as a part of his redaction of his sources.[6] These descriptions were not present in Mark's account, but Luke elected to place them in his own.

The principal argument advanced by the supporters of the political apologetic position is that Luke describes Pilate affirming Jesus' innocence more emphatically than Mark does and also shows Pilate playing a less important role in Jesus' actual execution. However, as we have pointed out in Chapter Five, these alterations represent only one dimension of Luke's passion account; and, instead of expressing Luke's apologetic concerns, they very likely represent his efforts to be more precise about the major responsibility that the chief priests and their allies had in securing Jesus' death.

One other alteration that Luke makes of a Markan passage also indicates that he was not concerned with political apologetic. If Luke's objective was to establish Jesus' loyalty and "safeness" for the Roman order, the last thing he would have wanted to do was to show him in the company of Zealots; yet, as we observed in Chapter One, he does. In describing the twelve disciples, Mark had described Simon with the somewhat obscure designation "the Canaanean." Luke, however, sought to be more precise about Simon's background; he altered Mark's description and plainly designated Simon as the disciple "who was called the Zealot."

Notes

Chapter One

1. For an extended discussion of the various factors (the same level of proficiency in Greek, the consistency of style, the common motifs, etc.) that indicate that the same person was the author of both Luke and Acts, see H. Cadbury, *The Making of Luke-Acts* (London: SPCK, 1958).

2. Standard commentaries on Luke's gospel such as E. Ellis, *The Gospel of Luke* (London: Nelson, 1966), and W. Grundmann, *Das Evangelium nach Lukas* (Berlin: Evangelische Verlagsanstalt, 1971), provide good discussions of the history of the question regarding Luke's sources.

3. Ellis, *Gospel of Luke*, pp. 22–24, indicates that while there is disagreement over whether or not "Q" was a written source (Ellis believes it was not), the dominant opinion is that Luke and Matthew did share a "Q" source. However, he also indicates that there is support for the position advanced by A. Farrer and others that Luke actually had access to Matthew's gospel. Grundmann *Evangelium nach Lukas*, p. 10, believes that "Q" was a written source for Luke and Matthew.

4. B. Throckmorton, *Gospel Parallels: A Synopsis of the First Three Gospels* (London: Nelson, 1967), presents the parallel texts in English. Kurt Aland, *Synopsis of the Four Gospels* (Stuttgart: Wurttembergische Bibelanstalt, 1970), presents them in Greek and English. For suggestions in making comparisons between the various gospels, see. F. Beare, *The Earliest Records of Jesus* (New York: Abingdon, 1962).

5. N. Perrin, *What is Redaction Criticism?* (Philadelphia: Fortress, 1974), provides a brief, but extremely helpful introduction. More comprehensive is J. Rohde, *Rediscovering the Teaching of the Evangelists* (Philadelphia: Westminster, 1968).

6. Perrin, *What Is Redaction Criticism?* pp. 21–22, indicates that the work of scholars such as R. H. Lightfoot paved the way for redaction

criticism, but that this discipline came to full expression during the 1950s in the works of G. Bornkamm, H. Conzelmann, and W. Marxsen.

7. Since there is no source that served Luke for Acts in the way that Mark served him for his gospel, Acts is a much less fruitful ground for redaction criticism. However, for a discussion of the sources that Luke may have had available to him for Acts, see E. Haenchen, *The Acts of the Apostles* (Philadelphia: Westminster, 1971), pp. 81–90.

8. In his work *Eschatology in Luke* (Philadelphia: Fortress, 1971), p. 3, n. 6, E. Ellis states that since Luke "shows himself quite capable of altering his sources, it is doubtful that he includes anything, however traditional, with which he explicitly disagrees." In the text itself Ellis states, "All of the material in Luke is in some sense 'Lukan' from the fact that Luke includes it. If the traditional material has acquired a Lukan shape, the editorial material also may have a traditional character. In choosing sources, as much as in *ad hoc* elaboration, Luke is expressing his concerns and preferences."

In his article "Lukan Eschatology," *New Testament Studies* 16 (1970): 345, Wilson expresses a similar position: "Moreover, who can say that because Luke transmits some material unchanged this does not represent his own view? Surely the very fact that he transmits this material shows, at the least, that it was not objectionable to him; had it been, he would have omitted it."

9. M. Tolbert, *The Broadman Bible Commentary: Luke* (Nashville: Broadman Press, 1970), p. 1.

10. J. M. Creed, *The Gospel According to St. Luke* (New York: Macmillan, 1960), p. xi.

11. In his essay "Luke's Place in the Development of Early Christianity," *Studies in Luke-Acts*, ed. L. Keck and J. Martyn (New York: Abingdon, 1966), p. 298, Conzelmann reiterates his earlier position that the phrasing and description of Luke 21:20–24 indicate that Luke knows of the destruction of Jerusalem.

12. H. Cadbury, *Making of Luke-Acts*, pp. 346 and 359, concludes from the prologue that Luke, while indicating that he was not an eyewitness to the events of Jesus' ministry, may have been affirming some first-hand contact with the events described in the later parts of Acts.

13. Cadbury's companion study, *The Book of Acts in History* (New York: Harper, 1955), contains a chapter dealing with Luke's sensitivity to Greek culture and Greek social patterns. In *The Making of Luke-Acts*, pp. 244–45,

he discusses Antioch as one of the likely possibilities for having been Luke's home city.

14. Relying on a passage from Tacitus (*Annals* 15, 44), H. Workmann, *Persecution in the Early Church* (London: Epworth, 1923), pp. 52–53, concludes that Nero's persecution was in fact directed against Christians. However, he concedes that this is a disputed issue and notes that other Roman historians do not support Tacitus on this point. Workmann cites Neumann, Lightfoot, Mommsen, Hardy, and Ramsay as historians who agree that persecution was definitely taking place under Domitian. G. Braumann, "Das Mittel der Zeit," *Zeitschrift für die Neutestamentliche Wissenschaft* 54 (1964): 117–45, argues that Luke was well aware of the persecutions besetting the early Christian communities and sees this awareness strongly reflected within Luke's gospel.

15. Flavius Josephus, *The Jewish War* (New York: Loeb Classical Library, 1928), VI. 6.2. We shall have more to say regarding these concessions in Appendix I.

16. B. Easton, *The Purpose of Acts* (London: SPCK, 1936), pp. 11–12, argues that the Romans did not usually distinguish among the various theological positions and groupings within Judaism. He believes that one of Luke's purposes in Acts was to establish that Christianity was a "party" or "way" within Judaism; thus perceived, Christianity might itself be accorded the privileges that Judaism had as a *religio licita*, a "recognized" religion. Haenchen, *Acts of the Apostles*, p. 102, expresses a similar view. However, in his review of the third German edition of Haenchen's work, an essay entitled "Geschichte, Geschichtsbild und Geschichtsdarstellung bei Lukas," *Theologische Literaturzeitung* 85 (1960): 241–50, Conzelmann argues against the position that Luke was trying to secure a place for Christianity under Judaism's *religio licita* umbrella. Conzelmann believes that Luke had apologetic purposes, but he believes that Luke sought to achieve them by distancing Christianity from Judaism. He asserts that Luke could not have operated on the basis of a *religio licita* concept because that was a concept first enunciated by Tertullian. However, such an argument does not rule out the possibility that the *reality* of *religio licita* might have been in effect even if the terminology for describing it came later.

17. One example of a punitive measure taken against the Jews outside of Palestine was the stipulation that the tax that they had formerly collected for the support of the Temple in Jerusalem was now to be paid to the Roman state.

18. A.J.B. Higgins, "The Preface to Luke and the Kerygma in Acts," *Apostolic History and the Gospel*, ed. W. Gasque and R. Martin (Grand Rapids: Eerdmans, 1970), p. 79, indicates that the majority view is that Luke's preface to the gospel is intended as a preface to both works. (This interpretation was pioneered by Cadbury who argued that, like Josephus and other ancient historians, Luke rededicated his work to Theophilus at the beginning of the second volume.)

19. The interpretation that Luke wrote to persuade educated Gentiles (Theophilus) to become Christians is strongly argued by J. O'Neill, *The Theology of Acts* (London: SPCK, 1961), pp. 168ff.

20. H. Cadbury, "The Purpose Expressed in Luke's Preface," *The Expositor* 8 (1921): 439–40.

21. E. Goodspeed, "Some Greek Notes: Was Theophilus Luke's Publisher?" *Journal of Biblical Literature* 73 (1954): 84.

22. The book is dedicated to Theophilus in the same sense that a modern author might dedicate a book to a person or group. Thus, the dedication is a means for honoring or thanking the particular person or group, but the work itself is written for broader purposes.

23. M. Dibelius, *Studies in the Acts of the Apostles* (New York: Scribner's, 1956), p. 103. Also Easton, *Purpose of Acts*, p. 5.

24. As noted above, this view is strongly argued by J. O'Neill, *Theology of Acts*, pp. 168ff.

25. Easton, *Purpose of Acts*, pp. 5–6, thinks that Luke's awareness that his work would be read aloud influenced his presentation in Acts: for example, he allowed somewhat repetitious material to stand in his final draft.

26. Cadbury, *The Making of Acts*, p. 337. Cadbury has pointed out that Luke's own Christianity permeates the work as a whole and cites Harnack's reference to Luke as "an enthusiast for Christ."

27. Conzelmann, *The Theology of St. Luke* (New York: Harper, 1961), p. 14.

28. Ibid., p. 16.

29. Ibid., p. 136.

30. Ibid., pp. 139–40 and 188–89.

31. Ibid., p. 149.

32. H. Flender, *St. Luke: Theologian of Redemptive History* (Philadelphia: Fortress, 1967), and W.C. Robinson, Jr., "The Way of the Lord: A Study of History and Eschatology in the Gospel of Luke" (University of Basle doctoral dissertation, 1960) have followed Conzelmann's general approach to Luke's gospel. Each study recognizes the breakthrough that Conzelmann has achieved but criticizes the general interpretation of Luke's theology that Conzelmann has given. What is of particular importance for our own study is that both Flender and Robinson tend to concur with Conzelmann's approach on political apologetic. For a listing of the various articles responding to Conzelmann's approach and conclusions, see C. Talbert, "The Redaction Critical Quest for Luke the Theologian," *Perspective* (1970): 171–222.

33. Cadbury, *Making of Luke-Acts*, pp. 254–58, provides a careful treatment of the subject, comparing the universalism expressed in Luke's gospel with that expressed in the other gospel accounts. Cadbury points out that there are elements of universalism and particularity in all the accounts.

34. See the bibliographical references in subsequent chapters.

35. See the extended article by G. Lampe, "The Holy Spirit in the Writings of St. Luke," *Studies in the Gospels*, ed. D. Nineham (Oxford: Blackwell, 1955), pp. 159–200.

36. Cadbury, *Making of Luke-Acts*, p. 269.

37. C. Talbert, *Luke and the Gnostics: An Examination of the Lucan Purpose* (New York: Abingdon, 1966).

38. It is important to note that in many discussions about Luke's role as a historian, the meaning of the term "historian" is frequently not precisely defined. M. Dibelius, *Studies in the Acts*, pp. 136–37, speaks of the ancient historian as not wishing "to present life with photographic accuracy, but rather to portray and illumine what is typical"; he believes that such an understanding of the historian's role is what enables the author of Acts "partly to omit, change, and generalize what really occurred." The implication is that Luke could have operated according to the standards of an ancient historian while not necessarily meeting those of a modern historian. However, if Dibelius's distinction between "ancient" and "modern" historians is accepted, then the issue is whether or not Luke was a historian in the modern sense. Dibelius does not clearly and explicitly address himself to this issue, although the implication is that he would not attribute such a degree of "technical" accuracy to Luke.

39. The position that the process by which the gospels were formed has rendered them unreliable sources for points of history has a long tradition behind it. R. Bultmann's two works, *The History of the Synoptic Tradition* (New York: Harper and Row, 1972), and *Theology of the New Testament* (London: SCM, 1959) have been extremely influential in this regard.

40. C. Ogg, "The Quirinius Question Today," *Expository Times* 79 (1968): 231–36, provides a summary of the various positions regarding Luke's accuracy in this passage. H. Moehring, "The Census in Luke as an Apologetic Device," *Studies in the New Testament and Early Christian Literature* (Leiden: Brill, 1972), pp. 146–47, provides a summary of the chief objections against Luke's account.

41. Flavius Josephus, *Jewish Antiquities* (New York: Loeb Classical Library, 1928), XVII. ll.5; XVIII. 1.1; XVIII. 2.1.

42. Drawing upon ideas advanced by Grundmann and others, Moehring, "Census in Luke," pp. 157–60, argues that although he knew that it was historically incorrect to place Jesus' birth at the time of the census in A.D. 6–7, Luke had theological reasons for doing so. Luke knew that the uprising against the census had been one of the chief moments in the development of the revolutionary movement led by the Zealots. Thus, for apologetic reasons he portrayed Joseph and Mary not only as having nothing to do with the violent opposition to the census, but as actually being so loyal to the emperor's decree that they travelled to Bethlehem to conform to its requirements.

43. In *Antiquities*, XX.5.1, Josephus tells of the uprising that Theudas led when Cuspius Fadus was governor of Judea (c. A.D. 44–46). In the very next paragraph, XX.5.2, Josephus refers to an event that had happened much earlier, i.e., the uprising of Judas in A.D. 6–7 at the occasion of Quirinius' census. In the argument against Luke's accuracy it is suggested that he read Josephus' account hurriedly and did not realize that, while Josephus mentioned the uprising of Judas after that of Theudas, he actually indicated that it had happened much earlier.

44. This essay is contained in *Studies in Luke-Acts*, L. Keck and J. Martyn (New York: Abingdon, 1966), pp. 258–78. Haenchen had already adopted this basic outlook in the original German editions of his *Acts of the Apostles*. However, in this essay he develops his objections more thematically.

45. Ibid., p. 260.

46. Ibid., pp. 262–65.

47. Ibid., pp. 265–68.

48. Ibid. See also *Acts of the Apostles*, pp. 112–16.

49. Ibid., pp. 273–75.

50. Ibid., p. 278.

51. S.G.F. Brandon, *The Trial of Jesus of Nazareth* (London: Batsford, 1968). See also *Jesus and the Zealots: A Study of the Political Factor in Early Christianity* (Manchester: Manchester University Press, 1967).

52. Brandon, *Trial of Jesus*, pp. 75–76.

53. Ibid., p. 124. See below for our own interpretation of the description that Luke gives of Pilate.

54. Ibid., p. 63.

55. Our term "empire history" has a range of meaning comparable to what W. Ramsay, *Was Christ Born at Bethlehem?* (New York: Putnam's, 1898), calls "general history." Our reason for choosing a term with the word "empire" in it is to emphasize that the Roman empire was the controlling frame of reference in Luke's day and that information concerning important social and political patterns and events circulated widely. When they established their dynasty, Vespasian and Titus gave prominence to their personal successes in the Jewish war. (The construction of the Arch of Titus, the minting of new coins, and indeed the publication of Josephus' *The Jewish War* all witness to their concern to publicize their achievements.) Thus it is likely that even more information than usual regarding Judea and Palestine would have been in general circulation throughout the empire.

56. Luke also provides numerous references to empire history in Acts. In addition to his descriptions of Roman officials and Roman trial procedures, he makes reference to the famine that occurred during Claudius' reign (11:38) and mentions Claudius' edict expelling the Jews from Rome (18:2). In 12:20 we have the following description of Herod Agrippa's relations with neighboring powers: "Now Herod was angry with the people of Tyre and Sidon; and they came to him in a body, and having persuaded Blastus, the king's chamberlain, they asked for peace, because their country depended on the king's country for food."

57. See in particular A. N. Sherwin-White, *Roman Society and Roman Law in the New Testament* (Oxford: Clarendon Press, 1963).

58. A. N. Sherwin-White, "The Trial of Christ," *Historicity and Chronology in the New Testament* (London: SPCK, 1965), p. 101.

59. Sherwin-White, *Roman Society and Roman Law*, pp. 144–62.

60. Creed, *Gospel According to St. Luke*, pp. 28–29.

61. J. Finegan, *Handbook of Biblical Chronology* (Princeton: Princeton University Press, 1964), pp. 235–38, cites the relevant passages from Tacitus and Josephus and also reconstructs a tentative chronology for the Roman governors of Syria. Finegan believes that the existing evidence admits of the possibility that Quirinius could have served as governor in Syria after he had successfully directed Rome's forces in the Homanadensian war and before he served as advisor to Gaius Caesar in Armenia. According to this sequence, he was then reappointed as governor in A.D. 6.

A. N. Sherwin-White, *Roman Society and Roman Law*, p. 166, states that "uncertainty still prevails about the legate of Syria in the very last years of Herod's reign, to which the alternative versions assign the nativity. Quintilius Varus took office in 6 B.C. and held it until at least 4 B.C. If his tenure then ended, his successor down to the arrival of Gaius is unknown."

An important article, not yet published, "Lysanias and Quirinius: A New Solution Through Micrographics," by Dr. Jerry Vardaman of Mississippi State University, has recently come to my attention. Dr. Jack Finegan made his copy available to me, and Dr. Vardaman has agreed that I might refer to several of its main points. Accordingly, I wish to express my thanks to both of these scholars.

Using techniques that he has developed, Vardaman has deciphered many faint letterings that he found on the surfaces of coins, seals, weights, and sculpture from the Greco-Roman period. According to Vardaman, these letterings show that Quirinius served as *proconsul* of Syria and exercised supreme authority over Cilicia and other Eastern territories from 11 B.C. until after 4 B.C. Vardaman also finds that Titus, Saturnius, Varus, and other Roman officials in the East were under Quirinius' authority even though they held the title of "Legate."

Vardaman's findings will have to overcome a significant amount of contrary evidence in order to prevail with respect to his finding that Quirinius was serving as proconsul. The traditional view (for a discussion on this point, see G. Vermes, F. Millar, and E. Schürer, *The History of the Jewish People in the Age of Jesus* [Edinburgh: Clark, 1973], p. 255), is that during this period Syria was an imperial province, a province directly under Augustus and administered by his legate. Vardaman's finding would seem to require that Syria was actually a senatorial province, one administered by a proconsul that the senate appointed. His findings that Varus and others were actually serving under Quirinius and that Quirinius exercised supreme authority over Cilicia, a territory with its own king, also faces a considerable amount of countervailing evidence.

As a result of his investigations Vardaman concludes that, just as Luke states, Quirinius was in office at the time when Jesus was born. The publication of his manuscript will therefore be an event of considerable importance.

62. J. Schmid, *Das Evangelium nach Lukas* (Regensburg: Pustet, 1960), pp. 66–70. Schmid refers to the evidence concerning censuses taken by the Romans in Egypt, Syria, and elsewhere at approximately this time. The census that Luke describes differs considerably from any of these, but Schmid believes that there are similarities that make Luke's description conceivable.

63. F. F. Bruce, *The Acts of the Apostles* (London: Tyndale Press, 1952), p. 147.

64. At the time of Herod the Great's death, three of his sons journeyed to Rome seeking to receive dominion over Herod's territories.

65. O. Cullmann, *The State in the New Testament* (New York: Scribner's 1956), p. 15.

Chapter Two

1. Questions about Luke's understanding of Jesus' identity are important, and various interpretations have been put forward. In our view, there are grounds for believing that Luke describes Jesus' birth and life as a unique divine intervention into human history, that he situates him in terms of several Old Testament prophetic and apocalyptic traditions, that he portrays Jesus as a millennial figure who announced that a new age had dawned, and that he viewed him as the long-awaited Christ, a messiah who accomplished the "redemption" not only of Israel, but of all peoples. To this list other elements might be added.

However, our objective is not definitively to resolve the various questions surrounding Jesus' identity in Luke's account. Instead, we will assume that the elements we have listed are important characteristics in Luke's portrait of Jesus, and we will attempt to determine just how Luke shows Jesus relating to the social patterns and political conditions around him. Does Luke show Jesus endorsing or criticizing the existing social patterns? Was he submissive and deferential to Herod Antipas, the chief priests, and the Romans, or not? These are the kinds of questions that we are primarily concerned with.

2. At the turn of the century, Albert Schweitzer and others advanced the interpretation that Jesus expected the final days to come within his lifetime. Schweitzer then argued that Jesus' own teaching and conduct

(and that which he recommended to the disciples) were premised upon the "imminent coming of the kingdom" and did not have relevance for later generations of Christians. Few scholars now defend Schweitzer's interpretation without making considerable modifications; this is particularly true of commentators on Luke's gospel. Indeed, as we saw in our first chapter, Hans Conzelmann's view is that Luke addressed the problem of the "delay" by showing that there were definite stages in salvation history. (Since Conzelmann is more concerned to interpret Luke's eschatological outlook than to analyze the outlook that Luke attributes to Jesus, we do not have his precise position on this latter question; however, it is clear that he does not believe that Luke shows Jesus as expecting an imminent coming.)

However, even if Schweitzer's improbable interpretation were assumed to be correct, our own study would not be seriously affected. We could grant that Luke's Jesus expected the final days to come within his lifetime and still go on to inquire about precisely how he related to the social patterns and the political conditions around him. Regardless of whether Jesus believed that the end was near or not, did he treat the established political authorities with deference?

With respect to Schweitzer's "interim ethic" and the "impossible ideal" of Reinhold Niebuhr, Amos Wilder's *Eschatology and Ethics in the Teaching of Jesus* (New York: Harper, 1939) provides a helpful perspective. Wilder's insights need to be confirmed through redaction critical analyses, but his argument that the gospels evidence a belief in the enduring validity of Jesus' teachings is a significant one.

3. In an effort to give a systematic and concise presentation of the social stance that Luke attributes to Jesus, we have structured our presentation around a number of the important subject areas that Luke's account touches upon: Jesus' concern for the poor and the infirm, his approach regarding material possessions, his stance regarding the use of violence against persons. Such an approach runs the risk of abstracting Luke's individual descriptions from the setting that they occupy within the gospel as a whole; this is a risk we will strive to be mindful of. In almost all cases we will provide a description of the context of the passage with which we are concerned, and we will seek to avoid introducing concepts and categories that are not consistent with the passages in question and with Luke's presentation throughout the gospel as a whole.

4. For reasons of style, particularly when a cumbersome sentence structure would result, we will occasionally refer to "Jesus' social stance," "Jesus' outlook toward the poor," etc. In all of these instances, we continue

to mean "the social stance that Luke describes Jesus as having," "the outlook toward the poor that Luke attributes to Jesus," etc.

Also we will be primarily concerned with analyzing the portrait of Jesus that emerges in Luke's finished account. In the notes (and occasionally in the text when doing so will particularly illumine the meaning embodied in Luke's final version) we will frequently present interpretations regarding the process that Luke very likely followed in ordering and formulating his material, but these interpretations are not as important to our project as is the analysis of what Luke's finished gospel actually states about Jesus' social and political stance.

5. The fiery notes contained in Mary's Magnificat have frequently, but not always, gone unnoticed. According to a Dantean legend (cited by Walter Rauschenbusch), King Robert of Sicily recognized the revolutionary ring present in Mary's prayer and thought it well that the Magnificat be sung only in Latin.

6. Luke's accounts of Jesus' baptism (3:15–22) and his temptations (4:3–13), particularly the second temptation in which the devil shows Jesus the kingdoms of the world and offers to give him "all this authority and their glory," also contain material relevant to an interpretation of Jesus' social and political stance.

7. Mark (6:1–6; see also Matt. 13:54–58) describes a similar visit by Jesus to Nazareth, but Luke goes considerably beyond Mark by reordering the sequence of events and by including an extended quotation from Isaiah along with other additions. Luke also departs from Mark's framework by placing Jesus' visit at the beginning of his public ministry. This positioning may indicate that Luke intended Jesus' identification with Isaiah's mission and his advertence to the Gentiles to stand as a "program statement" for Jesus' overall ministry. For a helpful discussion on these and other related points, see A. Leaney, *A Commentary on the Gospel According to St. Luke* (London: Black, 1958), pp. 50–54.

8. Leaney, ibid., pp. 51–52.

9. Ibid., p. 53. See also W. Grundmann, *Das Evangelium nach Lukas* (Berlin: Evangelische Verlaganstalt, 1971), p. 121.

10. Whether or not Jesus' words "Today this scripture is fulfilled in your hearing" carried messianic implications, they assuredly had the force of associating him with Isaiah's mission. This aspect of the passage has all too frequently been overlooked by commentators. Since Luke probably viewed the events at Nazareth as indicative of the "program" of Jesus'

subsequent ministry (see Grundmann, *Evangelium nach Lukas*, p. 119), Jesus' identification with Isaiah's themes is all the more significant.

We have not based our analysis of Jesus' stance toward oppression upon his association of himself with Isaiah's mission "to proclaim the acceptable year of the Lord." However, it is also significant since it implies a commitment to the new social beginnings that the original sabbatical year was designed to foster. For a helpful treatment along these lines, see J. Yoder, *The Politics of Jesus* (Grand Rapids: Eerdmans, 1972), pp. 34–40 and 64–77.

11. J. Schmid, *Das Evangelium nach Lukas* (Regensburg: Pustet, 1960), p. 112. After stating that the verses originally referred to a liberation from material suffering, Schmid takes the position that Luke has endowed them with a "spiritual-symbolic" meaning. As we have indicated, we disagree with this latter assertion. See Grundmann, *Evangelium nach Lukas*, pp. 120–21.

12. In addition to the paragraphs immediately following in the text, see also our analysis in the following section of this chapter.

13. We refer to the collection of Jesus' teachings in Luke 6:20–49 as the "Great Sermon." This Lukan compilation is also described as the "Sermon on the Plain" or as Luke's version of the "Sermon on the Mount."

14. Matthew's "sermon" occupies Chapters 5 through 7 in his gospel and is much longer than Luke's. He includes a large body of material that Luke presents in other places throughout his gospel. However, both sermons begin with the beatitudes and both end with the comparison of the two builders; and, with the exception of the "woes," much of the material that Luke includes in his sermon has its counterpart in Matthew. Since much of this material is not to be found in Mark, many scholars believe that Luke and Matthew drew their material from the "Q" source. See J. Creed, *The Gospel According to St. Luke* (New York: St. Martin's Press, 1960), pp. 89–90. For a statement of the position (held by a number of scholars in Britain and the United States) that Luke had access to Matthew, see A. Farrer, "On Dispensing with 'Q,' " *Studies in the Gospels*, ed. D. Nineham (Oxford: Blackwell, 1955).

15. 4:33–37; 4:38–39; 5:12–14; 5:17–25; 6:6–11; 7:1–10; 7:11–17; 8:26–33; 8:40–56; 9:37–43; 11:14; 13:10–13; 14:1–6; 17:11–19; 18:35–43.

16. 4:40–41; 5:15; 6:17–19; 7:21; 8:2.

17. 7:1–10; 8:26–33; 17:11–19. The last-mentioned healing (of the Samaritan leper) occurs only in Luke's account. While Luke generally follows Mark's outline faithfully, his omission of a number of passages from Mark's sixth and seventh chapters is well known. One of the passages

omitted contains Mark's account of how Jesus healed the daughter of a Syro-Phoenician woman. One possible explanation for this omission is that Mark's description shows Jesus initially responding to the woman adversely, stating that it was not right to take the children's bread and throw it to the dogs. See Mark 7:24–30 and Matt. 15:21–28.

18. The healings in 7:11–17 and 13:10–13 occur only in Luke's account.

19. Among those that Jesus calls is Levi, a tax collector (5:27–28). Since Levi was collecting customs in Herod Antipas' territory, he was likely in Herod's employ and not quite the target of the Zealots' wrath that he would have been if he were directly in the service of the Romans. Nevertheless, the fact that Simon, one of the apostles, had, or once had, a Zealot affiliation (6:16) indicates that Jesus drew his followers from both poles of the political spectrum. Also, Jesus included a considerable number of women among his intimate circle.

20. 6:29–32; 14:1–7; 19:1–10.

21. 7:1–10; 8:40–56.

22. The three instances in which Jesus reprimands the disciples will be analyzed in the next chapter in the section entitled "Jesus and Violence."

23. As we shall see below, when all of Luke's passages are adverted to, Jesus emerges as someone who called for (and practiced) a simple style of living and gave definite advice to the rich to divest themselves of their possessions. Since Jesus himself retained at least enough to live on and seemingly allowed his disciples to retain a minimum, we have interpreted his position to be that of opposing *surplus* possessions.

The question that immediately arises is which possessions are surplus and which are essential. Luke's gospel does not provide any specific answers, but the general impression is that almost all possessions are to be questioned.

24. This parable occurs only in Luke's account. Because it focuses so directly and critically upon the *accumulation* of wealth, it might well be referred to (anachronistically) as the "anti-capitalist parable."

25. The similarity between Luke's account of the mission of the twelve in 9:1–6 and his description of the mission of the seventy (or seventy-two) in 10:1–24 has led some commentators to conclude that Luke incorporated into his account material from Mark and also similar material from "Q." Luke's description of the mission of the seventy follows closely Mark's description in 6:7–13, and most of his description of the mission of the twelve has parallels in Matthew. A further relationship to be noted is that

in 22:35–36, Luke presents Jesus as referring to the instruction that he gave to the disciples in 10:4. See Creed, *Gospel According to Luke*, pp. 124–26 and pp. 143–50.

26. Although Luke depicts Jesus as occasionally accepting hospitality from the rich, he does not ever present him as indulging himself in high living. In 7:33–35 Jesus refers to the criticism that some have made of him as "a glutton and a drunkard, a friend of tax collectors and sinners"; but he matter of factly dismisses this criticism.

27. Shortly after the beginning of Jesus' journey to Jerusalem, Luke presents a series of Jesus' sayings on the subject of discipleship (this material is paralleled in Matt. 8:19–22); the words we cited appear in this context. The primary meaning of these words may be to underline the demanding character of the journey and to emphasize that Jesus' disciples have to be prepared to give up many conventional forms of security. However, Jesus' words also indicate that he does not have much in the way of material possessions. (If he did, it would be inappropriate for him to stress the rigors and hardships involved in following after him.)

Jesus' earlier words concerning simplicity were addressed to the twelve and the seventy. Here they are addressed to a potential disciple. The persons and circumstances may vary, but Jesus stressed the same theme whether he was addressing large numbers of people, instructing the disciples, or conversing with an individual person.

28. Mark (10:17–23) and Matthew (19:16–23) also describe this meeting. Several of the alterations that Luke introduces into Mark's version are relevant to our analysis. In the first place, Luke states that the person who approached Jesus was a "ruler," where Mark indicates only that he was "a man." Second, Luke omits Mark's report that after the man had replied, "Jesus looking upon him loved him."

Third, whereas in Mark's account Jesus tells the man, "Go, sell what you have and give to the poor," in Luke's version Jesus tells him to "sell *all* that you have." Thus, in Luke's account Jesus' counsel to the ruler to sell all of his possessions clearly forecloses any half-hearted compliance. Fourth, while Mark (and Matthew) state that the man became disheartened at Jesus' words and went away sorrowful, Luke states only that he became sad; in effect he thus softens the outcome of the encounter.

29. J. Creed, *Gospel According to Luke*, pp. 201–3, provides a good general discussion of the parable. J. Fitzmyer, "The Story of the Dishonest Manager," *Theological Studies* 25 (1964): 23–42, interprets the actions that the parable attributes to the steward against the background of the economic powers that such stewards may have enjoyed. Fitzmyer holds

that while the steward had previously been irresponsible and dishonest in his stewardship, he was not dishonest in summoning the debtors and granting them a reduction in their debts. Rather, as his employer's duly constituted agent, he had the power to act according to his own discretion in handling his employer's affairs.

Second, as an agent he also was entitled to a substantial commission; but in this instance realizing that he was to be dismissed from service, he decided to forego this commission. Thus, not only was this action legal, it was a prudent step to take given the circumstances. And even though his employer was in the process of firing him for his previous irresponsibility, the employer could still commend the steward's astuteness in trying to prepare for the future.

Fitzmyer also provides a helpful treatment of the comments that Jesus appends to the parable, although he does not assess them from the standpoint of Luke's other passages concerning wealth and possessions.

30. The Revised Standard Version translates *mamona tes adikias* as "unrighteous mammon." This is a somewhat bulky and cumbersome expression, but it does preserve well the meaning that "mammon" is not morally neutral for Jesus, but rather "unrighteous." If we regard mammon as referring to surplus possessions, it is clear why this would be the case. Since Luke has shown Jesus as strongly criticizing surplus possessions, it is clear that he views such extra possessions as "unrighteous." They can, however, be used to benefit the poor, and for a person to use them in this way is commendable. For the meaning "illgotten gains," see F. Hauck, "mamonas," *Theological Dictionary of the New Testament*, 4:388–90.

31. Mark's version is in 4:1–20 and Matthew's in 13:1–23.

32. This criticism occurs only in Luke's gospel.

33. This parable is peculiar to Luke's gospel. Creed, *Gospel According to Luke*, pp. 208–10, interprets it, especially the first part, as emphasizing the contrast in the conditions of the rich man and Lazarus in this life and then the sharp reversal of their situations in the next life. However, he fails to appreciate that the parable itself provides reasons for understanding why the rich man was punished. Schmid, *Evangelium nach Lukas*, pp. 264–268, is somewhat better in this regard, but still interprets the parable in terms of the concept of "reversal." Grundmann, *Evangelium nach Lukas*, pp. 325–30, follows an approach similar to Schmid's.

The parable indicates that the rich man knew Lazarus. (Lazarus was close to his gate during his lifetime, and in the afterlife he knows his name.) Second, the parable indicates that the rich man loved his possessions and disdained Lazarus. (Note that even though Lazarus is now under the care of Abraham, the rich man still takes a superior attitude toward him and attempts to have him do his bidding.) The point of the parable is, therefore, not that striking reversals of roles often take place in the life after death. Rather, it is that the rich who live a life of luxury indifferent to the poor around them will come to no good end. Seen from this perspective, the parable is thoroughly consistent with virtually all the other teachings regarding the rich and the poor that Luke attributes to Jesus. (Note the similarities between this rich man and the rich fool who sought to build additional barns.)

In their interpretations of Luke's gospel, many commentators have remarked on the Lukan theme of "reversal" and, by way of example, they have cited Mary's words ("he has filled the hungry with good things, and the rich he has sent empty away"), Jesus' words in the Great Sermon ("Blessed are you poor, for yours is the kingdom of God, . . . but woe to you who are rich for you have received your consolation"), and the present parable. While such an interpretation draws attention to Jesus' questioning whether the position of the rich is very good, it fails to appreciate the depth of Jesus' criticism of the rich and the rationale upon which it is grounded.

34. Luke here takes over a Markan passage (12:41–44) with minor modifications in it. However, one of these modifications is significant. Whereas Mark shows Jesus watching while many people, including some who were rich, contributed to the temple, Luke mentions only two kinds of contributions: those made by the rich and that made by the widow. He thus focuses more attention on the rich than Mark and heightens the contrast between what the widow is contributing and what they are contributing. See Schmid, *Evangelium nach Lukas*, p. 301.

The position that Jesus adopts fits well with the stance he takes toward the rich and their possessions elsewhere in Luke's gospel. Because Jesus has called upon the rich to divest themselves of all of their surplus possessions, he is not impressed by incidental contributions that they might make. Such contributions still leave them with the bulk of their possessions.

35. Grundmann, *Evangelium nach Lukas*, pp. 354–55, is typical of many commentators who explain these words and the passage as a whole in terms of the failure of the rich to be "detached" from their possessions. To the extent that it leaves open the possibility that the rich might still keep their possessions while remaining "spiritually detached" from them, such an interpretation misreads the position that Luke shows Jesus adopting. Jesus consistently advocates that the rich give up their possessions. He recognizes, though, that it is extremely difficult for the rich to do so.

36. In this report, Luke again follows the main lines of Mark's account while introducing minor modifications. He adds "wife," omits "sisters," gives "parents" for "mother and father," and omits "lands" in describing Jesus' words to the disciples concerning what they have left behind.

37. Matthew also reports Jesus' praise of John (11:8). While the two accounts are closely parallel, Luke does present Jesus as speaking slightly more sarcastically regarding those who wear soft clothes. In Luke's version Jesus states: "Behold, those who are gorgeously appareled and live in luxury are in kings' courts," whereas in Matthew's version Jesus states: "Behold, those who wear soft raiment are in kings' houses."

38. This again is material particular to Luke's account.

39. The closest that Jesus comes to indicting the rich for exploiting the poor is when he assails the scribes (20:47) for devouring the houses of widows. In this respect, Jesus' response to his situation differed from that which the Old Testament prophets such as Amos and Micah made in their own circumstances. Amos censures the rich and the powerful for trampling upon the needy and cheating them with falsely weighted scales (8:4–6). Micah accuses them of stealing the houses and fields of the defenseless (2:1–2) and also of cheating at the marketplace (6:11).

40. Commentators have frequently stated that the gospels do not attribute a social program to Jesus. This is correct in that the gospels do not describe Jesus as presenting a systematic and comprehensive program similar to that which a contemporary political party or governmental agency might develop. However, the real question is whether or not the evangelists (in this case Luke) show Jesus taking a position with respect to the social and political patterns around him. The evangelists do show Jesus following and recommending a specific approach and, in this sense, it is possible to speak of his having a social program.

41. Creed, *Gospel According to Luke*, p. 190; Schmid, *Evangelium nach Lukas*, pp. 243–44.

42. Both 5:29–32 and 15:1–3 are relevant in this regard.

43. The descriptions of the early Christians that Luke gives in Acts shows them practicing a community life based upon the concept of sharing: "And all who believed were together and had all things in common; and they sold their possessions and goods and distributed them to all, as any had need" (Acts 2:44–45); "now the company of those who believed were of one heart and soul, and no one said that any of the things which he possessed was his own, but they had everything in common" (Acts 4:32).

The fact that Luke's description of the Jerusalem community's attitude toward material possessions coincides so well with his description of Jesus' own teaching regarding possessions is noteworthy. Luke probably wished to indicate that the disciples were taking Jesus' teachings seriously and putting them into practice.

Chapter Three

1. Luke derives this passage from Mark (see Mark 12:40).

2. This parable is proper to Luke alone. W. Grundmann, *Das Evangelium nach Lukas* (Berlin: Evangelische Verlaganstalt, 1971), p. 347, hypothesizes that the dispute in question may have been over an inheritance or a mortgage.

3. There are important differences between Mark's account (11:11, 15–19) and Luke's account of Jesus' actions at the temple. In Mark Jesus entered the temple, looked around, and then returned to Bethany for the night. He returned to the temple the next day and began to drive out those who sold "and those who bought in the temple and he overturned the tables of the money-changers and the seats of those who sold pigeons; and he would not allow anyone to carry anything through the temple." Jesus then said that instead of being a house of prayer, the temple had been turned into a den of robbers.

In Luke, by contrast, Jesus made only one entry into the temple (his description of Jesus' entry into Jerusalem is also different from Mark's) and immediately started to drive out those who sold. Luke omits the part of Mark's description that we have cited above and closes with Jesus' criticism that the temple has been made into a den of robbers.

H. Conzelmann, *The Theology of St. Luke* (New York: Harper & Row, 1960), pp. 77-78, believes that Luke's whole description (beginning with Jesus' approach to the city and continuing through verse 47, "And he was teaching daily in the temple") is designed to emphasize that Jesus "takes possession" of the temple. To achieve this emphasis Luke has modified Mark and constructed his account as he has. In Conzelmann's view, Luke shows Jesus taking possession of the temple (and making it a fit place for him to be and to teach) by "cleansing" it; but the cleansing has a different significance for Luke than it does for Mark, for whom it is more an "eschatological sign." Grundmann, *Evangelium nach Lukas*, pp. 369–70, follows Conzelmann on this point and accordingly refers to this passage in Luke as Jesus' "occupation" *(Besitzergreifung)* of the temple.

Here the principle that a given passage can have several dimensions of meaning is of considerable importance. On the basis of this principle, it is possible to accept an interpretation such as Conzelmann's and Grundmann's and simultaneously affirm that Luke wanted to indicate that Jesus took aggressive action against the economic abuses that were taking place at the temple. Thus, while Luke has modified Mark's account on several points, he has still preserved the heart of Mark's description of Jesus' actions against those responsible for the prevailing economic practices.

4. The term "protest" highlights the challenging and confronting nature of Jesus' actions and, in our view, gives a more accurate description of what took place than does the traditional term "cleansing." "Protest" signifies that Jesus disrupted the normal pattern of temple activities to witness against them. The term does not imply that he succeeded in ending these practices or even that he thought he had a chance of doing so. Since the term does not necessarily imply violence to persons (it may signify only that vigorous action was taken, possibly even without damage to property), it also effectively represents the nonviolent character of Jesus' actions.

5. See, for example, 6:1–11; 11:37–46, 52; 13:10–17; 14:1–6.

6. Grundmann, *Evangelium nach Lukas*, pp. 319–20, thinks that Luke may have drawn upon "Q" for this material (see Matt. 5:13) or may have received it from one of his own sources. J. Creed, *The Gospel According to Luke* (London: Macmillan, 1930), pp. 207–8, provides a helpful analysis of the differences between Luke's description of Jesus' teaching and those given by Matthew and Mark (see Mark 10:11–12). Creed also examines the various practices that were in effect with respect to marriage.

7. This incident is recorded only by Luke.

8. In his description of Jesus' crucifixion, Luke indicates that "all his acquaintances and the women who had followed him from Galilee stood at a distance and saw these things" (23:49). A few verses later he states that "the women who had come with him from Galilee followed, and saw the tomb, and how his body was laid" (23:55). While Mark (15:40–41 and 15:47) and Matthew (27:55–56 and 27:61) both mention that the women who had accompanied Jesus from Galilee were present at his crucifixion and burial, they do not refer earlier to the fact that these women were accompanying Jesus. Also, while Mark and Matthew do indicate that the women they name had ministered to Jesus, their reports are not nearly as concrete or striking as Luke's when he states that the women "provided for *them* out of their means."

9. Mark (9:33–37) and Matthew (18:1–5) also indicate that the disciples quarreled and describe Jesus' response stressing humility. In Luke's ver-

sion, Jesus emphasizes the same points as in Mark's, but Luke's version arranges them differently, perhaps to develop the main theme more clearly.

10. This "parable" is proper to Luke. Note that Luke later (18:14) presents Jesus closing the parable of the publican and the Pharisee with virtually the same words as he closes this parable; R. Morgenthaler comments on Luke's tendency to parallel and repeat various words and concepts in his work *Das Zweiheitsgesetz im Lukanischen Werke* (Zurich: Zwingli-Verlag, 1949).

11. Only Luke reports this teaching. J. Schmid, *Das Evangelium nach Lukas*, 4th ed. (Regensburg: Pustet, 1960), p. 271, comments that "in this parable we have the best description of and foundation for Christian humility."

12. This criticism is addressed to the Pharisees and can be compared with Jesus' criticism of the Pharisees in Matt. 23:6–7. There are considerable differences in the contents of the two criticisms, however.

13. This criticism follows Mark 12:38–39 almost word for word. It is also similar to Jesus' earlier criticism against the *Pharisees* (see the preceding note). Grundmann, *Evangelium nach Lukas*, p. 377, suggests that Luke may have utilized material from "Q" and from his own sources when he reported Jesus' criticism of the Pharisees and then followed Mark's account (Mark having preserved material somewhat similar to that which Luke had derived from his other sources) in reporting this criticism of the scribes.

14. Jesus' reply here has some similarity with the reply that Mark depicts him giving to the disciples in another context (10:41–45; see also Matt. 20:25–28. In Mark's version, Jesus and the disciples are journeying together, and James and John's request to Jesus provokes resentment from the other disciples.) However, Schmid, *Das Evangelium nach Lukas*, p. 267, believes that the differences in the two accounts are such as to warrant the conclusion that Luke was making use of his own material. Schmid and A. Leaney, *A Commentary on the Gospel According to St. Luke* (London: Black, 1958), p. 269, both affirm that Jesus' use of the term "benefactors" was strongly sarcastic and Schmid supplies helpful information regarding the various ways in which this term was used in the ancient world. One point that he makes is particularly relevant for subsequent parts of our study. According to Schmid, "benefactor" was one of the titles that Augustus and other Roman emperors used in reference to themselves.

15. G. Sharp, *The Politics of Nonviolent Action* (Boston: Sargent, 1973)

provides a comprehensive treatment of the various forms of nonviolent responses.

16. That Jesus knew of John's death follows from the conversation that Luke describes taking place between Jesus and the disciples in 9:18–21. If Jesus did not know of John's death, their report that some people believe that Jesus is John or one of the prophets would not make sense.

17. We will consider both of these passages in greater detail in our next chapter.

18. See, for example, 11:21–22; 12:47–48; 14:31–33; 19:27.

19. In 6:35 Jesus again calls for love toward enemies and bases his appeal on the example of God in showing kindness to the ungrateful and the selfish. In the concluding section of this chapter we will advert more explicitly to the fact that Jesus' social stance is strongly related to what he believes about God.

20. For a brief comment on the differences between the wording of this petition in Luke's account and the wording in Matthew's, see Grundmann, *Evangelium nach Lukas*, p. 233.

21. This passage has fairly close parallels in Matt. 18:15 and 18:21–22. Jesus intertwines the concepts of forgiveness and repentance in three parables (the lost sheep, the lost drachma, and the forgiving father-prodigal son) in Luke 15:4–32.

22. The first part of the passage that we have cited is proper to Luke, but the verses beginning with "Do you think that I have come to give peace . . ." are paralleled in Matt. 10:34–36. Schmid, *Evangelium nach Lukas*, pp. 225–26, emphasized that Jesus' statements here underline that there can be no neutrality with respect to his coming. Our own interpretation goes beyond Schmid's to suggest that Jesus is referring to the fact that his teachings (such as that requiring the rich to divest themselves of their possessions) will inevitably cause great divisions between those who accept them and those who do not.

In our view, the purpose of the teachings is not division (rather, their purpose is the true well-being of all); but it is reasonable to conjecture that divisions will result from them. Grundmann, *Evangelium nach Lukas*, p. 270, discusses the various interpretations of Jesus' words about casting fire upon earth. The difficulty with almost all of these interpretations is that they do not advert to the fact that Jesus' teachings were highly challenging to the people and the society of his day.

23. In Luke's gospel, the greater part of the teachings and events of

Jesus' public ministry occur within a journey to Jerusalem that Jesus undertakes with his disciples. This "journey" lasts from 9:51 to 19:28. Scholars consider it to be one of the main literary and theological concepts that Luke uses in structuring his account. See, for example, C. Ogg, "The Central Section of the Gospel According to St. Luke," *New Testament Studies* 18 (1971):39–53; also F. Stagg, "The Journey Toward Jerusalem in Luke's Gospel," *Review and Expositor* 64 (1967):499–512.

24. The enmity between the Jews and the Samaritans was long-standing; one explanation of it was that the Samaritan peoples refused to accept the temple in Jerusalem and continued to worship at Mt. Gerizim. In *Antiquities*, XX.6.1., Josephus describes some of the conflicts that took place when Jews from Galilee attempted to reach Jerusalem by travelling through Samaria.

25. Creed, *Gospel According to Luke*, p. 141, sees this whole passage as a practical illustration of the teaching that Jesus had given about not responding to evil with violence. He notes the contrast between the approach that Luke shows Jesus following and that followed by Elijah when he called down fire upon the men that King Ahaziah sent out against him (2 Kings 1:9–16).

26. From another standpoint, Schmid, *Evangelium nach Lukas*, pp. 293–94, holds that Jesus' sadness and his reproach to the city arise because he foresees that Jerusalem will, tragically, fail to recognize him as the Messiah.

27. John's gospel indicates that Jesus fashioned a whip of cords and overturned the tables of the money-changers (2:14–16), but also stops short of stating that Jesus harmed anyone. The argument of Brandon and others is that the gospels give distorted accounts of what Jesus actually did and, thus, cannot be relied upon. In our own study, though, we are less concerned with Brandon's position than we are with that of scholars who mistakenly conclude (through a lack of close attention to the text) that Luke's gospel itself describes Jesus doing physical violence to others.

28. F. Hauck, *"ballo, ekballo," Theological Dictionary of the New Testament* (Grand Rapids: Eerdmans, 1964), 1:527–28, analyzes the use of this word in the New Testament. He indicates that it is used with several shades of meaning and that none of these expresses physical violence to others.

W. Bauer, *A Greek-English Lexicon of the New Testament and Other Early Christian Literature* (Chicago: University of Chicago Press, 1957), takes a contrary position holding that *ekballo's* primary meaning is *"drive out, expel*, lit. *throw out* more or less forcibly." However, the New Testament passages that he cites to illustrate this use of the term are precisely those passages that have to do with Jesus' actions at the temple. Bauer has presumed that the evangelists report Jesus using physical force when that is the very question under discussion. Bauer gives "without the connotation of force: *send out*" as a second meaning for *ekballo*, and it is our contention that this is the meaning that the word has in Luke's description. This interpretation is also supported by H. Liddell and R. Scott, *A Greek-English Lexicon*, New edition by H. Jones (Oxford: The Clarendon Press, 1940). This work gives *throw out, cast out, banish*, and *turn out* as leading meanings for *ekballo* and does not indicate that this term implies the use of force.

E. Ellis, *The Gospel of Luke* (London: Nelson, 1966), p. 231, makes the point that Luke's sense is that Jesus' actions are not viewed by Jesus' opponents, or by Jesus himself, as a breach of the peace. (It should be noted that Luke follows his account of Jesus' actions with the statement that Jesus was teaching daily in the temple.) Grundmann, *Evangelium nach Lukas*, Schmid, *Evangelium nach Lukas*, Leaney, *Commentary on Luke*, and Creed, *Gospel According to Luke*, do not address themselves to the nonviolent or violent character of Jesus' actions.

29. This teaching is proper to Luke's account. In the first part of the passage Jesus refers to the instructions that he gave to the seventy disciples (10:4). See note 25 in Chapter Two.

30. We should also note that on an earlier occasion Jesus counselled the disciples not to fear death: "I tell you, my friends, do not fear those who kill the body, and after that have no more that they can do. But I will warn you whom to fear: fear him who, after he has killed, has power to cast into hell; yes I tell you, fear him!" (12:4–5) Luke has this saying in common with Matthew.

31. See particularly, Grundmann, *Evangelium nach Lukas*, p. 409, and Schmid, *Evangelium nach Lukas*, pp. 334–35.

32. By referring to Isa. 53:12 and indicating that this prophecy will find fulfillment in him, Jesus indicates to the disciples his own premonition about the outcome of coming events. Because he considers an unfavorable outcome likely, he calls upon them to strengthen themselves that they might remain faithful to his way and teachings. However, they misunderstand what he is saying, particularly his symbolic reference to the need for swords.

33. Luke's version of Jesus' arrest follows the general lines of Mark's (14:41–50; see Matt. 26:47–55), but there are important differences. (For this reason, a number of scholars believe that Luke had a second passion

account that he used along with Mark's.) Of particular concern to us are the disciples' asking whether or not they should strike with the sword (one of them does before receiving Jesus' reply), and the emphatic negative reply from Jesus.

34. We have focused on Jesus' clear and explicit response to the disciples' question and the significance of his action in healing the ear of the high priest's servant. However, Luke's description of the other events surrounding Jesus' arrest provides us with one further note that is also important.

Luke reports that Jesus comments to those who arrested him (22:52–53): "Have you come out as against a robber, with swords and clubs? When I was with you day after day in the temple, you did not lay hands on me. But this is your hour and the power of darkness." Jesus' surprise here may be because his enemies did not take advantage of better opportunities to apprehend him, but it is more likely because they had apparently thought it necessary to arm themselves. Since he had taken such a definite stand against the use of violence, Jesus would have had a more than adequate basis for the surprise and indignation that he here displays.

35. Luke is the only evangelist to record these words. Since some of the early manuscripts omit this passage, some scholars dispute its authenticity. In addition to the various textual considerations in favor of its authenticity, the strong similarity between Stephen's prayer in Acts 7:60 and Jesus' prayer here suggests that Luke may have wished to indicate that Stephen's response paralleled Jesus'.

36. Given the complexities involved, we will not attempt a comprehensive analysis of Jesus' understanding of the kingdom of God in Luke. However, passages such as 4:43; 9:2; 9:11; 9:60; and 10:9–11 indicate that Jesus viewed his ministry and that of the disciples in terms of announcing (and furthering?) the kingdom of God. Luke 18:24–25, for example, indicates how closely Jesus' position on surplus possessions was related to his understanding of the kingdom of God.

37. Luke 3:21, 6:12, and 22:41–46 describe Jesus praying at critical moments. Cf. also 9:18, 9:29, and 22:32.

Chapter Four

1. See Appendix I.

2. This material appears only in Luke. This passage comes well after Jesus' journey to Jerusalem has begun (9:51); but since it seems to imply

that Jesus is still within the territory over which Herod has dominion, it is difficult to be sure just where Luke believes that this interchange took place. J. Creed, *The Gospel According to Luke* (London: Macmillan, 1930), p. 186, believes it likely that the incident took place in Galilee. This is also the opinion of H. Hoehner, *Herod Antipas* (Cambridge: Cambridge University Press, 1972), p. 218.

3. We have not chosen to press this interpretation, but we believe that there is much to recommend it. In Luke's account, Jesus has already done significant teaching before Antipas decides to proceed against him. As we have seen, Jesus' teachings with respect to surplus possessions were controversial and could well have been the cause of divisions within families and households.

4. Since Jesus sends the Pharisees back to Herod, W. Grundmann, *Das Evangelium nach Lukas* (Berlin: Evangelische Verlaganstalt, 1971), p. 288, believes it likely that these Pharisees were actually Herod's messengers. It is indeed true that Luke often shows the Pharisees opposing Jesus. However, there were very likely various groupings within the Pharisaic movement, and it is possible that some Pharisees may have been more favorably disposed toward Jesus' ministry. In Acts 5:34–39 Gamaliel takes a position favorable to the disciples, and Gamaliel was a Pharisee and a well-respected teacher of the law.

5. Grundmann, *Evangelium nach Lukas*, p. 288, Hoehner, *Herod Antipas*, p. 220, and Creed, *Gospel According to Luke*, p. 187, believe that the sense of Jesus' reply is to indicate his defiance of Herod's wishes. Creed accepts Wellhausen's reconstruction and proposes the following meaning: "I shall continue my work for the present; nevertheless I shall shortly go on my way—not because Herod threatens, but because a prophet must not perish outside Jerusalem."

Although H. Conzelmann, *The Theology of St. Luke* (New York: Harper & Row, 1960), refers to this passage more than half a dozen times, he does not once comment upon Jesus' defiance of Herod. It is understandable that Conzelmann wants to assess the meaning of the passage from the standpoint of Luke's journey motif and from the standpoint of eschatology. However, since the concept of a "political apologetic" is an important part of his general thesis, and since Antipas played a role of some importance as a Roman vassal and collaborator, Conzelmann's failure to take account of Jesus' criticism of him is a serious oversight.

If Luke was motivated by political apologetic, why did he show Jesus taking such a critical stance toward a ruler who functioned as a representative of Roman interests? (This passage was not even present in Mark's account.) Conzelmann gives further testimony about the nature of his basic oversight: "The passage 13,31ff shows the death of Jesus to be that of a prophet and—according to Luke—non-political" (p. 139).

6. H. Hoehner, *Herod Antipas,* pp. 343–47, provides an appendix analyzing the various meanings that the term "fox" had in biblical and other ancient literature. He cites Ezek. 13:4 as evidence that the fox was considered a destructive animal; he also cites several ancient fables that portray the fox as a creature of secondary rank, not equal to the lion. Creed, *Gospel According to Luke,* p. 186, also believes it likely that Jesus used the term with this meaning in mind.

7. Hoehner, *Herod Antipas,* p. 221 and p. 347. See also Grundmann, *Evangelium nach Lukas,* p. 288.

8. Luke 6:7–8 and 11:53–54, for example, show the Pharisees conspiring against Jesus during the time of his pre-Jerusalem ministry.

9. The chief priests' principal allies are the scribes and the elders. Although the great majority of the scribes were Pharisees (and thus not sympathetic to the Sadducean priests), there were also some who supported the Sadducean position. Assuming that the scribes to whom Luke refers here were Sadducean, it is plausible for them to have been working in partnership with the chief priests against Jesus. It may also be that Jesus' criticism of scribes who devour the property of widows (20:47) is a criticism of these Sadducean scribes.

10. In Mark's version, the chief priests plot to kill Jesus immediately after he has acted at the temple. Creed, *Gospel According to Luke,* p. 242, thinks that Luke's statement that Jesus taught daily in the temple weakens the connection between Jesus' demonstration at the temple and the chief priests' plot against him. However, Luke also may have wished to suggest that some of Jesus' teachings intensified the hostility of the chief priests without obscuring the fact that Jesus' aggressive actions supplied them with their primary motivation.

11. If the temple protest was an attack on economic abuses, then the events that eventually led to Jesus' death were set in motion by his stance against an economic injustice. As we shall see below, numerous other factors intensified the chief priests' opposition to Jesus and strengthened them in their resolve to see their plot through to an end.

12. In Mark's account, the chief priests, the scribes, and the elders (11:27) ask Jesus the first question and then they send some Pharisees and some Herodians (12:13) to ask him the tribute question. In contrast, while

he indicates that it was the chief priests and elders who asked Jesus the question regarding authority, Matthew states that it was the Pharisees who were responsible for asking him the tribute question. He states that the Pharisees sent some of their disciples and the Herodians for this purpose (22:15–16).

13. Since, as Luke himself states (20:27), the Sadducees did not believe in the resurrection, it is clear that their question was not a sincere one. In light of the fact that the principal members of the Sadducean party were the chief priests and the influential laity, there are good grounds for affirming that the chief priests were in back of this question as well as the other two. Indeed, as we shall see below, Luke indicates that, from the time of the demonstration at the temple, the chief priests were unrelenting in their efforts to kill Jesus.

14. Luke (20:27–40) follows the main outline of Mark's description (12:18–27; see also Matt. 22:23–33) of the interchange between the Sadducees and Jesus, but he introduces enough changes that commentators such as Grundmann, *Evangelium nach Lukas*, p. 374; T. Schramm, *Der Markus-Stoff bei Lukas* (Cambridge: Cambridge University Press, 1971), pp. 170–71; and V. Taylor, *Behind the Third Gospel* (Oxford: Clarendon Press, 1926), pp. 99–100, have concluded that he drew upon another source as well. Luke's principal departure from Mark occurs in vv. 34b–36. Mark (vv. 24–25) says: "Jesus said to them, 'Is not this why you are wrong, that you know neither the scriptures nor the power of God? For when they rise from the dead, they neither marry nor are given in marriage, but are like angels in heaven.' " Luke substitutes: "And Jesus said to them, 'The sons of this age marry and are given in marriage; but those who are accounted worthy to attain to that age and to the resurrection from the dead neither marry nor are given in marriage, for they cannot die any more, because they are equal to angels and are sons of God, being sons of the resurrection.' "

Exactly why Luke chose to omit Jesus' question to the Sadducees found in Mark is difficult to determine (Grundmann, Schramm, and Taylor do not take a position on this matter), but. F. Reinecker, *Das Evangelium des Lukas* (Wuppertal: Brockhaus, 1959), p. 476, believes that Luke omits the question because he is more concerned that Jesus give an "objective refutation" of the false premise underlying the Sadducees' dilemma than that Jesus expose the Sadducees themselves. (Luke also later omits Mark's closing phrase [27b]: "You are quite wrong.") Since Luke follows a similar approach in his rendering of Jesus' response to the spies who ask him about tribute, we ourselves are inclined to concur with Rienecker's opinion. (In

Luke 20:23 Jesus does not directly challenge his questioners; however, in Mark 12:15 and Matt. 22:15 he does.)

Since most scholars do not approach this passage to determine exactly how Jesus' response fits with the Sadducees' original question, we do not find a great number of opinions on this issue. Creed, Schmid, Grundmann, Schramm, and Taylor do not comment on this point. This is our concern since we are seeking to determine whether Luke shows a pattern in Jesus' responses to his various questioners.

There are, however, at least three scholars whose comments do touch on this point and their opinions provide support for our position. E. Ellis, *The Gospel of Luke* (London: Nelson, 1966), p. 235, states, "By asserting a fundamental difference in sexual relationships in 'that age' Jesus dismisses their immediate question as irrelevant." Similarly, N. Geldenhuys, *Commentary on the Gospel of Luke* (Grand Rapids: Eerdmans, 1952), p. 511, states that Jesus "pointed out to them that their question was based on altogether wrong hypotheses." See also G. Caird, *The Gospel of Saint Luke* (London: Penguin Books, 1963), p. 224.

Further, if we place the conclusions that many scholars reach about Jesus' response alongside the original question (which these scholars do not do), our own interpretation finds additional support. For example, W. Manson, *The Gospel of Luke* (New York: Smith, 1930), p. 140, states that an important feature of Jesus' reply is his criticism that "the Sadducees overlook the total difference between the present life and life in the world to come."

15. This parable is common to Mark (12:1–9) and Matt. (21:33–41). Luke introduces minor alterations into Mark's version, which make the murder of the owner's son more of a climax.

16. In Chapter Three we noted that Luke's report in 20:47 implies that scribes were manipulating the legal and judicial system to take advantage of widows. We noted that Jesus' parable about the woman who persevered in seeking a just verdict (18:1–8) also suggests that judges sometimes abused their positions.

17. This material occurs only in Luke. The report given to Jesus indicates that Pilate had killed these Galileans while they were getting ready to offer sacrifice. (As Grundmann, *Evangelium nach Lukas*, p. 276, notes, we would be in a better position to assess the meaning of the report if Luke had indicated who—Pharisees, Zealots, etc.—brought it to Jesus.) Since the Jerusalem temple was the officially designated place for sacrifices, the implication is that Pilate's massacre took place there. If this was the case, it would have been a particular outrage against Jewish customs and sensitivities.

Jesus does not comment on Pilate's actions but rather asks those who brought him the news whether these particular Galileans were worse sinners than all other Galileans simply because they suffered this fate. (Continuing his reflection over who brought Jesus this news, Grundmann conjectures that it may have been Pharisees because, he believes, the Pharisees affirmed that people suffered their ultimate fate because of their own sins.) Jesus then denies that this would have been the case and issues a call for repentance. The entire incident, including another reference to a mass death, is recorded by Luke in the following way: "There were some present at that very time who told him of the Galileans whose blood Pilate had mingled with their sacrifices. And he answered them, 'Do you think that these Galileans were worse sinners than all the other Galileans, because they suffered thus? I tell you, No; but unless you repent you will all likewise perish. Or those eighteen upon whom the tower in Siloam fell and killed them, do you think that they were worse offenders than all the others who dwelt in Jerusalem? I tell you, No; but unless you repent you will all likewise perish' " (13:1–5).

18. In Mark's version (and, to some extent, in Matthew's) Jesus' questioners present their question with greater emphasis than they do in Luke's. They ask whether it is lawful to pay taxes and then repeat, "Should we pay them or should we not?" (12:15) C. Giblin, "The Things of God in the Question Concerning Tribute to Caesar," *Catholic Biblical Quarterly* 33 (1971): 520, argues that Luke emphasizes that Jesus' reply has substance. This may explain why Luke does not have the question repeated.

In Mark and Matthew the term used for tribute is *kensos*, while in Luke it is *phoros*. E. Stauffer, *Christ and the Caesars* (Philadelphia: Westminster, 1955), p. 115, holds that both terms refer to poll taxes or *tributum capitis* (see Appendix I).

Mark and Matthew present Jesus explicitly confronting his questioners. Mark states that Jesus knew their hypocrisy and said to them, "Why put me to the test?" (12:15b). Matthew states that Jesus was "aware of their malice" and said to them, "Why put me to the test, you hypocrites?" (22:18). Luke states only that "he perceived their craftiness," and he does not present him confronting them directly.

19. In Luke's version Jesus' way of requesting the coin is simpler than it is in Mark and Matthew. (There are minor differences between Mark and Matthew on this and other points.) Also in Luke's version Jesus refers to the coin and asks whose likeness and inscription "has it?" In Mark and Matthew he asks, "Whose likeness and inscription *is this*?"

Finally, in Luke's version, Jesus starts his reply with the word "then."

In Mark he simply starts, "Render to. . . ." In Matthew he begins, "Render, *therefore*, to Caesar. . . ."

20. Giblin, "Things of God," pp. 510–14, discusses a number of the interpretations recently put forward, but confines his attention almost exclusively to interpretations that have Jesus' support for the payment of tribute as a part of their conclusion. Among the recently published interpretations which have this feature in common are those by G. Bornkamm, R. Völkl, R. Schnackenburg, P. Bonnard, W. Grundmann, and E. Ellis. Giblin himself also reaches a conclusion with this element in it.

21. Representative scholars holding that Jesus was advocating opposition to the tribute are S. Brandon, *Jesus and the Zealots* (Manchester: Manchester University Press, 1967), and S. Kennard, *Render to God* (New York: Oxford University Press, 1950). Kennard's position is well argued and provides some extremely helpful information regarding the Jewish prohibition against images and the Roman and Tyrian coins in circulation at the time. His conclusion that Jesus viewed the silver in the denarius as belonging to God exaggerates the point. (He holds that such a position would have been consistent with the general Jewish view regarding God's sovereignty in the Holy Land; see pp. 123–25.) But as we shall argue, it is important to recognize Jesus' belief that God had dominion over all of creation.

Our first reason for rejecting the interpretation that Jesus refused payment is based on Luke's description of the reaction (confusion) that Jesus' questioners had to his answer. Second, on his subsequent description of the charges that the chief priests prefer against Jesus when they bring him before Pilate, Luke implies that the charges are distortions of Jesus' position and essentially false. One of the charges is that Jesus counselled against the payment of tribute; if he had actually done so, then the chief priests would not have been falsifying his position.

22. In this interpretation, since he knew that the final times were close at hand, Jesus was not interested in what obligations were owed to the state. Giblin, "Things of God," p. 510, cites A. Schweitzer, S. Kierkegaard, and M. Dibelius as maintaining interpretations along this line.

23. S. Kennard, *Render to God*, p. 54, holds that the Jews normally paid tribute in the Attic drachma and that no denarii were minted in the East after 18 B.C. As a consequence, in asking specifically for a denarius, Jesus was asking for a coin that was not commonly in circulation, and he was asking specifically for a coin that bore the image and inscription of a Roman emperor (Augustus or Tiberius).

24. See S. Kennard, "Judaism and Images," *Crozer Quarterly* 23 (1946): 259–65. Kennard also includes additional relevant information at various points in *Render to God*. The three principal coinages that we need to keep track of are the Attic drachma, the coin in which the Jews normally paid Roman tribute, the Tyrian shekel, in which they normally paid the temple tax, and the denarius. (As we noted above, Kennard does not believe that the denarius circulated widely in Judea; he states that it was principally used to pay the wages of the Roman troops; see p. 155.)

Kennard believes that the images and inscriptions on the denarius were a means of furthering the cult of the emperor and that the Jews would therefore resist these coins much more vigorously than they would the Attic drachmas and the Tyrian shekels whose images were less offensive and less dangerous. Assuming the correctness of Kennard's view, Jews who saved denarii or handled them regularly may well have been looked down upon by dedicated Jews. It should be noted, though, that Luke does not indicate whether the spies themselves possessed a denarius or whether they procured it from some other source and brought it to him. Interpreters have frequently presumed that Jesus' questioners themselves possessed and used denarii, but none of the gospel accounts actually state this.

25. Some scholars prefer to stop short of commenting on the second part of Jesus' reply and simply state that the primary meaning of the passage is that Jesus showed his superiority to his questioners and indicated that they were not in good faith. See, for example, J. Schmid, *Das Evangelium nach Lukas*, 4th ed. (Regensburg: Pustet, 1960), p. 297. In our view, there is a similarity between Jesus' response to the tribute question and that which he gave to the question concerning the resurrection. Although he does not answer the original question in either instance, he does proceed to give teachings that are relevant for the general topic that the questioners had brought up.

26. Despite his considerable learning in a number of the disciplines that relate to New Testament studies, E. Stauffer's personal bias in favor of imperial regimes leads him to take a number of positions that are not only foolish but also dangerous. In addition to concluding that Jesus was calling for unqualified support for both empire and temple, he also attempts to reconstruct why Jesus felt that the Jews owed such allegiance to the empire. In his analysis there are several elements that are particularly regrettable. The following passages occur on pp. 131–32 of his work, *Christ and the Caesars*: "So far we have spoken negatively of what was not permitted. But Jesus held up the coin before His questioners in order to give them a positive and imperative lesson about the duty which the people of God owed to the empire. This is not just a recommendation to be loyal

to one's nearest superior (as the Talmud speaks of 'not attempting to evade taxes'). But is an affirmation of the *Imperium Romanum*, of the foreign master-race with its polytheistic emperor, an unsentimental and undialectical affirmation in the true succession of the prophetic and apocalyptic theology of history. . . .

"To pay the imperial tax means to fulfill God's will for history—and is at the same time a contribution to the prayers and sacrifice for the emperor. For the imperial tax clearly provided in the time of Jesus the means for the daily sacrifice for the welfare of the Roman emperor. In brief, the tax to Caesar was the contribution of the people of God to the maintenance of the empire which involved not only financial and political considerations, but also theological views about imperial history."

27. In the view of a number of scholars (see C. Giblin, "Things of God," p. 511), Jesus was primarily concerned with disassociating himself from the Zealots and from all those who were taking the question of tribute as the sole or primary question that dedicated Jews should be concerned about. Some hold that Jesus did this by reminding his hearers that they should not forget to render to God at the same time that they were rendering to Caesar by paying tribute. Others hold that Jesus went even farther and emphasized that the things of God were far more important than the things of Caesar. Therefore, Caesar should be rendered to in the minimum way possible (the minimum was to pay tribute), and much greater attention should be given to rendering to God the things of God. Note that both groups of scholars assume that Jesus accorded to the Roman empire autonomy in its own sphere. In our view, such an assumption cannot be justified.

28. Those scholars who view Jesus as teaching that rendering to God was more important than rendering to Caesar still believe that he intended for Caesar to be rendered to and, accordingly, for tribute to be paid.

29. Our assertion that Jesus did not ascribe to the Roman empire any independent standing apart from God's dominion can be substantiated, we believe, from the rest of Luke's gospel and from the larger gospel traditions. In the concluding section of Chapter Three, we noted that Luke describes Jesus as believing that all human activity took place under God.

In the Great Sermon, Jesus teaches his hearers to love their enemies on the basis that God cares for the ungrateful and the wicked (6:35). In the Lord's Prayer, Jesus suggested that his disciples pray to God for their daily bread (11:2). In the passage about God's providence (12:22–32), Jesus reminded them that God cares even for the birds of the air and the flowers of the fields. In admonishing some Pharisees for their false virtuousness, he stated that God knew their hearts and that God was not impressed with what was, humanly speaking, well thought of.

In all of the above and in the rest of the synoptic tradition there is virtually nothing that would justify the assumption that there is a "temporal," "secular," or "political" sphere that possesses an autonomy of its own or somehow stands outside of God's creation. Thus, for Jesus to be holding in the tribute passage that God has granted the Roman empire its own sphere of influence would mean that he was introducing an entirely new teaching that was at least potentially at variance with his previous teaching.

30. When they bring him before Pilate, the chief priests charge Jesus with opposing the payment of tribute (23:2), and the implication is that Jesus himself does not pay it. However, as we have already begun to see, the chief priests are committed to destroying Jesus and are not scrupulous about the means that they use to do so. Our own view is that all three charges that the chief priests make against him distort Jesus' actual positions. For them to tell Pilate that Jesus opposed the payment of tribute is a lie. However, the priests' lying does not establish what Jesus' actual position was. They would have been lying if he had recommended paying tribute, but they would also be lying if he had not actually indicated his own personal stance.

The fact that Jesus' response on the subject of tribute was not the response of the Zealots should also be taken account of. If the Zealots had been asked the question that Jesus was asked, they would have given a clear and explicit denunciation of Roman rule and Roman taxes. In comparison, although it provides the possibility for criticizing the Roman order, and although it leaves the way open for tax resistance, Jesus' response was not such as to challenge the Romans in the way that the Zealots' response would have.

31. See Chapter Three, note 14.

32. These verses are peculiar to Luke. The second warning that Luke portrays Jesus giving to the disciples is paralleled in Mark and Matthew, but this is not.

33. This passage comes within a discourse about the end times, frequently referred to as the "synoptic apocalypse," that appears in all three synoptic accounts. Scholars differ over whether Luke has substantially followed Mark's version of this discourse or whether he has drawn extensively upon "Q" material and his own personal material. (See Grundmann, *Evangelium nach Lukas*, pp. 377–78, for a discussion of the various

opinions.) There is, however, general agreement that Luke's version contains a number of emphases and perspectives that are not present in the same way in Mark's account. Two are noticeable in the passage we have cited.

First, in Luke's version Jesus prefaces his warning to the disciples with the phrase, "but before all this." He thereby indicates that the disciples' time to suffer persecution and give testimony will precede the time when "nation will rise against nation and kingdom against kingdom" (21:10). In Mark, Jesus describes the disciples' hardships as happening at virtually the same time as the other cataclysmic events. Second, in Luke's account Jesus envisions a favorable outcome to the trials that the disciples will be facing. In Luke, Jesus explicitly predicts that the disciples' adversaries will not be able to withstand or contradict their testimony, whereas in Mark's version he does not make such a prediction. (As both accounts go forward, the different emphasis is maintained: Mark shows Jesus offering hope, but in Luke's version he offers it more explicitly.)

Other differences on specific points should also be noted. In Mark's version the disciples will be delivered up to councils and beaten in synagogues. In Luke there is no mention of their being delivered up to councils, but Jesus does indicate that they will be delivered up to synagogues (instead of being beaten in them) and delivered up to prisons. In Mark, Jesus states that the disciples will "stand before governors and kings for my sake," while in Luke Jesus states that they "will be brought before kings and governors for my name's sake." Instead of Mark's next verse, "And the gospel must first be preached to all the nations," Luke's next verse is, "This will be a time for you to bear testimony." Both Mark and Luke then indicate that the disciples will be supported in what they are to say. In Mark, it is the Holy Spirit; in Luke, it is Jesus himself who will support them.

Numerous scholars (see, for example, A. Stoger, "Eigenart and Botschaft der lukanische Passionsgeschichte," *Bibel und Kirche* 24 [1969]: 7) have pointed out that Luke subsequently shows Jesus being brought before a tetrarch and a governor, a fate similar to that which he had predicted for the disciples. Luke also shows the disciples recalling that Jesus had been brought before Herod and Pilate when they themselves are later suffering persecution (see Acts 4:23–31).

34. A traditional explanation is that the disciples would suffer for affirming their faith in Jesus himself. This is consistent with Luke's text. We would also focus upon the disciples' commitment to observe Jesus' teachings regarding material possessions, nonviolence, the status of women, etc. In this view, Jesus foresees that the political authorities will

have little tolerance for those who observe such teachings. They will persecute the disciples just as they have persecuted Jesus himself.

Chapter Five

1. Since the accuracy of various passages in Luke's trial narrative has been subject to heavy criticism, and since (at least on a first reading) there is tension between Jesus' lack of deference to Pilate and Herod and their verdict that he is innocent of the charges against him, it is appropriate that we recall our commitment to work with Luke's account as it stands. Our primary purpose is to achieve an understanding of what Luke's account tells us, and we will not attempt to resolve the various questions concerning the accuracy of Luke's descriptions and interpretations. Thus, we shall not debate whether the hearing before Herod that Luke describes could have taken place as he reports it, and we shall not debate whether Luke's portrait of a Roman governor who bowed to the pressures brought to bear by the Jerusalem chief priests is a historically plausible one. In the first chapter we argued that Luke is amazingly accurate with regard to terms, dates, and events that pertain to empire history; but, at that time, we did not rule out the possibility that he could have constructed situations for the purpose of stressing various theological themes. However, as we have indicated, we do not believe that Luke's gospel reflects a concern to achieve a "political apologetic."

2. Luke's reports concerning the chief priests' actions in arresting and beating Jesus are contained in his twenty-second chapter. In our assessment of the chief priests' responsibility for Jesus' death, we will cite the specific references for all their activities against him.

3. J. Schmid, *Das Evangelium nach Lukas*, 4th ed. (Regensburg: Pustet, 1960), pp. 315–19, provides a helpful discussion of the differences between Mark's account and Luke's and of various theories to explain these differences. Particularly important for our study is that the sanhedrin hearing does not have the same importance in Luke's account as it does in Mark's. In Mark the sanhedrin hearing is formal (witnesses give testimony against Jesus and a formal verdict is reached) and is almost a self-contained event. In contrast, Luke does not indicate the presence of witnesses, and the council members do not enact a formal condemnation of Jesus. There are also other differences in the accounts: e.g., Mark shows two meetings of the sanhedrin—the principal one on the night of Jesus' arrest, and the second the following morning; Luke shows only an early morning session.

4. Luke reports that Jesus prophesied the destruction of the temple

(21:5–7); this may have fueled the chief priests' hostility against him. However, in Luke's account, the chief priests do not refer to this prophecy and, even more significantly, they do not refer to his protest at the temple. The charges that Luke shows them preferring are charges to which the Roman governor would be more likely to respond.

5. W. Grundmann, *Das Evangelium nach Lukas* (Berlin: Evangelische Verlaganstalt, 1971), p. 420, believes that in the first part of his answer Jesus denies that he is the Christ in the sense that the sanhedrin members are using the term (a political messiah who intends to throw off Roman rule), but affirms that he is the Christ in another, more transcendent sense. In our view, such an interpretation reads too much into Jesus' answer.

Grundmann and other commentators fail to appreciate the pattern of Jesus' responses to the chief priests and their allies. When the chief priests questioned Jesus about his authority for acting as he had at the temple, he countered with a question about John the Baptist and then refused to give them an answer. Similarly, he refused to answer the question that *their* spies asked him about tribute payments, and likewise the question that *their* allies, the Sadducees, asked him about life in the resurrection. This pattern continues in the two questions that they now ask him; as we shall see, Luke indicates that Jesus was no more cooperative in his answer to Pilate's question and in his refusal to answer any of Herod's questions.

6. When he replies that he would receive vindication from God, Jesus referred to himself as "the Son of man." The council members seem to have understood Jesus' answer to express a claim to the exalted rank of "the Son of God," for in their second question they ask him, "Are you the Son of God, then?"

7. As we observed in note 5 above, Grundmann believes that Jesus cooperated with the questions that were put to him. In this instance, Grundmann holds that Jesus replied in the affirmative, and Schmid, *Evangelium nach Lukas*, p. 341, concurs in this judgment. However, in our estimation such an interpretation requires ascribing a meaning to Jesus' words that they do not literally have. Jesus has replied, "You say that I am" (in the Greek, *humeis legete oti ego eimi*), and such a reply does not indicate either agreement or disagreement.

J. Creed, *The Gospel According to Luke* (London: Macmillan, 1930), p. 279, states that the exact meaning of this phrase is doubtful and that "there is no unquestioned evidence that it was an accepted formula of assent." While Creed himself leans toward the interpretation that Jesus' answer implies assent, he goes on to relate Jesus' words here to the answer he gives Pilate, stating: "But the personal pronoun (*su, humeis*) must be significant:

'the statement is yours,' *i.e.*, a certain protest against the question is implied."

In Mark's account, Jesus gives a clear affirmative answer to the high priest's question, "Are you the Christ, the Son of the Blessed?" He replies, "I am; and you will see the Son of man sitting at the right hand of Power, and coming with the clouds of heaven" (Mark 14:61–62). Thus, if Luke had intended to show Jesus dignifying the council members' question with a direct, cooperative answer, he certainly had a precedent for doing so.

8. Although Jesus did not answer either of the questions that the Sanhedrin put to him, they can say that they have gone through the process of holding a hearing, so they proceed on to Pilate. As we shall see, the charges they prefer against Jesus do not reflect the answers that Jesus gave to the question concerning tribute that their spies asked him. They are fully committed to giving false statements about Jesus' activities.

9. Luke goes considerably beyond Mark and Matthew in showing the chief priests making such an orderly presentation of the charges. In Mark (15:1–2) and Matthew (27:11) the priests and their allies simply bring Jesus to Pilate and Pilate begins to interrogate Jesus.

10. Grundmann, *Evangelium nach Lukas*, p. 422; Schmid, *Evangelium nach Lukas*, p. 342.

11. The three charges interrelate. The primary assertion is that Jesus wants to throw off Roman rule and set himself up as king over the Jews. To this end, he is misleading the people and counselling them not to pay tribute. It is not clear whether the Zealots advocated that a Jewish king rule Palestine. (They may have envisioned theocratic rule by a legitimate high priest, and they may have been prepared to support the ascendancy of a reconstituted sanhedrin of which they themselves would undoubtedly be members.) Nevertheless, if he had been trying to establish himself as a king, Jesus would have agreed with the Zealots on the point of throwing off Roman rule. Thus in the eyes of the Romans, the position that the chief priests were attributing to Jesus would not have seemed to differ greatly from that of the Zealots.

12. The Revised Standard Version translates *diastrephonta* as "perverting." W. Bauer, *A Greek-English Lexicon of the New Testament and Other Early Christian Literature* (Chicago: University of Chicago Press, 1957), gives "make crooked," "pervert" as the first meaning of *diastrepho*, but gives "mislead (someone)" as the second meaning. H. Liddell, R. Scott, and H. Jones, *A Greek-English Lexicon* (Oxford: Clarendon Press, 1940), gives "turn different ways," "twist about" as the first meaning and "distort," "pervert" as the second meaning.

13. For a more extended analysis of why Pilate represented Jesus' best chance of staying alive, see the section "Jesus' Responses to His Judges" below.

14. Mark (15:2) and Matthew (27:11) show Pilate asking this same question and portray Jesus giving the same answer. In the Greek, Jesus' answer is *su legeis*. As we indicated in note 7 above, J. Creed sees a connection between Jesus' reply in this instance and his reply to the sanhedrin members' second question. Creed believes that both replies focus attention on the person(s) asking the question and that they imply a protest against the question. In his note commenting on Jesus' answer to Pilate's question, Creed refers to his earlier note and thereby avoids explicitly taking a position on whether Jesus' reply in this instance is affirmative or negative. However, as we have noted above, Creed leans toward holding that Jesus' reply to the sanhedrin members was (despite the note of protest that it embodied) in the affirmative. Thus, although he does not declare himself explicitly with respect to Jesus' reply to Pilate, implicitly he would seem to hold that Jesus answered affirmatively.

However, since Luke shows Pilate following Jesus' answer with a declaration that he is innocent, there are grave problems in affirming that Jesus' reply could have been affirmative. Grundmann, *Evangelium nach Lukas*, p. 422, recognizes this and therefore holds that Jesus' reply was negative. However, since he has previously stated that Jesus answered the sanhedrin members' second question affirmatively, Grundmann is left in the position of having to maintain that when Jesus answered, "You say that I am," he meant yes; and, when he answered, "You have said so," he meant no.

Schmid, *Evangelium nach Lukas*, pp. 341–43, also has difficulty in achieving a satisfactory explanation to provide for Jesus' answers in both instances. Schmid holds that Jesus answered the council members' question affirmatively, and he is inclined to hold that Jesus also answered Pilate's question affirmatively. He accounts for the fact that Pilate then declares Jesus innocent by holding that although Jesus has replied affirmatively, Pilate does not understand him to be admitting to anything criminal.

Our own position is that Jesus did not answer the council members' question either affirmatively or negatively. Instead, just as he had previously done, he refused to cooperate with them by giving a direct answer to their question. Our argument is that Luke shows Jesus taking this same approach toward Pilate and toward Pilate's question. He does not answer the question one way or the other, and the manner in which he responds implies a certain lack of deference.

15. We will make a more extended analysis of Pilate's verdict in the last section of this chapter.

16. Mark and Matthew do not show Herod Antipas playing any role in Jesus' trial.

17. Earlier (9:9), Luke indicated that Herod was eager to see Jesus and his present statement that Herod "had long desired to see him" carries through this earlier reference. As we have noted, Luke here makes no mention of the Pharisees' report (13:31) that Herod was seeking to kill Jesus.

18. Grundmann, *Evangelium nach Lukas*, p. 425, believes that Jesus' silence is that of a "servant of God" and adds that, in the Hellenistic world, such a silence was deemed to be a sign of godliness. In his article, "Das Schweigen Jesu," *Theologie und Unterricht*, K. Wegenast, ed. (Gütersloh: Mohn, 1969), J. Schreiber analyzes the reports of all four gospels concerning Jesus' silence. Schreiber believes that Luke portrays Jesus' death as that of a martyr and he holds that Jesus' silence is a martyr's silence (see pp. 84–85). However, in trying to explain why Jesus is silent only before Herod, Schreiber runs into considerable difficulty and ends up theorizing that Luke fails to differentiate clearly between Herod the Great, Herod Antipas, and Herod Agrippas I.

Schmid, *Evangelium nach Lukas*, p. 344, believes that Jesus' silence provoked Herod but that instead of reacting with an outburst of anger, he responded with a joke. He dressed Jesus in the garments of a "mock" king and ridiculed him. By sending him back to Pilate in this way, Herod also indicated (Schmid believes) that he did not see any real substance in the chief priests' charges against Jesus.

19. The fact that the chief priests follow Jesus to Herod's quarters provides another indication of how intent on seeking Jesus' death they were. We shall see below that Luke shows them to be unrelenting in their efforts against Jesus.

20. When we provide a more extended analysis below of Jesus' response to Herod and Herod's verdict concerning Jesus, we will again refer to the fact that Luke has presented Pilate as according a certain respect to Herod and displaying a regard for Herod's ability to judge concerning Rome's interests.

21. See Chapter One for our presentation of H. Conzelmann's theory concerning Luke's purposes for making such an "apology."

22. We have already analyzed many of Luke's descriptions concerning the chief priests and their allies (see Chapter Four), but here we consider their full range. In this instance (19:47–48), Luke's report contains approximately the same material that Mark's does. In 11:18 Mark states that the chief priests and the scribes (Luke also includes "the principal men") sought to destroy Jesus after his protest at the temple.

23. Luke 20:19. Mark (12:12) states that "they" sought to arrest Jesus, but the groups referred to are the chief priests, the scribes, and the elders (see Mark 11:27).

24. Luke 20:20. In Mark (12:13) it is the chief priests, the scribes, and the elders who are behind the tribute question, but Mark states that they sent "some of the Pharisees and some of the Herodians" to entrap Jesus. As we have noted, Luke indicates that the chief priests and the scribes sent "spies."

25. Luke 22:1–5. Luke's account follows Mark's fairly closely in describing the chief priests' continued interest in destroying Jesus and Judas' dealings with them. Luke adds the note that Satan had entered into Judas, and this is a point to which H. Conzelmann attaches a great deal of importance. Earlier in the gospel (4:13) Luke stated, "And when the devil had ended every temptation he departed from him until an opportune time," and Conzelmann believes that Satan's re-emergence indicates that the "Satan-free" period of Jesus' ministry is now over and that his passion will soon begin.

26. Mark (14:43) indicates that the ones who arrested Jesus were Judas and a crowd who had been sent by the chief priests, scribes, and elders. In contrast, Luke (22:52) indicates that the "chief priests and captains of the temple and elders" themselves arrested Jesus.

27. Mark (14:65) and Matthew (26:67) indicate that a similar beating transpired after the sanhedrin members reached their verdict, but they do not report such mistreatment before the hearing itself.

28. See Appendix I and Appendix III for our analysis of the groups who comprised the sanhedrin.

29. When they sent spies to entrap Jesus over the tribute question, Luke indicates that it was the chief priests' intention "to deliver him up to the authority and jurisdiction of the governor" (20:20). He now shows them hurrying through a sanhedrin meeting and remitting Jesus to Pilate without enacting a formal verdict against him. They have kept to their original plan (Mark and Matthew do not mention such a plan) and now they have to persuade Pilate to cooperate with their purposes.

30. We have noted that the chief priests are the ones who prefer the charges against Jesus. Mark indicates that the chief priests "accused him of many things" (15:3), but he does not subsequently show them actively pressing the case against Jesus to the degree that Luke does (see Luke 23:5 and 23:13).

31. In repeating their general charge, the priests emphasize that Jesus has been active as far away as Galilee (23:5). The implication is that Pilate will be remiss if he underestimates the serious threat that Jesus constitutes.

32. Since only Luke includes an account of the events before Herod (23:6–16), this further testimony to the chief priests' efforts against Jesus does not have a counterpart in Mark or Matthew.

33. Luke indicates that after Herod returned Jesus to him, Pilate called together "the chief priests and the rulers and the people" (23:13); it is this group that now clamors for Barabbas' release (23:18). The sense of Luke's description is that while others have now joined them, the chief priests and their allies are still the central persons in the efforts to pressure Pilate. Mark indicates (15:11) that the chief priests stirred up the crowd to ask for Barabbas' release.

34. In comparison with Mark's report (15:13) that they cried out, "Crucify him," Luke's description (23:21) conveys the sense of a chant being mounted: "Crucify, crucify him."

35. Luke's description (23:23) indicates that more pressure was brought to bear upon Pilate than Mark's description (15:14) does.

36. As we have previously indicated, the Pharisees do not appear in Luke's account after Jesus has entered Jerusalem.

37. Since Mark indicates that Judas and a crowd came to arrest Jesus, Judas has a more prominent role in Mark's description of this scene than he has in Luke's. In Luke (22:47–51) Judas leads the crowd to Jesus and draws near to kiss him. (Mark indicates that Judas kissed Jesus; but in Luke Jesus stops him from doing so by asking if he will betray him with a kiss.) But it is the chief priests, the captains of the temple, and the elders who actually arrest him.

In his report of Jesus' words at the Last Supper about the one who would betray him (22:21–23), Luke omits Mark's verse (14:21) in which Jesus says in reference to the betrayer (Judas): "It would have been better for that man if he had not been born." In addition, just before Judas and the crowd draw near to arrest him in Mark (14:42) Jesus says, "See, my betrayer is at hand." Luke omits this reference.

38. In addition to stating that Satan had entered into Judas (22:3), Luke also portrays Jesus subsequently telling Peter (22:31–32) that Satan had demanded to have Peter and sift him like wheat, but that Jesus has prayed that Peter will be strengthened.

39. See note 33.

40. Luke's account shows Pilate more frequently and explicitly affirming Jesus' innocence than Mark's account does. In Luke, Pilate initially announces that he finds no guilt in Jesus (23:4); he announces that he and Herod do not find him guilty (23:14–15); he addresses the chief priests and the others on Jesus' behalf (23:20); and he again states that he does not find Jesus guilty (23:22). In Mark, Pilate initially proposes to release Jesus (15:9); he asks the crowd—after they had pressured for Barabbas' release—what he should do about Jesus (15:12), and he expresses his reluctance to crucify Jesus (15:14) since he has committed no crime. Luke also shows Pilate playing a less prominent role in the actual crucifixion.

Commentators who hold to the political apologetic position generally notice that Luke shows Pilate affirming Jesus' innocence more emphatically than Mark does, and they then conclude that Luke presented this revised portrait in order to make it easier for the Christians of his own day to gain the approval of the Roman authorities. However, *in addition to overlooking the other passages in Luke's gospel which run counter to such an interpretation*, these scholars fail to appreciate the larger patterns that are present within Luke's passion account itself. In concentrating on Luke's description of Pilate's involvement, they fail to take account of how this description blends with Luke's other descriptions.

Our own view is that Pilate's more emphatic proclamation of Jesus' innocence and his lessened involvement in Jesus' actual crucifixion are both a part of Luke's larger effort to describe the persons and groups who played a role in Jesus' death. Beyond Luke's description of Pilate, what are the other elements in his passion account that pertain to the question of who has "responsibility" for Jesus' death?

The first point to be noted in this regard is that in addition to greatly diminishing Pilate's role in Jesus' death, Luke also greatly diminishes the role of Judas (see note 37 above). Second, Luke also significantly diminishes the role of the Jerusalem crowds (see note 41 below). Third, Luke's account accords a degree of responsibility to Satan, whereas Satan plays no role in Mark's version (see note 38 above). Finally, as we have indicated, Luke greatly increases the role that the chief priests and their allies play in the proceedings. Indeed, it can be argued that the diminished role of Pilate, Judas, and the Jerusalem crowds have further accentuated the fact that the chief priests are centrally involved.

Given the presence of these other patterns in Luke's account, it is far more likely that Luke diminished Pilate's role as a part of a general effort to indicate how dominant the chief priests were in securing Jesus' death than it is that he did so in order to gain later Christians safe passage in the Roman empire. The political apologetic position takes account of only one feature of Luke's passion account, whereas the interpretation we are advancing recognizes the other elements present in Luke's trial narrative and is, in addition, consistent with Luke's other descriptions throughout his writings. (In addition to the gospel passages we have already cited, see 24:20; in Acts, see especially 4:8–10 and 5:27–33.)

41. As we have indicated, Luke portrays some of the populace joining with the chief priests and their allies in clamoring for Jesus' death (as shown in note 33 and note 40, the Jewish crowds have a less important role in Luke's account than they do in Mark's). However, Luke also indicates that a number of people, including a number of women, followed Jesus on the way to the crucifixion and "bewailed and lamented him" (23:27; this passage does not occur in Mark). Luke also shows a group of people present at the crucifixion (23:35); and these people, in contrast with the jeering rulers (presumably the chief priests or their allies), seem to be sympathetic to Jesus (in Mark's account the people who walk by the cross deride and mock Jesus; see 14:29–30).

In 23:39–41 Luke also indicates (in contrast with Mark 15:32 and Matt. 27:44) that one of the criminals who was crucified with Jesus spoke kindly to him and affirmed his innocence. Finally, in his description of Joseph of Arimathea (23:50–52), Luke specifically states that, "He was a member of the council, a good and righteous man, who had not consented to their purpose and their deed, and he was looking for the kingdom of God." Mark mentions (15:43) that Joseph was a member of the council and was looking for the kingdom of God, but he does not explicitly state that Joseph had not consented to the action taken by the other sanhedrin members. Matthew (27:57) merely states that Joseph was a rich man and a disciple of Jesus. Taken together, the above passages clearly establish that Luke does not consider the Jewish populace as a whole to have been responsible for Jesus' death.

42. Except for implying that it was, at least to some degree, under the authority of the Roman governor, Luke's narrative does not give us much information concerning the sanhedrin's status. While other sources indicate that the sanhedrin had a great deal of influence within the Judaism of Jesus' day (see Appendix I) its decisions did not represent "the will of the people" in the sense that the decisions of modern democratically-elected

bodies (to a greater or lesser degree) reflect the will of the constituents they serve.

43. To speak generally about "Jewish responsibility" is to be careless where Luke is precise. Moreover, given the fact that anti-Semitism continues to be a contemporary social problem of considerable magnitude, generalizations about "Jewish guilt," "Jewish hate," "Jewish responsibility," or "Luke's concern to shift responsibility from the Romans to the Jews" have more than academic importance; see, for example, Grundmann, *Evangelium nach Lukas*, pp. 419, 421; P. Benoit, *The Passion and Resurrection of Jesus Christ* (New York: Herder and Herder, 1969), pp. 99, 143, 146; Schmid, *Evangelium nach Lukas*, pp. 342, 345; A. Stöger, "Eigenart und Botschaft der Lukanishchen Passionsgeschichte," *Bibel und Kirche* 24 (1969): 4–8, p. 7.

44. Commenting on this verse, Creed, *Gospel According to Luke*, p. 283, observes that Luke almost seems to suggest that "the Jews" (*sic*) took Jesus away to be crucified.

45. P. Parker, "Crucifixion," *The Interpreter's Dictionary of the Bible*, 1:746–47. H. Cohen, *The Trial and Death of Jesus* (New York: Harper and Row, 1971), pp. 208–17, provides a well-argued response to the view that Jewish leaders also used crucifixion as a form of execution. He emphasizes the importance of differentiating between crucifixion and the other forms of hanging.

46. P. Parker, "Inscription on the Cross," *The Interpreter's Dictionary of the Bible*, 2:705–6.

47. F. Gealy, "Centurion," *The Interpreter's Dictionary of the Bible*, 1:547–48. Grundmann, *Evangelium nach Lukas*, p. 435, considers it likely that the centurion was actually supervising the crucifixion.

48. See note 41 for an indication of how Luke's description of Joseph of Arimathea differs from Mark's.

49. According to Luke's reports, despite his initial inclinations to the contrary, Pilate has bowed to the chief priests' pressure and has ordered Jesus' crucifixion. He did so on the grounds (which he, Pilate, did not believe) that Jesus had sought to throw off Roman rule and establish himself as king over the Jews.

50. See note 5 above.

51. See note 7 above.

52. See note 14 above.

53. Luke does not indicate the sanhedrin's exact composition, but in 22:66 he conveys the impression that the chief priests and the scribes were its leading members. From his subsequent report about Joseph of Arimathea (23:50–51), we do know, however, that not every member of the council followed the lead of the chief priests.

54. See Chapter Four and the relevant sections in Chapter Three. The remainder of the present section draws heavily upon our earlier analysis.

55. Before Pilate and before Herod, Jesus is neither as forceful or as articulate as Luke has shown him to be in other situations. However, these interrogations occur after he has suffered a beating at the hands of the chief priests or their supporters; and he has also, presumably, been without sleep.

56. As we have seen, Luke indicates that Antipas had married his brother Philip's wife and had imprisoned John when John criticized this action (3:19–20). Luke subsequently indicates that Herod killed John (9:9) and shows the Pharisees bringing Jesus a report that Herod is seeking to kill him (13:31). He has also shown Jesus receiving a report about Pilate's massacre of some Galileans (13:1).

57. In their plan to send spies to entrap Jesus on the tribute question "so as to deliver him up to the authority and jurisdiction of the governor" (20:20), Luke shows the chief priests operating on the assumption that Pilate will take action against anyone who counsels against the payment of tribute. Similarly, in his declaration that Herod too has found Jesus innocent of the priests' charges (23:15), Luke shows Pilate assuming that Herod was capable of making a good judgment about what was needed to keep Roman rule in operation.

58. See the section on "Jesus and Violence" in Chapter 3.

59. Since Mark 15:10 (similarly also Matt. 27:18) states that Pilate "perceived that it was out of envy that the chief priests had delivered him up," there are grounds for arguing that Luke believed this was the motive for which Pilate and Herod acquitted Jesus. It is also possible that one of Luke's other sources indicated to him that Pilate and Herod were ill-disposed toward the chief priests on other grounds that had nothing to do with Jesus. In this case, Luke may have seen Pilate and Herod's failure to cooperate with the chief priests' plans to get rid of Jesus as a part of their general refusal to cooperate with the chief priests in anything at all.

Chapter Six

1. See Chapter Two, Section 1.

2. See Chapter Two, Section 2.

3. Jesus' teachings and conduct could constitute a threat to the Romans even if he was not contravening a pattern or practice that was particularly sacred to them. For example, the Romans might not feel themselves directly threatened by Jesus' advocating a radical approach to the use of material possessions, or by his allowing women to assume new social roles. Nevertheless, since Jesus' teachings would be disrupting the existing social order, and since the Romans stood at the head of this order and wanted to avoid turbulence and upheaval, they might well eventually find themselves threatened by what Jesus was doing.

Second, inasmuch as Jesus' teachings regarding service and humility related much more directly to the issue of whether any group, the Romans included, should dominate over another group, the threat that he posed was proportionately greater. There were, therefore, (indirect and direct) ways in which Jesus' social positions could prove threatening to Roman rule.

4. See Chapter Three, Section 1.

5. See Chapter Three, Section 2.

6. For the extent to which violence was present in the society of Jesus' day, see Appendix III, Section 3. For the way in which the Roman empire was premised upon violence and the threat of violence, see Chapter Four, Section 3.

7. See Chapter 3, Section 3.

8. See Chapter Three, Section 2, and Chapter Four, Section 4.

9. See Chapter Four, Section 4.

10. For Jesus' response to Herod, see Chapter Four, Section 1, and Chapter Five, Section 3. For his reply to Pilate, see Chapter Five, Section 2.

11. For Luke's description of Jesus' protest at the temple, see Chapter Three, Section 3. For his reply to the chief priests' initial question and the criticism that he made of them, see Chapter Four, Section 2. For his replies to the sanhedrin members, see Chapter Five, Section 1.

12. In Luke's gospel, Jesus gives more of his time and attention to advocating new patterns in social relationships that he does to opposing Roman rule. Although the Romans were maintaining the undesirable patterns, Jesus does not engage in an anti-Roman polemic. In contrast, the Zealots had the overthrow of Roman rule as their primary objective. However, even though Luke does not describe Jesus as anti-Roman, he does describe him advocating social relationships that explicitly or implicitly undermined the domination and exploitation that the Roman empire was premised upon. In Luke's account, Jesus advocates radically new social practices and is critical of all those, *including the Romans*, whose behavior is inconsistent with these new practices.

13. The material in the present section is taken from the following works by Mohandas K. Gandhi: *An Autobiography: The Story of My Experiments with Truth*, trans. M. Desai (Boston: Beacon Press, 1957); *Economic and Industrial Life and Relations*, 3 vols., comp. and ed. V. Kher (Ahmedabad: Navijivan, 1957); *Gandhiji and International Politics*, comp. and ed. P. Chaudhury (Ahmedabad: Navijivan, 1970); *Gandhi: Selected Writings*, ed. R. Duncan (New York: Harper and Row, 1971).

Two other works, L. Fischer, *The Life of Mahatma Gandhi* (London: Cape, 1951); and J. Bondurant, *Conquest of Violence: The Gandhian Philosophy of Conflict* (Berkeley: University of California Press, 1967), help to place Gandhi's own writings and narratives in perspective. I am also grateful to Dr. Mark Juergensmeyer for several helpful suggestions regarding parallels between Gandhi's stance and the stance which Luke ascribes to Jesus.

14. A. Richardson, *The Political Christ* (Philadelphia: Westminster, 1973), p. 47.

15. Like Martin Hengel (see below), Richardson is concerned that radical students and others have held that the revolutionary leader Che Guevara closely resembles Jesus. Richardson, therefore, strongly emphasizes that Jesus was not a Zealot, that is, he did not support violent revolution. However, his rejection of violence is only one aspect of Jesus' social and political stance in Luke. Luke shows Jesus calling for radically new social patterns and criticizing the political authorities who maintain the existing patterns; this Richardson does not adequately emphasize.

16. R. Schnackenburg, *The Moral Teaching of the New Testament* (New York: Seabury, 1971), p. 111.

17. See Chapter Four, Section 4.

18. In *Was Jesus a Revolutionist?* (Philadelphia: Fortress, 1971), p. 33,

Hengel states that Jesus was not one to justify the status quo; to support this statement he refers to Jesus' progressive attitude toward Gentiles and Samaritans and the way in which Jesus contradicted the Jewish law when it stood in the way of genuine human relations. However, both of these positions could be adopted without posing a serious challenge to the existing social order, particularly those aspects about which the Romans were most concerned.

In referring to Jesus' response to the tribute question, Hengel states that Jesus' answer shows that he did not hold a "conservative attitude of faithfulness to the state," but he then goes on to say that in Jesus' answer "world power is neither justified nor condemned." The result is that Hengel portrays Jesus adopting a "neutral" stance toward Roman rule in Palestine and throughout the world. However, the consequence of "neutrality" is that the Roman social order continues to operate.

19. If Jesus himself was not presenting a challenge to the Roman-controlled social order, and if he was counselling dissidents like the Zealots not to take up arms against the Romans, the combined effect would be indirect support for the Romans. Such is the logical consequence of Hengel's interpretation of Jesus' stance.

20. O. Cullmann, *The State in the New Testament* (New York: Scribner's, 1956), p. 18.

21. As we have previously stated, our own interpretation is that Luke does not show Jesus attempting to overthrow Roman rule in Palestine (or in the empire itself). Rather, Luke shows him espousing social practices and patterns that would have, if they became widely accepted, brought about the demise of the Roman empire.

22. O. Cullmann, *Jesus and the Revolutionaries* (New York: Harper and Row, 1970), p. 27.

23. As we indicated in Chapter Two, Section 3, our own view is that it is possible to use the term "program" in speaking about Jesus' response to poverty (or, by extension, about his responses to other social questions). Luke does not describe Jesus as having an administrative program for dealing with social problems in the way that a modern governmental agency or political party has; however, Luke does show Jesus making a response to these problems, and the elements present in his response do constitute the broad outlines of a "program."

In Luke's account, when Jesus calls his disciples, he calls them into a new way of life that includes a new stance toward God and a new social and political stance to the society around them. As we have seen in

Chapters Two and Three, Luke shows Jesus asking those who would be his disciples (among other things) to share their surplus possessions, adopt patterns based on humility and service, and reject the use of violence against persons. These are not separate from Jesus' call; and, inasmuch as they constitute the outlines of a "social program," Jesus is calling upon his followers to support such a program.

M. Hengel, *Victory Over Violence* (Philadelphia: Fortress, 1973), pp. 47–51, adopts an approach similar to Cullmann's and posits a dichotomy between Jesus' call to "conversion" and any social reform program. In our estimation part of the reason Cullmann and Hengel adopt such a position is that they are overreacting to the statement that, like Che Guevara and other revolutionary leaders, Jesus established a specific social program. However, to hold that Jesus was only (or even primarily) interested in "personal conversion" is a distortion of Luke's reports comparable to that made by those who say that Jesus operated as Che Guevara did.

Appendix I

1. G. Vermes and F. Millar's updating of E. Schürer's classic work, *The History of the Jewish People in the Age of Jesus Christ* (Edinburgh: Clark, 1973) provides an extensive survey of the various sources and auxiliary sciences that contribute to our understanding of the period of the Herods and the Romans. We will refer to these authors as Vermes-Millar/Schürer.

2. Since he actually participated in many of the events that he narrates, and since he had access to many documents and reports concerning the preceding history, Josephus' works, *The Jewish War* (New York: Loeb Classical Library, 1928); *Jewish Antiquities* (New York: Loeb Classical Library, 1930); *The Life* and *Against Apion* (New York: Loeb Classical Library, 1926), are our most important sources for Jewish history during this period. We will refer to *The Jewish War* as *War* and to *Jewish Antiquities* as *Ant.*

Josephus lived from A.D. 38 until somewhere around the turn of the first century. He came from a priestly family, had a wide experience with various aspects of Jewish life, and eventually served as the commander of the Jewish forces in Galilee during the war against Rome in A.D. 66. However, the fact that he subsequently became a convert to the Roman cause and a court historian for several of the Roman emperors often influences his presentation of events and groups. Despite his new allegiance to the Roman cause, Josephus retained a certain degree of loyalty to his own people and sought to present Jewish customs and institutions in such a way that they would be favorably viewed by the other peoples of the empire. For an analysis of these and other similar "tendencies" in Josephus' writings, see F. Jackson, *Josephus and the Jews* (London: SPCK, 1930).

To a lesser degree, similar considerations also apply to the writings of Philo Judeus, a Jewish philosopher who lived in Alexandria from approximately 20 B.C. until around the middle of the first century, and Tacitus, a Roman historian who lived from A.D. 56 until sometime in the reign of the emperor Hadrian (A.D. 117–138).

3. The principal sources for the history of this period are the books of the Maccabees and Josephus' works. See 1 Macc. 1–9:22, 2 Macc. 4–15, *War*, I. 1. 1–6. 4, and *Ant.*, XII. 3. 3—XIV. 3.1.

4. Even though the Hasmoneans initially enjoyed popular support, the Jewish commitment to the law requiring that the high priest be of Zadokite descent was still strong. Thus, the approval for the Hasmoneans to take over the high priestly offices was given only conditionally, or as 1 Macc. 14:41 puts it: "until a trustworthy prophet should arise." After the Seleucids had deposed and killed his father, the legitimate Zadokite heir had fled to Egypt and established a temple there; thus there was no direct Zadokite alternative at the time that the Hasmoneans assumed the office. However, Herod the Great and then the Zealots both had occasion to revive the concept of a Zadokite succession.

5. Given the extremely important role that religion played in Jewish life, the person who held the office of high priest could frequently exercise a great deal of influence upon the public life of the Jewish community. It was thus clearly to the advantage of the Hasmoneans to establish an arrangement whereby the person who held secular, princely power likewise held the office of high priest. Not only did such an arrangement reinforce the prince's secular power, but it also removed the possibility that anyone could use the office of high priest to criticize or subvert the policies of the reigning prince. Those who were critical of the Hasmoneans, particularly those concerned that the Jewish laws pertaining to ritual purity be carefully observed, disliked such an arrangement because they believed that the high priest would be more susceptible to ritual impurity or to personal corruption as a result of his involvement in secular affairs.

6. The Hasmonean house had previously had contact with the Romans when Judas Maccabeus had sent two of his sons to Rome to enlist the support of the Romans against the Seleucids. Since it was to their own interests to see the Seleucids weakened, the Romans signed a treaty of friendship with the Hasmoneans; but, apart from sending a warning letter

to the Seleucid leaders, they did not directly intervene on the Hasmoneans' behalf.

7. At the beginning of his reign Herod sought to convey the impression that he was a Jew by birth and thoroughly committed to the observance of the Jewish law. Since his mother was not Jewish, and since Josephus describes his father, Antipater, as an Idumean, there is reason to doubt whether Herod was Jewish by birth. However, even if Herod did claim to be a Jew by birth, he still did not have any hereditary qualifications for ruling over his fellow Jews; he was neither of Hasmonean nor of priestly background.

8. Since his ears had been mutilated to prevent him from exercising the office of high priest, the Romans could not have appointed Hyrcanus II to that position. However, they could have made him king and installed another member of the Hasmonean family as high priest. A second possibility was that they could have installed Aristobulus, Hyrcanus' grandson, as both king and high priest. Herod's own hope may thus have been that, by reason of his marriage to Mariamme and his own abilities, he would still be able to function as a behind-the-scenes power.

9. *War*, I.17.8; *Ant.*, XIV.16.1.

10. The various measures that Herod took to establish his position extended over a considerable length of time and were intertwined with one another. Thus, in order to simplify our presentation, we are rearranging the actual chronological sequence.

11. *War*, I.22.2; *Ant.*, XV.3.3–4.

12. *War*, I.22.1.; *Ant.*, XV.6.1–4.

13. *Ant.*, XIV.9.4; XV.1.2.

14. *Ant.*, XVI.2.3–5; XII.3.2. In some of the Greek cities within the empire, the local officials were attempting to require that the Jewish inhabitants worship idols as a condition to their being admitted to full citizenship within the city. Herod and his counsellor intervened and got the Roman authorities to guarantee both the civil rights and the religious rights of Jews throughout the empire.

15. When a severe famine struck in 25 B.C., Herod took extraordinary steps to secure supplementary grain for the people (*Ant.*, XV.9.1–2). Also in 20 B.C. Herod cut taxes by a third (*Ant.*, XV.10.4) and in 14 B.C. he reduced them by a quarter (*Ant.*, XVI.2.5).

16. *War*, I.21.1; V.15.1–8; *Ant.*, XV.11.1–6.

17. *Ant.*, XIII.8.4.

18. *Ant.*, XIV.10.6. indicates that the policy of exemption was established by Julius Caesar. Vermes-Millar/Schürer, *History*, p. 362 conclude, on the basis of other references sprinkled throughout Josephus' writings, that later Roman emperors continued this exemption.

19. V. Scramuzza, "The Policy of the Early Roman Emperors Towards Judaism," *The Beginnings of Christianity*, ed. F. Jackson and K. Lake (London: Macmillan, 1933), 5:283–84.

20. Philo Judeus, *The Embassy to Gaius* (New York: Loeb Classical Library, 1942), 23 and 40, indicates that Augustus paid for these sacrifices out of his own revenue. Josephus, *War*, II.10.4; II.17.2–3, indicates that the Jews paid for them out of temple revenues.

21. Philo, *Embassy*, 40; Josephus, *Ant.*, XVI.6.2–7.

22. In 30 B.C. Augustus increased Herod's kingdom by giving him control over several additional territories including Samaria (*Ant.*, XV.7.3; *War*, I.20.3). He made Herod similar gifts in 23 (*War*, I.20.4; *Ant.*, XV.10.1) and 20 B.C. (*War*, I.20.4; *Ant.*, XV.10.3).

23. Herod put to death the wife whom he loved the most, Mariamme, and three of his sons, Aristobulus, Alexander, and Antipater. He also put to death his sister's second husband and others. As described by Josephus, the web of intrigues became so complicated that it was impossible for anyone to know whom to trust. Even though we are not basing our analysis of the socio-political situation at the time of Jesus upon the writings of the New Testament, it is still worth noting in passing that it is Herod the Great to whom Matthew's gospel ascribes the destruction of the children of Bethlehem (Matt. 2:16).

24. In his work, *The Jews Under Rome* (New York: Putnam's, 1902), p. 90, W. Morrison cites Macrobius, "Saturnal," 2.4. The Latin is: "Melius est Herodius porcus esse, quam filius."

25. Solomon Zeitlin, "Herod, A Malevolent Maniac," *Jewish Quarterly Review* (1964).

26. *War*, I.14.4; *Ant.*, XIV.14.4. The Parthians were an Iranian tribal group that emerged in the East as the Seleucid empire went into decline. They subsequently built their own empire in the territory between the Euphrates and the Indus rivers. Since their western-most territories bordered on the eastern frontiers of the Roman empire, there were frequent conflicts between the two powers.

27. Mercenaries from such places as Thracia, Gaul, and Germany served in Herod's armies (*War*, I.33.9; *Ant.*, XVII.8.3). In addition Herod may also have conscripted from Idumea and the other non-Jewish sections of his kingdom and may have drawn Jewish recruits from the Diaspora. See A. Momigliano, "Herod of Judaea," *Cambridge Ancient History*, ed. S. Cook and others (Cambridge: Cambridge University Press, 1963), 10:327.

28. Josephus' accounts of the arguments put forward by Archelaus and Antipas and the Jewish delegation are given in *War*, II.6.1–2; *Ant.*, XVII.11.1–3. It is also interesting to note the affinities between Luke's version of the parable of the pounds (Luke 19:12–27) and Josephus' reports of the Jewish delegation's efforts to oppose Archelaus. Luke intersperses the following notes as he recounts the parable: "A nobleman went into a far country to receive a kingdom and then return. . . . But his citizens hated him and sent an embassy after him saying, 'We do not want this man to reign over us.' "

29. *War*, II.94–100; *Ant.*, XVIII.318–24.

30. Vermes-Millar/Schürer, *History*, p. 333, n. 12, provides a good analysis of the relative status and power of each of these ranks.

31. In *War*, II.6.3, Josephus indicates that Archelaus was to receive an income of four hundred talents, but in *Ant.*, XVII.11.4, he puts the amount at six hundred talents.

32. *War*, II.7.3; *Ant.*, XVII.13.2.

33. "Assessment" is the term that Josephus uses. Luke, as we have seen, uses the term "census." Given the protest that the Jews had made regarding Herod the Great's high taxes, and given the turbulence which characterized the period after Herod's death and the period of Archelaus' rule, it is not likely that Augustus was considering the imposition of additional taxes. Thus, the assessment was probably to bring the tax-collecting mechanism that Herod had established (and Archelaus continued) into line with Roman administrative procedures.

34. On the basis of the information that Josephus supplies in *War*, II.8.1; *Ant.*, XVII.13.5; and *Ant.*, XVIII.1.1, we know that Quirinius, the Syrian governor, was of consular rank, while Coponius, the new Judean governor, was of equestrian rank. Since the former consuls were men of considerable influence, it is likely that they would have had precedence over those who had recently come into an administrative position out of a military, or equestrian, background.

35. T. Tucker, "The Extent and Nature of the Roman Empire at the Birth of Christianity," *The History of Christianity in the Light of Modern Knowledge* (London: Blackie, n.d.), pp. 7–11.

36. T. Burkhill, "Sanhedrin," *Interpreter's Dictionary of the Bible*, ed. G. Buttrick (New York: Abingdon, 1962), 4:215.

37. H. Mantel, *Studies in the History of the Sanhedrin* (Cambridge: Harvard Press, 1961), pp. 55–101, provides a helpful discussion of the contrasting pictures of the sanhedrin given by Greek sources on the one hand and rabbinic sources on the other.

38. Vermes-Millar/Schürer, *History*, p. 377. While the Roman governors entrusted the sanhedrin with a great variety of responsibilities, it is not clear whether the responsibility for collecting taxes was among them.

39. Burkhill, "Sanhedrin," p. 216.

40. Vermes-Millar/Schürer, *History*, p. 378. The term "political" is here used to describe those offenses that would have constituted a threat to Roman rule and to the order that Rome was seeking to establish.

41. In *War*, II.8.1, Josephus states that when Augustus sent Coponius to Judea, he sent him "with full power, including the infliction of capital punishment," and it is therefore clear that the Roman governors had the authority to put a criminal to death. However, the fact that the governors possessed this power does not preclude the possibility that the sanhedrin may also have possessed it, and scholars have argued persuasively on both sides of this question.

Because of its relevance to the statements in the gospels about the trial(s) of Jesus, this matter is important. If the sanhedrin did have the power of capital punishment, then the sanhedrin members have less "responsibility" for Jesus' death since the gospels report that the sanhedrin handed Jesus over to Pilate and did not execute him themselves. On the other hand, if the sanhedrin did not have the authority for capital punishment, then, according to the gospel reports, it may have done everything within its power to bring about Jesus' death. P. Winter, *On the Trial of Jesus* (Berlin: DeGruyter, 1961) believes that the sanhedrin did possess the authority to inflict capital punishment. J. Blinzler, *The Trial of Jesus* (Westminster, Maryland: Newman, 1959) believes that the sanhedrin could pronounce the death sentence, but did not have the authority to execute it.

42. J. Jeremias, *Jerusalem in the Time of Jesus* (Philadelphia: Fortress, 1967) provides a good discussion of the persons and groups who served on the sanhedrin.

43. As we have remarked above, Herod was particularly concerned with establishing his "Jewish credentials" with his Jewish subjects and, especially at the outset, emphasized his loyalty to the Jewish law. Later on, however, when his own political position was firmly established, Herod occasionally chose to disregard the law in order to fulfill other objectives, e.g., to enhance his standing as a patron of Hellenistic culture, he ornamented the Jerusalem temple with a great golden eagle. However, that Herod did possess a basic understanding of the law and was capable of observing its finer points is clear.

44. Herod would have likely passed on to his sons something of his own sense for the Jewish law and for the political benefits that could attend to its proper observance. In addition, the fact that Galilee (which had a substantial Jewish population) was relatively calm under Antipas' rule (except for John the Baptist's criticism of Antipas' marriage to Herodias), indicates that he knew how to respect the religious sensitivities of his subjects.

45. Josephus is particularly critical of the conduct of the later governors (*War*, II.14.1–2; *Ant.*, XVIII.1.6).

46. As indicated in note 34 above, the "equestrian" governors had been promoted to the office out of a previous background in military service. Consequently, they would not have been as well suited for adapting to new cultural patterns as would governors who took office after extensive senatorial and administrative experience.

47. As noted above, the Roman emperors made several important concessions to the Jews. We shall see a further example of an emperor's willingness to accommodate Jewish religious sensitivities in Tiberius' response to news of one of Pilate's blunders.

48. In his article, "Judaism and Images,"*Crozer Quarterly* 23 (1946): 259–65, S. Kennard notes that the annual temple tax was to be paid in Tyrian coinage and observes that these Tyrian coins were almost always embossed with figures drawn from mythology. Kennard argues that committed Jews were able to justify this exception on the basis that Tyre did not constitute a political threat to the Jewish community of Palestine, and was not in a position to impose idolatrous practices upon believing Jews. The situation was quite different with respect to the Herods and *a fortiori* with respect to the Romans. That is why the Jews remained so adamant against any Herodian-Roman practices that contained any suggestion of emperor worship or other forms of idolatry.

49. In *War*, I.33.2, and *Ant.*, XVII.6.2–3, Josephus describes how two "doctors" denounced the golden eagle that Herod had erected over the

main gate to the temple and incited some of their followers to lower themselves from the temple roof to chop the eagle loose from its position. In *Ant.*, XVII.2.4, he describes how a large group of Pharisees refused to participate in swearing an oath of loyalty to the emperor. In both of these cases, Herod had many of those who took part in the protests killed.

50. F. Madden, *History of Jewish Coinage and of Money in the Old and New Testament* (New York: KTAV, 1967). However, since gold and silver coins were not minted in the province (and since many of these coins bore images or inscriptions that were offensive to Jewish sensibilities), the situation was not one of complete "purity of observance." This bears upon the incident concerning the "tribute money" which Luke and the other Synoptic writers report.

51. *War,* II.9.2–3; *Ant.*, XVIII.3.1.

52. To protest to Pilate, the Jews would have had to travel to Caesarea. Although they maintained troops in Jerusalem and themselves went up to Jerusalem for the major festivals (staying in the palace that Herod the Great had built), the Roman governors' official place of residence was in Caesarea.

53. Neither Josephus nor other reliable historical sources tell us anything about Pilate's subsequent fate. There are, however, a number of legends that purport to present information concerning Pilate's subsequent activities as well as new information about his role in Jesus' trial. Some of these legends are favorable to Pilate, tend to minimize his role in the verdict against Jesus, and even go so far as to proclaim him a saint. S. Brandon, *Jesus and the Zealots* (Manchester: Manchester University Press, 1967) cites these legends to illustrate his theory that subsequent Christian tradition sought to minimize Roman involvement in Jesus' death. However, there are also several legends distinctly unfavorable to Pilate, e.g., that he committed suicide and his body was transported by evil spirits to Mt. Pilatus near Lucerne. For a listing of both kinds of legends, see Vermes-Millar/Schürer, *History*, p. 387, note 144.

54. Philo, *Embassy*, 38.

55. This evaluation is actually made by Agrippa I in a letter which Philo reproduces. For a comment in support of Agrippa's credibility, see Vermes-Millar/Schürer, *History*, p. 384.

56. *Ant.*, XVIII.4.6.

57. *War*, II.9.1; *Ant.*, XVIII.2.3.

58. *War*, II.9.1; *Ant.*, XVIII.2.1. The name of this city was later changed to Julias.

59. In our description of Antipas' dealings with Vitellius, we have followed the chronology and particulars given by Josephus in *Ant.*, XVIII.4.5—5.3. However, Vermes-Millar/Schürer, *History*, p. 351, point out that Suetonius, Cassius Dio, and Tacitus contradict Josephus' chronology. If Josephus did err in his chronology, then Vitellius' reluctance to fight the Nabateans on Antipas' behalf was not due to his pique over Antipas' message to Rome.

60. *Ant.*, XVIII.5.1.

61. *War*, II.9.6; *Ant.*, XVIII.7.1–2.

62. Vermes-Millar/Schürer, *History*, pp. 373–75 and 401–3, provide an exceptionally clear analysis of Rome's general taxing policies and their specific application in the territories of Palestine. See also A. Büchler, "The Priestly Dues and the Roman Taxes in the Edicts of Caesar," *Studies in Jewish History*, pp. 1–23.

63. *War*, I.8.5; *Ant.*, XIV.5.4.

64. Vermes-Millar/Schürer, *History*, p. 375.

65. O. Michel, "telones," *Theological Dictionary of the New Testament*, ed. G. Kittel (Grand Rapids: Eerdmans, 1964–74), 8:94. Michel cites the work of S. deLaet on this point.

66. Vermes-Millar/Schürer, *History*, p. 375.

67. *Ant.*, XVII.11.2.

68. The other principal argument that Herod did pay tribute is that Pompey had placed Judea under tribute, and evidence that this policy was changed when Antony and Augustus established Herod in office is lacking. Thus A. Schalit, *König Herodes* (Berlin: DeGruyter, 1969), pp. 271–72, and A. Momigliano, "Herod," p. 330, defend a continuous policy of tribute. However, Vermes-Millar/Schürer, *History*, p. 317, S. Perowne, *The Life and Times of Herod the Great* (London: Hodder and Stoughton, 1958), p. 94, and others argue that Herod's standing as a friendly client king (along with his good personal relationship with Augustus) would have exempted him from tribute.

69. *Ant.*, XVI.5.4.

70. Tacitus, *Annals* (New York: Loeb Classical Library, 1942), II.42.

71. *Ant.*, XVIII.4.3.

Appendix II

1. J. Jeremias, *Jerusalem at the Time of Jesus* (Philadelphia: Fortress Press, 1967), p. 205.

2. H. Hoehner, *Herod Antipas* (Cambridge, England: Cambridge University Press, 1972), pp. 52–53. Hoehner also provides an appendix (pp. 291–97) in which he discusses the problems in computing the population figures for Palestine in general and Galilee and Perea in particular.

3. C. McCown, "Palestine, Geography of," *The Interpreter's Dictionary of the Bible*, 3:637.

4. Ibid., p. 636.

5. Jeremias, *Jerusalem*, p. 27.

6. Hoehner, *Herod Antipas*, pp. 65–68.

7. McCown, "Geography," p. 637.

8. Hoehner, *Herod Antipas*, pp. 69–70; Jeremias, *Jerusalem*, pp. 31–51.

9. McCown, "Geography," p. 637. McCown's judgments about the social and economic conditions that prevailed in Palestine tend to correlate with the conditions that many sociologists believe to be usual in agrarian societies. See, for example, G. Lenski and J. Lenski, *Human Societies*, 2nd ed. (New York: McGraw-Hill, 1974), pp. 207–62.

10. The degree to which the various Mosaic laws were actually observed is a much controverted question. If the laws preserved in the Pentateuch only represented the vision of persons far removed from the realities of everyday life, then the values that were expressed and the directives that were given may not have exercised a very influential role in ongoing Jewish life. Our position is that the Mosaic laws generally exercised a significant influence upon the practice of the Jewish community. This conclusion is suggested by Josephus' various reports that the Jews resisted idolatrous practices, paid the annual temple tax, etc. Regarding the overall observance of the laws relating to socio-economic practices, see our treatment of the probosol in section 3 of this Appendix and in note 17 below.

11. W. Harrelson, "Law in the Old Testament," *The Interpreter's Dictionary of the Bible*, 3:77.

12. Protests against injustice and oppression constitute one of the main

themes of the prophetic writings, and the fact that these writings were revered and eventually incorporated into the Jewish canon indicates that social responsibility was an important part of Judaism's heritage. Nevertheless, while the prophetic writings were highly esteemed within the Judaism of Jesus' day, it was the Mosaic law that supplied the basis for the ongoing life of the community. The prophetic traditions were extremely important and served to elaborate the law and encourage its practice, but it was the law that provided the foundation for the positions taken by the prophets. For a complementary analysis on this point, see the section of Harrelson, "Law," p. 88, entitled "Law as the Dominant Reality Within Judaism."

13. Exod. 21:2–6; 23:10–11. Deut. 15:1–18. Lev. 25:2–7; 18–24. In several aspects, the seventh year as a year of "release" paralleled the concept of the seventh day of the week as a day of "rest."

14. R. DeVaux, *Ancient Israel* (London: Darton, Longman, Todd, 1965), p. 75.

15. The rationale and effects of this probosol are analyzed by J. Neusner, *From Politics to Piety* (Englewood Cliffs: Prentice-Hall, 1973), pp. 14–19. The rabbinic source is Sifre, Dt. 113.

16. Ibid., pp. 42–43.

17. In his three-volume work, *The Rabbinic Traditions Before 70* (Leiden: Brill, 1971), Jacob Neusner analyzes the various rabbinic traditions in great detail. His general conclusion is that much of what the traditions report about pre-70 situations is suspect; however, he holds that the traditions about the laws, including the probosol, are the most reliable (3:287–91; see also 1:301). Thus, even though Hillel may not have been responsible for the probosol, it is extremely likely that the controversies that gave rise to it were taking place within the Judaism that existed before the destruction of the temple.

In this instance, we have used a rabbinic report to establish that questions concerning social responsibility were being discussed and deliberated in the Judaism of Jesus' day; the same point can also be established by references to Josephus' writings. For instance, in *Ant.*, XIV.10.6, Josephus reports a decree of Julius Caesar that the Jews "shall pay a tax for the city of Jerusalem, Joppa excluded, every year except in the seventh year, which they call the sabbatical year, because in this time they neither take fruit from the trees nor do they sow." We can be sure that the Romans would never have made such a concession if the sabbatical year practices had not been widely observed. See also *Ant.*, XIV.16.1, and XV.1.2.

18. Our account of the conditions under which sacrifice was offered and of the emergence of the Jerusalem temple (also its reconstruction after the exile) is based upon DeVaux, *Ancient Israel*, pp. 289–99 and 415–32.

19. Josephus supplies us with significant information regarding Herod's renovation and enlargement of the second temple. *War*, V.5.1–6, and *Ant.*, XV.11.1–6, are the two most important passages, but there are a number of others. For a diagram of the temple area (and also various models) based upon Josephus' reports and other sources, see W. Stinespring, "Temple, Jerusalem," *The Interpreter's Dictionary of the Bible*, 4:534–60.

20. Jeremias, *Jerusalem*, p. 84.

21. Ibid., pp. 21–57, 82.

22. DeVaux, *Ancient Israel*, p. 403. DeVaux also indicates that the kings could draw upon the temple treasury to meet their own emergencies (p. 124).

23. Ibid., p. 404.

24. Ibid.

25. Ibid. G. Moore, *Judaism* (Cambridge: Harvard University Press, 1950), 2:70–72, also provides a helpful analysis of tithes and the other forms of revenue that the priests received.

26. *Ant.*, XX.8.8, 9.2. In both of these instances Josephus criticizes the priests for confiscating the tithes and not allowing the lower clergy the nine-tenths that was rightfully due them.

27. According to Josephus, Herod reproached those who had torn down the golden eagle for failing to appreciate how much money he had spent on the temple. Such a statement suggests that Herod had financed part of the reconstruction, perhaps the major part, out of his own funds. However, the construction that continued subsequent to Herod's death would have had to be financed from the temple treasury. In addition, it seems likely that Herod would have asked the chief priests, men he had appointed, to commit temple funds for a percentage of the initial expenses.

28. Philo, *Embassy*, 40; *Ant.*, XVI.6.2–7.

29. Exod. 30:11–16; Neh. 10:33–35. DeVaux, *Ancient Israel*, p. 403, describes the history of this tax.

30. H. Hamburger, "Money," *The Interpreter's Dictionary of the Bible*, 3:428.

31. *War*, VI.6.2.

32. *Ant.*, XIV.4.5; XIV.7.2; *War*, II.14.6.

33. Our treatment of the synagogue follows closely upon W. Schrage, "sunagogue," *The Theological Dictionary of the New Testament* 7:810–28.

34. Ibid., pp. 821–25.

35. Ibid., pp. 822–23.

36. After the destruction of the temple and the city, rabbinic schools at Jamnia and later at Tiberias came to exercise a central influence within Judaism. The oral tradition to which the Pharisees had long adhered was eventually written down and became steadily more important within the life of the Jewish community. In many respects, then, the premises upon which the synagogue was based eventually became the foundation for subsequent Judaism. Or, to put it another way, the Judaism that survived and developed from the ruins of Jerusalem was the Judaism of the Pharisees. The first two chapters of S. Sandmel, *The First Christian Century in Judaism and Christianity* (New York: Oxford University Press, 1969) make a further analysis along this line.

37. *Ant.*, XVII.11.2.

38. *Ant.*, XVII.11.5.

39. Hoehner, *Herod Antipas*, p. 70.

40. *Ant.*, XVIII.1.1., 2.1

41. *Ant.*, XVII.2.3.

42. Jeremias, *Jerusalem*, p. 99.

43. Ibid., p. 49.

44. *Life*, 76.

45. Jeremias, *Jerusalem*, p. 99, cites rabbinic references concerning the priest Eleazar B. Harsum.

46. Ibid., p. 97, cites several rabbinic sources that narrate this episode.

47. *War*, II.21.2; *Life*, 13.

48. *Ant.*, XIII,10.6.

49. Jeremias, *Jerusalem*, p. 111, indicates that it was a serious matter if a day laborer could not find work on a given day. To illustrate this, he cites a rabbinic report describing how Hillel faced this situation when he was a day laborer.

50. Hoehner, *Herod Antipas,* p. 79, estimates that if Jews living in Galilee under Antipas' rule faithfully paid both their religious and civil taxes, they ended up paying between 30 and 40 percent of their income in taxes.

51. Male scholars such as A. Oepke, "gyne," *The Theological Dictionary of the New Testament,* 1:776–89, and O. Baab, "Woman," *The Interpreter's Dictionary of the Bible,* pp. 864–67, present material that supports such a conclusion. It is to be hoped that women Scripture scholars will soon be in a better position to bring their sensitivities to bear upon this and related subjects.

52. Oepke, "gyne," p. 781.

53. DeVaux, *Ancient Israel,* pp. 25–26.

54. Oepke, "Gyne," p. 783. In *Ant.,* XV.7.10, Josephus indicates that Salome, Herod's sister, enacted a divorce against her husband, but he implies that this was an extraordinary occurrence.

55. DeVaux, *Ancient Israel,* p. 54.

56. Jeremias, *Jerusalem,* p. 363.

57. *Ant.,* XV.11.5.

58. Oepke, "gyne," p. 782.

59. Jeremias, *Jerusalem,* p. 375.

60. In *Ant.,* XVI.1.1, Josephus indicates that the reason the Jews were so strongly opposed to having Jews (even thieves) sold to pagan masters was because the law called for them to be released after six years; this would not occur if Jews were sold into slavery abroad.

61. Deut. 24:7; Lev. 25:47–54. In *Ant.,* XVI.1.1, Josephus reports that Herod the Great tried to deter thievery by establishing the policy that Jewish thieves would be sold into slavery abroad. However, such a strong popular outburst resulted that he had to abandon the proposal.

62. Exod. 21:5–6 envisions lifelong servitude as a possibility: "But if the slave plainly says, 'I love my master, my wife, and my children; I will not go out free,' then his master shall bring him to God, and he shall bring him to the door or the doorpost; and his master shall bore his ear through with an awl; and he shall serve him for life." See also Deut. 15:16–17 and Lev. 25:39–46.

63. R. North, *Sociology of the Biblical Jubilee* (Rome: Gregorian University Press, 1954), pp. 156–57.

64. Quoted by H. Daniel-Rops, *Daily Life in the Time of Jesus* (New York: Hawthorn, 1962), p. 167.

65. I. Mendelsohn, "Slavery in the Old Testament," *The Interpreter's Dictionary of the Bible,* 5:384, lists several Old Testament references and indicates that this was a common practice throughout much of the ancient world.

66. DeVaux, *Ancient Israel,* pp. 81–82.

67. Jeremias, *Jerusalem,* p. 111. Jeremias bases his position on an 1894 study by E. Riehm.

68. DeVaux, *Ancient Israel,* pp. 84–86.

69. Gentile slaves who converted to Judaism may have preferred full freedom as their first choice, but serving a Jewish owner until the next sabbatical year was undoubtedly far preferable to being sold to a Gentile owner where the conditions of service were more arduous and for life.

Appendix III

1. J. Jeremias, *Jerusalem in the Time of Jesus* (Philadelphia: Fortress, 1967), p. 163, describes the captain of the temple as responsible for the temple cultus and as supervising the entire body of officiating priests. Citing a rabbinic source, E. Schürer, *The Jewish People in the Time of Jesus Christ* (New York: Scribner's, 1891), p. 267, indicates that the captain had responsibility for the temple guards. (This and all subsequent references to Schürer refer to Volume 1, Division 2, of *The Jewish People in the Time of Jesus Christ.*)

2. Jeremias, *Jerusalem,* p. 166, states that a minimum of three priests served jointly as treasurers at any one time. Among their duties were responsibility for the produce and materials needed for the temple sacrifices, administration of the tribute money and the votive offerings, and general responsibility for the various other financial transactions in which the temple was involved. See also Schürer, *Jewish People,* pp. 260–64.

3. In contrast to Schürer, Jeremias, *Jerusalem,* p. 166, believes that the office of overseer was separate from that of treasurer and holds that the overseers were in charge of the various temple activities and departments such as music, doorkeeping, bakery, etc. He concludes, p. 172, that at any given time seven priests would have had the position and rank of overseer.

4. The directors of the weekly courses were immediately responsible for the conduct of sacrifices, purifications, etc., during the periods when

their particular group of priests came to Jerusalem from the outlying districts of Judea and Galilee. Although one rabbinic listing cited by Jeremias places them second to the temple captain in precedence, the fact that the directors lived in the outlying districts and were not permanent members of the temple staff would seem to have limited their influence over the daily activities in Jerusalem. See Jeremias, *Jerusalem*, p. 167.

5. For the reasons outlined in the paragraphs that follow, we have emphasized the given high priest's relationships to his peers. In their discussions, Jeremias and Schürer provide separate sections for the high priests on the one hand and the chief priests on the other; however, the emphasis that we have placed upon the *group* of chief priests (with the high priest as a leading member of that group) is consistent with the analyses of Jeremias and Schürer.

6. Chief among the high priest's prerogatives was the exclusive privilege to enter the innermost part of the temple, the holy of holies. See Jeremias, *Jerusalem*, pp. 151 and 160.

7. Schürer, *Jewish People*, pp. 181–82. Jeremias, *Jerusalem*, p. 151.

8. P. Gaechter, "The Hatred of the House of Annas," *Theological Studies* 8 (1948): 7, cites several rabbinic criticisms of the bribery extant during this period.

9. For a complete list of the high priests during this period, see Jeremias, *Jerusalem*, pp. 377–78.

10. Schürer, *Jewish People*, p. 202; Jeremias, *Jerusalem*, p. 157.

11. Schürer, *Jewish People*, p. 205; Jeremias, *Jerusalem*, p. 179.

12. In *Ant.*, XX.8.11, Josephus indicates that a priest who was a temple treasurer served on what seems to have been a sanhedrin delegation to Rome. Jeremias, *Jerusalem*, p. 179, believes that priests who had superior (temple captain) or comparable (overseer) positions also held sanhedrin seats.

13. During the Herodian-Roman period, there were twenty-five high priests who were not from Zadokite or Hasmonean background. Of this number, twenty-two clearly belonged to one of these four families, and Jeremias, *Jerusalem*, p. 194, believes that the three remaining priests were connected with one of these same four families in one way or another.

14. Jeremias, *Jerusalem*, p. 194.

15. Ibid.

16. *War*, IV.3.8. Josephus is negatively inclined to this step and criticizes Phanni as "such a clown that he scarcely knew what the high priesthood meant." Josephus may not have adverted to Phanni's Zadokite background and the significance that Zadokite descent had for the Zealots. Another consideration is that Josephus' own relatively prominent priestly background may have prejudiced him against the Zealots' efforts to remove the four leading families from their dominant position. Jeremias, *Jerusalem*, p. 193, indicates that there were other clans of Zadokite descent besides the Eniachin clan from which Phanni came.

17. F. Lang, "saddoukaios," *Theological Dictionary of the New Testament*, 7:35–43.

18. Ibid., p. 50.

19. Josephus describes the Pharisees and Sadducees in *War*, II.8.14; *Ant.*, XIII.10.6; *Ant.*, XVIII.1.3–4. Our treatment summarizes several of his principal points.

20. Jeremias, *Jerusalem*, pp. 229–30, emphasizes the influence of the lay aristocracy within the Sadducean party.

21. *Ant.*, XVIII.1.4.

22. We are not so much interested in the leverage that their seats on the sanhedrin gave the chief priests and their lay allies in matters of interpretation and doctrine. (Josephus conveys the impression that even with their high positions the approach followed by the Sadducees with respect to law and doctrine was not influential with the Jewish populace.) Rather, we are concerned with the likelihood that the chief priests were able to use their sanhedrin positions to further their political and economic aims and interests. For an analysis of how those with Sadducean and those with Pharisaic viewpoints interacted on the sanhedrin, see Schürer, *Jewish People*, pp. 174–79.

23. *Ant.*, XVIII.1.1.

24. *Ant.*, XVIII.3.2; see also *War*, II.9.4.

25. *War*, II.15.3–5; *War*, II.17.2.

26. *War*, II.17.5–6.

27. *War*, II.20.3–4. Jeremias, *Jerusalem*, p. 198, argues that the positions of responsibility that these chief priests held in the Jewish forces indicates that the Jews of Jerusalem and the surrounding territories were accustomed to look to them for political leadership; he sees this as another indication of the power that the priests possessed. However, such an

analysis fails to take into account the political loyalties of the chief priests themselves. One of them, Eleazar (the captain of the temple and the son of the reigning high priest), had indeed taken a leading role in the anti-Rome movement (see *War*, II.17.2), but he was an untypical representative of the political stance of the chief priests as a whole. Eleazar received support from the lower echelons of the clergy, but his chief priestly peers attempted to persuade him to turn back from his course. Having failed to persuade him and his followers and encouraged by reinforcements that they had received, "the leading men, the chief priests, and all the people who were in favor of peace occupied the upper city; for the lower city and the Temple were in the hands of the insurgents" (*War*, II.17.5).

It was only after the rebel forces had won an initial victory over Cestius, the Roman commander, and had returned to Jerusalem to persuade those Jews who were uncommitted that any of the other chief priests aligned themselves with the revolutionary effort. In effect they may still have been reluctant to take this step, but may have been forced to do so. In *War*, II.20.3, before he tells us that several of the chief priests accepted posts in the war effort, Josephus states: "The Jews who had pursued Cestius, on their return to Jerusalem, partly by force, partly by persuasion, brought over to their side such pro-Romans as still remained; and assembling in the Temple appointed additional generals to conduct the war."

28. In *War*, II.22.1, Josephus states that Ananus, one of the chief priests who had been placed in charge of military operations in Jerusalem, "nevertheless, cherished the thought of gradually abandoning these warlike preparations and bending the malcontents and the infatuated so-called zealots to a more salutary policy." See also *War*, II.19.5.

29. Jeremias, *Jerusalem*, pp. 148–49, explains why the high priest's vestments had great symbolic importance and sketches the turns that the dispute over them took under the various governors and emperors.

30. In *Ant.*, XX.8.5, Josephus states that Felix, the Roman governor, bribed one of the high priest's friends to arrange with brigands to have the high priest murdered. In *War*, II.13.3, he simply states that the high priest in question, Jonathan, fell victim to a group of brigands.

31. In the passage (*Ant.*, XX.8.5) we have just referred to, Josephus states that one of the reasons why Jonathan had been criticizing Felix's administration was because Jonathan "had requested Caesar to dispatch Felix as procurator of Judaea." Thus, he felt that his own standing with the Jewish populace was suffering as a result of Felix's ineptness. Schürer, *Jewish People*, p. 202, describes Jonathan's activities in some detail.

32. *Ant.*, XX.8.8.

33. *War*, II.17.6.

34. Pesachim f. 57, 1, *Tosefta Menachoth*. Cited in F. Farrar, *The Herods* (New York: Herrick, 1898), p. 117.

35. While we have concentrated our attention on the various reports describing the exploitation and abuse of office that the chief priests were guilty of, the strong likelihood that the high priests had to bribe the Roman governors (and the later Herods) in order to gain and maintain their office should also be emphasized. In addition to the rabbinic reports cited by P. Gaechter (see note 8 above), those contained in H. Strack and P. Billerbeck, *Kommentar zum Neuen Testament aus Talmud und Midrasch* (Munich: Beck'sche, 1924), 1:953 and 2:569, indicate that this was very likely the case.

36. *The Assumption of Moses* (London: Black, 1897), 7:3–10.

37. R. Meyer, "pharisaios," *Theological Dictionary of the New Testament*, 7:12. It may instead (or also) mean "interpret," "interpretation"; cf. J. Bowker, *Jesus and the Pharisees* (Cambridge: Cambridge University Press, 1973), pp. 20f.

38. Our own treatment of the Pharisees proceeds along relatively conventional lines (Meyer, Schürer, Jeremias); at the same time, it is important that we take account of Jacob Neusner's analysis in his three-volume study, *The Rabbinic Traditions About the Pharisees Before 70* (Leiden: Brill, 1971). Neusner maintains that scholars have all too frequently been prone to use the rabbinic texts at face value and have thereby arrived at descriptions of Pharisaism and portraits of leading rabbis that the texts will not substantiate if used critically.

Neusner also cautions about attempts to integrate the various references in Josephus, in the New Testament, and in rabbinic literature without being properly critical of the tendencies that are present in each of these sources. However, in his concluding summary (3:305), he does state that "the rabbinic tradition thus begins where Josephus' narrative leaves off and the difference between them leads us to suspect that the change in the character of Pharisaism from a political party to a sect comes with Hillel"; he thus conveys the impression that the rabbis described in the rabbinic literature are the same as the "Pharisees" described by Josephus.

Bowker, *Jesus and the Pharisees*, does not think that this was necessarily the case and points to passages in the rabbinic literature critical of "the Pharisees." The main thrust of Bowker's analysis is that without important qualifications the group which Josephus calls "the Pharisees," the group which the New Testament writings call "the Pharisees," and the group of rabbis designated in the rabbinic literature should not automatically be presumed to be the same group.

39. Meyer, "pharisaios," p. 15, discusses the possibility that temple priests who sought to popularize the concept of priestly holiness may have provided the original inspiration for the Pharisaic movement.

40. Ibid., p. 16.

41. Ibid. Jeremias, *Jerusalem*, p. 16, prefers to describe these groups as "communities" rather than as "societies."

42. Meyer, "pharisaios," p. 18.

43. *Ant.*, XIII.5.9.

44. Schürer, *Jewish People*, pp. 313–28, provides a helpful discussion on the origin and role of the scribes.

45. Jeremias, *Jerusalem*, p. 243, 256; Schürer, *Jewish People*, p. 319.

46. Jeremias, *Jerusalem* p. 235.

47. Ibid., p. 236; Schürer, *Jewish People*, p. 320.

48. Schürer, *Jewish People*, p. 315.

49. Meyer, "pharisaios," pp. 13–31, believes that a number of currents intermingled to produce the Pharisaic tradition.

50. *Ant.*, XV.1.1.

51. J. Neusner, *From Politics to Piety* (Englewood Cliffs: Prentice-Hall, 1973), p. 153, describes this shift of direction within the Pharisaic movement as a shift "from politics to piety." He maintains that during their "pietistic" phrase they gave their attention to their own observance of the law and the internal ordering of their own societies. However, in attributing such an inward-looking period to the Pharisees, it is important to emphasize that they were never indifferent to any breaches of the law that resulted from the actions of those who held political power. In his treatment of the Pharisees' political stance, Jeremias, *Jerusalem*, pp. 263–64, does not present them as decisively turning away from public life during the Roman period, but he does emphasize that they had very little political involvement or influence at that time.

52. *Ant.*, XVIII.1.1; XVIII.1.6; *War*, II.8.1.

53. M. Smith, "Zealots and Sicarii, Their Origins and Relations," *Harvard Theological Review* 64 (1971): 1–19, points out that there is no

substantial evidence that Judas himself or his immediate followers were ever called "Zealots" and argues that scholars have erred in attributing the creation of the formal Zealot party to Judas. Smith also emphasizes the evidence (from Josephus) that indicates that during the war the "Zealots" were only one of the factions in the anti-Roman effort. However, we are more interested in the moral continuity between the anti-Roman efforts that later marked the beginning of the war than we are in whether a single Zealot party or movement existed throughout the entire period. Josephus' references to the "fourth philosophy" as a continuing movement are one indication that there was moral continuity. Another is that one of Judas' sons, Menahem, emerged as one of the rebel leaders at the outbreak of the war (*War*, II.16.8).

54. *Ant.*, XVIII.1.1; *War*, II.8.1.

55. A. Stumpff, "zelo, zelotes," *Theological Dictionary of the New Testament*, 2:884.

56. Numerous scholars, including Meyer, "pharisaios," p. 27, have pointed out the similarities between the Pharisees and the Zealots on the basis of the high regard both groups had for the Jewish law. In fact, it is possible to interpret Judas' movement as an outgrowth of Pharisaism. Josephus tells us that Saddok, who joined Judas in leading the initial uprising, was a Pharisee (*Ant.*, XVIII.1.1); his statement that the fourth philosophy, the school established by Judas, "agrees in all other respects with the opinion of the Pharisees . . ." (*Ant.*, XVIII.1.6) offers further confirmation of this interpretation. Their different assessments of direct Roman rule was thus the crucial distinction between the Zealots and the Pharisees.

57. See especially *War*, V.1.1–3.1.

58. *War*, II.17.6.

59. Philo, *Embassy*, 38.

60. *Ant.*, XVIII.3.1; see also *War*, II.9.3.

61. Two of Josephus' most important references are *War*, II.8.2–13, and *Ant.*, XVIII.1.5. Philo's references occur in his work, *Hypothetica* 11.1–18, and *Every Good Man is Free*, 12–13.

62. Our brief summary of the Essenes' history follows largely along the lines of the sketch given by G. Vermes, *The Dead Sea Scrolls in English* (London: Penguin, 1973), pp. 53–68. Philo's account of the Therapeutae is contained in his work *On the Contemplative Life*.

63. Vermes, *Dead Sea Scrolls*, pp. 63–65.

64. W. Farmer, "Essenes," *Interpreter's Dictionary of the Bible*, 2:146.

65. Vermes, *Dead Sea Scrolls*, p. 71.

66. Ibid., pp. 29–30. Farmer, "Essenes," p. 146, cites several of Josephus' and Philo's passages on this point.

67. Vermes, *Dead Sea Scrolls*, p. 30. Farmer, "Essenes," pp. 147–48.

68. Vermes, *Dead Sea Scrolls*, pp. 124–48.

69. Ibid., p. 65.

70. Ibid., p. 252.

71. Ibid., p. 54.

72. *War*, II.8.10; *War*, II.20.4.

73. *Ant.*, XVII.2.4; *Ant.*, XVIII.1.5.

Appendix IV

1. H. Conzelmann, *The Theology of St. Luke* (New York: Harper & Row, 1960), pp. 188–89.

2. Conzelmann provides a further indication of his failure to grasp the nuances of Luke's passion account. As we saw in Chapter Five, Section 5, Luke provides four notes that indicate that the Romans executed Jesus and that Pilate retained jurisdiction over the proceedings; yet Conzelmann makes the following assertion: "But he [Pilate] does not condemn. Jesus does not die by the decision of the Roman judge—he is killed by the Jews [sic], to whom he is 'delivered' by the Romans (23:25). We cannot dismiss the 'absence' of the verdict in Luke to negligence, as Luke certainly read the condemnation in his source (Mark 15:15) and omitted it. Mark 15:12 is also omitted, because there Pilate appears as the one who carries out the verdict" (*Theology of St. Luke*, p. 87).

Conzelmann justifies his interpretation by adverting to the fact that Luke does not show Pilate pronouncing a verdict against Jesus as Mark does. However, as we have noted above, Luke very likely made this alteration in order to highlight the role that the chief priests played in securing Jesus' death. In our view, Luke wanted to emphasize the chief priests' role without absolving Pilate and the Romans. For this reason, he provides four indications of the Romans' involvement, but does so in the context of numerous descriptions that indicate that the chief priests had the major responsibility for Jesus' death.

3. Conzelmann states that Jesus' answer gave Pilate enough information to arrive at an "objective legal decision." However, Pilate's decision has an exceedingly strange character if Jesus answered that he was the king of the Jews and Pilate then immediately stated, "I find no crime in this man." Conzelmann says: "According to Luke, Jesus does not refuse to answer the Roman authorities. He gives the information they required and so enables them to arrive at the objective legal decision, which is in fact immediately done officially. The answer he gives is no fuller than in Mark, but there is no refusal to answer" (p. 86).

4. Conzelmann's position is similar to that of those scholars who hold that Jesus presumed the existence of two realms, Caesar's and God's, in his reply to the question concerning the payment of tribute. In Chapter Four, Section 4, we criticized this general interpretation for introducing a "dualistic" framework that is not consistent with Luke's general description of Jesus' outlook.

5. See Chapter Four, note 5, for an indication of Conzelmann's extremely limited response to the passage (13:31–33) in which Luke shows Jesus refusing to defer to Herod and referring to him as "that fox." Conzelmann also passes over or fails to provide an adequate treatment of the passage in which Luke shows Jesus criticizing the kings of the Gentiles for dominating their subjects (22:24–27) and the passage in which Luke describes Jesus' warning to the disciples that they will be brought before kings and governors (21:12–15).

6. Jesus' criticism of Herod occurs only in Luke's account. Similarly, Jesus' reference to the dominating practices of the kings of the Gentiles and the designation "benefactors" also occurs in a passage that Luke alone includes. As we noted in Chapter Four, Section 4, Mark shows Jesus warning the disciples that they will be persecuted by the political authorities, but Luke shows him doing this twice. As we have seen, Luke also goes beyond Mark in highlighting many of Jesus' controversial teachings with regard to various social practices.

Selected Bibliography

Ancient Sources

Aland, K., ed. *Synopsis of the Four Gospels*. Stuttgart: Württembergische Bibelanstalt, 1970.

The Assumption of Moses. Trans. R. Charles. London: Black, 1897.

The Dead Sea Scrolls in English. Trans. G. Vermes. London: Penguin, 1973.

Josephus. *Jewish Antiquities*. Trans. H. Thackeray and others. New York: Loeb Classical Library, 1930.

————.*The Jewish War*. Trans. H. Thackeray. New York: Loeb Classical Library, 1928.

————.*The Life and Against Apion*. Trans. H. Thackeray and others. New York: Loeb Classical Library, 1926.

The Mishnah. Trans. and intro. H. Danby. London: Oxford University Press, 1933.

The Odes and Psalms of Solomon. Ed. and trans. R. Harris. Cambridge: Cambridge University Press, 1909.

The Oxford Annotated Bible (Revised Standard Version). Ed. H. May and B. Metzger. New York: Oxford University Press, 1973.

Philo. *The Embassy to Gaius*. Trans. F. Colson. New York: Loeb Classical Library, 1942.

————. *Every Good Man Is Free*. Trans. F. Colson. New York: Loeb Classical Library, 1942.

————. *Hypothetica*. Trans. F. Colson. New York: Loeb Classical Library, 1942.

————. *On the Contemplative Life*. Trans. F. Colson. New York: Loeb Classical Library, 1942.

Strack, H., and P. Billerbeck. *Kommentar Zum Neuen Testament aus Talmud und Midrasch*. 2 Vols. Munich: Beck'sche, 1924.

Tacitus. *The Annals*. Trans. J. Jackson. New York: Loeb Classical Library, 1942.

Throckmorton, B., ed. *Gospel Parallels: A Synopsis of the First Three Gospels* (an English language [R.S.V.] version of the Huck-Lietzmann Synopsis, 9th edition). Camden, New Jersey: Nelson, 1967.

Critical Works on Luke and Acts

Baily, J.A. *The Traditions Common to the Gospels of Luke and John.* Leiden: Brill, 1963.

Baker, J. "Luke, the Critical Evangelist." *Expository Times* 68 (1956–57):123–25.

Barrett, C.K. *Luke the Historian in Recent Study.* London: Epworth, 1961.

Beare, F. *The Earliest Records of Jesus.* New York: Abingdon, 1962.

Blevins, J. "The Passion Narrative: Luke 19:28—24:53." *Review and Expositor* 64 (1967):513–22.

Blinzler, J. "Die Niedermetzelung von Galiläern durch Pilatus." *Novum Testamentum* 2 (1957):24–29.

————. "Passionsgeschehen und Passionsbericht des Lukasevangeliums." *Bibel und Kirche* 24, 1 (1969):1–4.

Braumann, G. "Das Mittel der Zeit." *Zeitschrift für die Neutestamentliche Wissenschaft* 54 (1963):117–45.

Brown, R.E. "The Beatitudes According to Luke." In *New Testament Essays.* Milwaukee: Bruce, 1965.

Brown, S. *Apostasy and Perseverance in ɪ ʋe Theology of Luke.* Rome: Pontifical Biblical Institute, 1969.

Bruce, F.F. *The Acts of the Apostles.* London: Tyndale Press, 1952.

————. *The New Testament Documents: Are They Reliable?* 5th ed. Grand Rapids: Eerdmans, 1960.

Bultmann, R. *The History of the Synoptic Tradition.* 2nd ed. Trans. J. Marsh. New York: Harper and Row, 1972.

————. *Theology of the New Testament.* Trans. K. Grobel. London: SCM, 1959.

Cadbury, H.J. *The Book of Acts in History.* New York: Harper, 1955.

————. *The Making of Luke-Acts.* London: SPCK, 1958.

————. "Commentary on the Preface of Luke." In *The Beginnings of Christianity,* 2:489–510. Ed. F.J.F. Jackson and K. Lake. London: Macmillan, 1933.

————. "The Purpose Expressed in Luke's Preface." *The Expositor* 8/21 (1921):431–41.

Caird, G.B. *The Gospel of St. Luke.* London: Penguin Books, 1963.

Conzelmann, H. *Die Apostelgeschichte.* Tübingen: Mohr, 1963.

————. *History of Primitive Christianity.* Trans. J.E. Steely. New York: Abingdon, 1973.

204   *Selected Bibliography*

———. *Jesus.* Translated by J. Raymond Lord. Philadelphia: Fortress, 1973.

———. *An Outline of the Theology of the New Testament.* Trans. J. Bowden. New York: Harper and Row, 1969.

———. *The Theology of St. Luke.* Trans. G. Bushwell. New York: Harper and Row, 1960.

———. "The First Christian Century as Christian History." In *The Bible in Modern Scholarship*, pp. 217–26. Ed. J.P. Hyatt. Nashville: Abingdon, 1965.

———. "Geschichte, Geschichtsbild und Geschichtsdarstellung bei Lukas." *Theologische Literaturzeitung* 85 (1960):241–50.

———. "History and Theology in the Passion Narratives of the Synoptic Gospels." *Interpretation* 24, 2 (1970):178–97.

———. "Luke's Place in the Development of Early Christianity." In *Studies in Luke-Acts*, pp. 298–316. Ed. L.E. Keck and J.L. Martyn. New York: Abingdon Press, 1966.

Creed, J.M. *The Gospel According to Luke.* London: Macmillan, 1930.

Danker, F.W. *Jesus and the New Age According to St. Luke.* St. Louis: Clayton, 1972.

———. *Luke.* Proclamation Commentaries. Philadelphia: Fortress, 1976.

Dibelius, M. *Studies in Acts.* Trans. M. Ling and P. Schubert. New York: Scribner's, 1956.

———. "The First Christian Historian (Luke)." *Religion in Life* 25 (1955): 223–36.

Easton, B.S. *The Purpose of Acts.* London: SPCK, 1936.

Edwards, R.A. "The Redaction of Luke." *Journal of Religion* 49 (1969): 392–405.

Ehrhardt, A. "The Construction and Purpose of the Acts of the Apostles." *Studia Theologica* 12 (1958):45–79.

Ellis, E.E. *Eschatology in Luke.* Philadelphia: Fortress, 1972.

———. *The Gospel of Luke.* London: Nelson, 1966.

Farrar, A. "On Dispensing with 'Q'." In *Studies in the Gospels.* Ed. D.E. Nineham. Oxford: Blackwell, 1955.

Fitzmeyer, J.A. "The Story of the Dishonest Manager (Luke 16, 1–13)." *Theological Studies* 25 (1964):23–42.

Flender, H. *Luke the Theologian of Redemptive History.* Trans. R. Fuller and I. Fuller. Philadelphia: Fortress, 1967.

Francis, F.O. "Eschatology and History in Luke-Acts." *Journal of the American Academy of Religion* 37 (1969):49–63.

Geldenhuys, N. *Commentary on the Gospel of Luke.* Grand Rapids: Eerdmans, 1952.

Goodspeed, E.J. "Was Theophilus Luke's Publisher?" *Journal of Biblical Literature* 73 (1954):84.

Grundmann, W. *Das Evangelium nach Lukas.* Berlin: Evangelische Verlaganstalt, 1971.

Haenchen, E. *The Acts of the Apostles: A Commentary.* Trans. B. Noble and others. Philadelphia: Westminster, 1971.

————. "The Book of Acts as Source Material for the History of Early Christianity." In *Studies in Luke-Acts,* pp. 258–78. Ed. L.E. Keck and J.L. Martyn. Nashville: Abingdon, 1966.

————. "Historie und Verkündigung bei Markus und Lukas." In *Die Bibel und Wir,* pp. 156–81. Tübingen: Mohr, 1968.

Higgins, A.J.B. "The Preface to Luke and the Kerygma in Acts." In *Apostolic History and the Gospel,* pp. 78–79. Ed. W.W. Gasque and R.P. Martin. Grand Rapids: Eerdmans, 1970.

Keck, L.E. "Jesus' Entrance Upon His Mission: Luke 3:1–4:30." *Review and Expositor* 64 (1967):465–83.

King, N.Q. "The 'Universalism' of the Third Gospel." In *Studia Evangelica,* 1:199–205. Ed. K. Aland et al. Berlin: Akademie, 1959.

Klein, G. "Lukas 1:1–4 als theologisches Programm." In *Zeit und Geschichte,* pp. 193–216. Tübingen: Mohr, 1964.

Kodell, J. "The Theology of Luke in Recent Study." *Biblical Theology Bulletin* 1 (1971): 115–44.

Lampe, G.W.H. "The Holy Spirit in the Writings of St. Luke." In *Studies in the Gospels,* pp. 159–200. Ed. D.E. Nineham. Oxford: Blackwell, 1955.

Leany, A.R.C. *A Commentary on the Gospel According to St. Luke.* London: Black, 1958.

Lightfoot, R.H. *History and Interpretation in the Gospels.* New York: Harper, 1935.

————. *Locality and Doctrine in the Gospels.* New York: Harper, 1938.

Lindsey, F. "Lucan Theology in Contemporary Perspective," *Bibliotheca Sacra* 125 (1968): 346–51.

Lohse, E. "Lukas als Theologe der Heilsgeschichte." *Evangelische Theologie* 14 (1954): 256–75.

Manson, W. *The Gospel of Luke.* New York: Smith, 1930.

Marshall, I. *Luke: Historian and Theologian.* Exeter, Devon: Paternoster, 1970.

————."Recent Study of the Gospel According to St. Luke." *Expository Times* 80 (1968): 4–8.

Mattil, A.J., "Luke as Historian in Criticism Since 1840." Dissertation at Vanderbilt University, 1959.

Milburn, R. L. *Early Christian Interpretations of History.* London: Black, 1954.

Moehring, H. "The Census in Luke as an Apologetic Device." In *Studies in New Testament and Early Christian Literature*, pp. 144–60. Leiden: Brill, 1972.

Morgenthaler, R. *Die Lukanische Geschichtsschreibung als Zeugnis.* 2 vols. Zurich: Zwingli Verlag, 1954.

———. *Das Zweiheitsgesetz im Lukanischen Werke.* Zurich: Zwingli Verlag, 1949.

Morton, A. Q., and G. H. C. MacGregor. *The Structure of Luke and Acts.* London: Hodder and Stoughton, 1964.

Ogg, G. "The Central Section of the Gospel According to St. Luke (9:51–19:28)." *New Testament Studies* 18 (1971): 39–53.

———. "The Quirinius Question Today (Luke 2:1–7)." *Expository Times* 79 (1957):231–36.

O'Neill, J. C. *The Theology of Acts in Its Historical Setting.* London: SPCK, 1961.

Perrin, N. *What Is Redaction Criticism?* Philadelphia: Fortress, 1969.

Piper, O. A. "The Purpose of Luke." *Union Seminary Review* 57 (1944–46):15–25.

Ramsay, W. M. *The Bearing of Recent Discovery on the Trustworthiness of the New Testament.* London: Hodder and Stoughton, 1915.

———. *Luke, the Physician and Other Studies in the History of Religion.* London: Hodder and Stoughton, 1908.

———. *Was Christ Born at Bethlehem? A Study on the Credibility of St. Luke.* New York: Putnam's, 1898.

Rengstorf, K. *Das Evangelium nach Lukas.* Göttingen: Vandenhoeck and Ruprecht, 1972.

Rienecker, F. *Das Evangelium des Lukas.* Wuppertal: Brockaus, 1966.

Robertson, A. T. *Luke the Historian in the Light of Research.* New York: Scribner's, 1920.

———. "Luke's Method of Research." *Biblical Review* 5 (1920): 171–95.

Robinson, W. C., Jr. "The Way of the Lord: A Study of History and Eschatology in the Gospel of Luke." Doctoral Dissertation: University of Basle, 1960.

Rohde, J. *Rediscovering the Teaching of the Evangelists.* Trans. D. Barton. Philadelphia: Westminster, 1968.

Schlatter, A. *Die Evangelien nach Markus und Lukas.* Stuttgart: Calwer Verlag, 1960.

Schmid, J. *Das Evangelium nach Lukas.* 4th ed. Regensburg: Pustet, 1960.

Schramm, T. *Der Markusstoff bei Lukas. Eine litterarische und redaktionsgeschichtliche Untersuchung.* New York: Cambridge University Press, 1971.

Stagg, F. "The Journey Toward Jerusalem in Luke's Gospel. Luke 9:51–19:27." *Review and Expositor* 64 (1967): 499–512.

Stöger, A. "Eigenart und Botschaft der Lukanischen Passionsgeschichte." *Bibel und Kirche* 24, 1 (1969): 4–8.

Stuhlmueller, C. "The Gospel According to Luke." In *Jerome Biblical Commentary*. Englewood Cliffs: Prentice-Hall, 1968.

Talbert, C. *Luke and the Gnostics: An Examination of the Lukan Purpose.* Nashville: Abingdon, 1966.

———. "The Lukan Presentation of Jesus' Ministry in Galilee: Luke 4:31–9; 50." *Review and Expositor* 64 (1967): 485–97.

———. "The Redaction Critical Quest for Luke the Theologian." *Perspective* 11 (1970): 171–222.

Taylor, V. *Behind the Third Gospel.* Oxford: Clarendon Press, 1926.

Tolbert, M.O. *Luke.* Nashville: Broadmann Press, 1970.

Tyson, J.B. "The Lukan Version of the Trial of Jesus." *Novum Testamentum* 3 (1959): 249–58.

Vögtle, A. "Was Hatte die Widmung des Lukanischen Doppelwerkes an Theophilos zu Bedeuten?" In *Das Evangelium und die Evangelien*, pp. 31–43. Dusseldorf: Patmos, 1971.

Wilckens, U. "Interpreting Luke-Acts in a Period of Existentialist Theology." In *Studies in Luke-Acts*, pp. 60–83. Ed. L.E. Keck and J.L. Martyn. Nashville: Abingdon, 1966.

Williams, C.S.C. "Luke-Acts in Recent Study." *Expository Times* 73 (1961): 133–36.

Williams, R.R. "Church History in Acts: Is It Reliable?" In *Historicity and Chronology in the New Testament*, pp. 145–59. London: SPCK, 1965.

Wilson, S.G. "Lukan Eschatology." *New Testament Studies* 16 (1969): 330–47.

Judea and Galilee Under Roman Rule

Abrahams, I. *Studies in Pharisaism and the Gospels.* New York: Ktav, 1967.

Allon, G. "The Attitude of the Pharisees to the Roman Government and the House of Herod." In *Scripta Hierosolymitana*, 7: 53–78. Ed. A. Fuks and I. Halpern. Jerusalem: Magnes, 1961.

Arnold, W.T. *The Roman System of Provincial Administration.* Oxford: Blackwell, 1914.

Baab, O. "Woman." In *The Interpreter's Dictionary of the Bible*, 4:864–67. Ed. G. Buttrick. New York: Abingdon, 1962.

Baron, S., *A Social and Religious History of the Jews.* New York: Columbia University Press, 1952.

Barrett, C. K., ed. *The New Testament Background*. New York: Macmillan, 1957.

Baumbach, G. "Die Zeloten—Ihre geschichtliche und religionspolitische Bedeutung." *Bibel und Liturgie* 41 (1968): 2–25.

———. "Zeloten und Sikarier." *Theologische Literaturzeitung* 90 (1965): 727–39.

Bevan, E. R. *Jerusalem under the High Priests*. London: Arnold, 1948.

Bishop, E. F. F. *Jesus of Palestine: The Local Background to the Gospel Documents*. 2 vols. London: Lutterworth, 1955.

Bouquet, A. C. *Everyday Life in New Testament Times*. New York: Scribner's, 1953.

Bowker, J. W. *Jesus and the Pharisees*. Cambridge: Cambridge University Press, 1973.

Braun, H. "The Qumran Community." In *Jesus in His Time*, pp. 66–74. Ed. H. J. Schultz. Trans. B. Watchorn. Philadelphia: Fortress, 1971.

Bruce, F. F. "Herod Antipas, Tetrarch of Galilee and Peraea." *The Annual of Leeds University Society* 5 (1963–65): 6–23.

Büchler, A. "On the History of the Temple Worship in Jerusalem." In *Studies in Jewish History*, pp. 24–63. Ed. I. Brodie and J. Rabbinowitz. New York: Oxford University Press, 1956.

———. "The Priestly Dues and the Roman Taxes in the Edicts of Caesar." In *Studies in Jewish History*, pp. 1–23. New York: Oxford University Press, 1956.

Burkill, T. A. "Sanhedrin." In *The Interpreter's Dictionary of the Bible*, 4:214–18. Ed. G. Buttrick. New York: Abingdon, 1962.

Colpe, C. "East and West," In *Jesus in His Time*, pp. 19–27. Ed. H. J. Schultz. Trans. by B. Watchorn. Philadelphia: Fortress, 1971.

Dalman, G. *Arbeit und Sitte in Palästina*. 5 vols. Gütersloh: Bertelsmann, 1928–42.

Daniel-Rops, H. *Daily Life in the Time of Jesus*. Trans. P. O'Brian. New York: Hawthorn, 1962.

Daube, D. *Civil Disobedience in Antiquity*. Edinburgh: Edinburgh University Press, 1972.

———. *The New Testament and Rabbinic Judaism*. London: University of London, 1956.

———. *Studies in Biblical Law*. Cambridge: Cambridge University Press, 1947.

Davies, W. D. "The Jewish Background of the Teaching of Jesus: Apocalyptic and Pharisaism." *Expository Times* 59 (1948): 233–37.

DeVaux, R. *Ancient Israel*. 2nd ed. Trans. J. McHugh. London: Darton, Longmann, Todd, 1965.

Dibelius, M. "Herodes und Pilatus." *Zeitschrift für die Neutestamentliche Wissenschaft* 16 (1915):113–26.

Dihle, A. "The Graeco-Roman Background." In *Jesus in His Time*, pp. 10–18. Ed. H.J. Schultz. Trans. B. Watchorn. Philadelphia: Fortress, 1971.

Duckworth, H.T.F. "The Roman Provincial System." In *The Beginnings of Christianity*, 1:171–217. Ed. F.J.F. Jackson and K. Lake. London: Macmillan, 1920.

Farmer, W.R. "Essenes." In *The Interpreter's Dictionary of the Bible*, 2:143–49. Ed. J. Buttrick. New York: Abingdon, 1962.

———. *Maccabees, Zealots, and Josephus*. New York: Columbia University Press, 1956.

Farrar, F.W. *The Herods*. New York: Herick, 1898.

Finegan, J. *Handbook of Biblical Chronology*. Princeton: Princeton University Press, 1964.

Fullerton, K., and J.P. Hyatt. "Slave, Slavery." In *The Interpreter's Dictionary of the Bible*, pp. 924–926. Ed. J. Hastings. New York: Scribner's 1963.

Gealy, F. "Centurion." In *The Interpreter's Dictionary of the Bible*, 1:547–48. Ed. G. Buttrick. New York: Abingdon, 1962.

Grant, F.C. *The Economic Background of the Gospels*. London: Oxford University Press, 1926.

———. "The Economic Background of the New Testament." In *The Background of the New Testament and Its Eschatology*, pp. 96–114. Ed. W.D. Davis and D. Daube. New York: Cambridge University Press, 1964.

Guignebert, C. *The Jewish World in the Time of Jesus*. Trans. S.H. Hooke. London: Routledge and Kegan Paul, 1939.

Guterman, S.L. *Religious Toleration and Persecution in Ancient Rome*. London: Aiglon, 1951.

Hamburger, H. "Money." In *The Interpreter's Dictionary of the Bible*, 3:423–35. Ed. G. Buttrick. New York: Abingdon, 1962.

Hardy, E.G. *Christianity and the Roman Empire*. New York: Macmillan, 1925.

Harrelson, W. "Law in the Old Testament." In *The Interpreter's Dictionary of the Bible*, 3:77–89. Ed. G. Buttrick. New York: Abingdon, 1962.

Higgins, A.J. "Sidelights on Christian Beginnings in the Graeco-Roman World." *Evangelical Quarterly* 41 (1969): 197–206.

Hoehner, H. *Herod Antipas*. Cambridge: Cambridge University Press, 1972.

Hoenig, S. *The Great Sanhedrin*. New York: Bloch, 1953.

Jackson, F.J.F. *Josephus and the Jews*. London: SPCK, 1930.

Jeremias, J. *Jerusalem in the Time of Jesus*. Trans. F.H. Cave and C.H. Cave. Philadelphia: Fortress, 1969.

Jones, A.H.M. *The Herods of Judaea*. Oxford: Clarendon Press, 1938.

Kennard, S. "Judaism and Images." *Crozer Quarterly* 23 (1946): 259–65.

Lang, F. "saddoukaios." In *Theological Dictionary of the New Testament*, 7:35–43. Ed. G. Kittel. Trans. and ed. G. Bromily. Grand Rapids: Eerdmans, 1964–1974.

Lightley, J. *Jewish Sects and Parties in the Time of Christ*. London: Epworth Press, 1925.

Loewe, H.M.J. *Render unto Caesar: Religious and Political Loyalty in Palestine*. Cambridge: Cambridge University Press, 1940.

Lohse, E. *Umwelt des Neuen Testaments*. Göttingen: Vandenhoeck und Ruprecht, 1971.

———."Temple and Synagogue." In *Jesus in His Time*, pp. 75–83. Ed. H.J. Schultz. Trans. B. Watchorn. Philadelphia: Fortress, 1971.

McCown, C.C. "Palestine, Geography of." In *The Interpreter's Dictionary of the Bible*, 3:626–39. Ed. G. Buttrick. New York: Abingdon, 1962.

Madden, F.W. *History of Jewish Coinage and of Money in the Old and New Testament*. Prolegomenon by M. Avi-Yonah. New York: Ktav, 1967.

Mantel, H. *Studies in the History of the Sanhedrin*. Cambridge: Harvard University Press, 1961.

Mendelsohn, I. "Slavery in the OT." In *The Interpreter's Dictionary of the Bible*, 4:383–91. Ed. G. Buttrick. New York: Abingdon Press, 1962.

Meyer, R. "pharisaios." In *Theological Dictionary of the New Testament*, 9:11–48. Ed. G. Kittel. Trans. and ed. G. Bromily. Grand Rapids: Eerdmans, 1964-1974.

Michel, O. "telones." In *Theological Dictionary of the New Testament*, 8:88–105. Ed. G. Kittel. Trans. and ed. G. Bromily. Grand Rapids: Eerdmans, 1964–1974.

Momigliano, A. "Herod of Judaea." In *Cambridge Ancient History*, 10:316–39. Ed. S.A. Cook and others. Cambridge: Cambridge University Press, 1963.

———. "Ricerche sull'Organizzazione della Giudea sotto Il Dominio Romano (63 A.C.–70 D.C.)." *Annali Della R. Scuola Normale Superiori di Pisa—Lettere, Storia e Filosofia*. Series (1934), 2:183–221, 347–96.

Mommsen, T. *The Provinces of the Roman Empire*. 2 vols. Trans. W.P. Dickson. New York: Scribner's, 1906.

———. *Romisches Staatsrecht*. 3 vols. Leipzig: Hirzel, 1887.

Moore, G.F. *Judaism in the First Centuries of the Christian Era*. Vol. 2. Cambridge: Harvard University Press, 1927.

Morison, F. *And Pilate Said: A New Study of the Roman Procurator.* London: Rich and Cowan, 1939.

Morrison, W. D. *The Jews Under Roman Rule.* New York: Putnam's, 1902.

Neusner, J. *From Politics to Piety: The Emergence of Pharisaic Judaism.* Englewood Cliffs, N.J.: Prentice-Hall, 1973.

————. *The Rabbinic Traditions About the Pharisees Before 70.* 3 vols. Leiden: Brill, 1971.

North, R. *Sociology of the Biblical Jubilee.* Rome: Pontifical Biblical Institute, 1954.

Oepke, A. "gyne." In *Theological Dictionary of the New Testament*, 1:776–89. Ed. G. Kittel. Trans. and ed. G. Bromily. Grand Rapids: Eerdmans, 1964–1974.

Parker, P. "Crucifixion." In *The Interpreter's Dictionary of the Bible*, 1:746–47. Ed. G. Buttrick. New York: Abingdon, 1962.

————. "Inscription on the Cross." In *The Interpreter's Dictionary of the Bible*, 2:705–6. Ed. G. Buttrick. New York: Abingdon, 1962.

Perowne, S. *The Later Herods: The Political Background to the New Testament.* London: Hodder and Stoughton, 1958.

————. *The Life and Times of Herod the Great.* London: Hodder and Stoughton, 1958.

Rees, W. "Archelaus, Son of Herod." *Scripture* 4 (1951): 348–55.

Reicke, B. "Galilee and Judaea." In *Jesus in His Time*, pp. 28–35. Ed. H.J. Schultz. Trans. B. Watchorn. Philadelphia: Fortress, 1971.

Rostovtzeff, M. *The Social and Economic History of the Roman Empire.* Oxford: Clarendon Press, 1957.

————. *The Social and Economic History of the Hellenistic World.* Oxford: Clarendon Press, 1941.

Sandmel, S. *The First Century in Judaism and Christianity: Certainties and Uncertainties.* New York: Oxford University Press, 1969.

————. *Herod: Profile of a Tyrant.* Philadelphia: Lippincott, 1967.

Schalit, A. *König Herodes: Der Mann und Sein Werk.* Berlin: DeGruyter, 1969.

————. "Herod and His Successors." In *Jesus in His Time*, pp. 36–46. Ed. H.J. Schultz. Trans. B. Watchorn. Philadelphia: Fortress, 1971.

Schrage, W. "sunagoge." In *Theological Dictionary of the New Testament*, 7:798–852. Ed. G. Kittel. Trans. and ed. G. Bromily. Grand Rapids: Eerdmans, 1964–1974.

Schürer, E. *The Jewish People in the Time of Jesus Christ.* 2 vols. Trans. S. Taylor and P. Christie. New York: Scribner's, 1891.

Scramuzza, V.M. "The Policy of the Early Roman Emperors Towards Judaism." In *The Beginnings of Christianity*, 5:277–97. Ed. F.J.F. Jackson and K. Lake. London: MacMillan, 1933.

Sherwin-White, A. N. *Roman Society and Roman Law in the New Testament.* Oxford: Clarendon Press, 1963.

Simon, M. *Jewish Sects at the Time of Jesus.* Trans. J. Farley. Philadelphia: Fortress, 1967.

Smith, M. "Zealots and Sicarii. Their Origins and Relation." *Harvard Theological Review* 64 (1971): 1–19.

Spence-Jones, H. D. M. *The Early Christians in Rome.* London: Methuen, 1910.

Stauffer, E. *Jerusalem und Rom im Zeitalter Jesu Christi.* Bern: Francke, 1957.

Stevenson, G. H. *Roman Provincial Administration.* Oxford: Blackwell, 1949.

Stinespring, W. F. "Temple, Jerusalem." In *The Interpreter's Dictionary of the Bible*, 4: 534–60. Ed. G. Buttrick. New York: Abingdon, 1962.

Stumpff, A. "zelo, zelotes." In *Theological Dictionary of the New Testament* 2: 877–88. Ed. G. Kittel. Trans. and ed. G. Bromily. Grand Rapids: Eerdmans, 1964–1974.

Tcherikover, V. *Hellenistic Civilization and the Jews.* Trans. S. Applebaum. Philadelphia: Jewish Publication Society of America, 1959.

Tucker, T. G. "The Extent and Nature of the Roman Empire at the Birth of Christianity." In *The History of Christianity in the Light of Modern Knowledge*, pp. 3–19. London: Blackie, n.d.

Vermes, G., F. Millar, and E. Schürer. *The History of the Jewish People in the Age of Jesus Christ.* Vol. 1. Edinburgh: Clark, 1973.

Vogt, Joseph. "Augustus and Tiberius." In *Jesus in His Time*, pp. 1–9. Ed. H. J. Schultz. Trans. B. Watchorn. Philadelphia: Fortress, 1971.

Wellhausen, J. *Die Pharisaer und die Sadduzaer: eine Untersuchung zu inneren Judischen Geschichte.* Hannover: Lafaire, 1924.

Winter, P. "Sadducees and Pharisees." In *Jesus in His Time*, pp. 47–56. Ed. H. J. Schultz. Trans. B. Watchorn. Philadelphia: Fortress, 1971.

Workman, H. B. *Persecution in the Early Church.* London: Sharp, 1923.

Zeitlin, S. *The Rise and Fall of the Judaean State.* 2 vols. Philadelphia: Jewish Publication Society of America, 1967.

————. "Herod: A Malevolent Maniac." *Jewish Quarterly Review* 54 (1964): 1–27.

————. "Zealots and Sicarii." *Journal of Biblical Literature* 81 (1962): pp. 395–98.

Jesus' Social and Political Stance

Allen, J. E. "Why Pilate?" In *The Trial of Jesus*, pp. 79–83. Ed. E. Bammel. London: SCM Press, 1970.

Barrett, C.K. "The New Testament Doctrine of Church and State." In *New Testament Essays*, pp. 1–19. London: SPCK, 1972.

Batey, R. *Jesus and the Poor: The Poverty Program of the First Christians.* New York: Harper and Row, 1972.

Benoit, P. *The Passion and Resurrection of Jesus Christ.* Trans. B. Weatherhead. New York: Herder, 1969.

Blinzler, J. *Herodes Antipas und Jesus Christus.* Stuttgart: Katholisches Bibelwerk, 1947.

———. *The Trial of Jesus.* Trans. I. and F. McHugh. Westminster, Maryland: Newman, 1959.

———. "The Trial of Jesus in the Light of History." *Judaism* 21, 1 (1971):49–55.

Bornhauser, D. "Die Beteiligung des Herodes am Prozesse Jesu. *Neue Kirchliche Zeitschrift* 40 (1929): 714–18.

Brandon, S.G.F. *Jesus and the Zealots.* Manchester: Manchester University Press, 1967.

———. *The Trial of Jesus of Nazareth.* London: Batsford, 1968.

———. "The Trial of Jesus." *Judaism* 21, 1 (1971): 43–48.

Bunn, L.H. "Herod Antipas and 'That Fox,' " *Expository Times* 43 (1932): 380–81.

Burkill, T.A. "The Condemnation of Jesus: A Critique of Sherwin-White's Thesis." *Novum Testamentum* 12 (1970): 321–42.

Cadbury, H.J. "The Social Translation of the Gospel." *Harvard Theological Review* 15 (1922): 1–13.

Caird, G.B. *Jesus and the Jewish Nation.* London: Athlone, 1965.

Cazelles, H. "Bible et Politique." *Recherches de Science Religieuse* 59 (1971): 497–530.

Chiavacci, E. "Non Resistenza ed Opposizione al Male nel Nuovo Testamento." In *La Pace: Reflessioni Bibliche*, pp. 111–40. Rome: A.V.E., 1971.

Cohn, H.H. *The Trial and Death of Jesus.* New York: Harper & Row, 1971.

———. "Reflections on the Trial of Jesus." *Judaism* 20, 1 (1971): 10–23.

Coste, R. *Evangile et Politique.* Paris: Aubier-Montaigne, 1968.

Cranfield, C.E.B. "The Christian's Political Responsibility According to the New Testament." *Scottish Journal of Theology* 15, 2(1962): 176–92.

Crespy, G. "Recherche sur la signification politique de la mort du Christ." *Lumière et Vie* 20, 101 (1970): 89–109.

Crivelli, D. "Gesu e la Rivoluzione." *Richerche Bibliche e Religiose* 6 (1971): 341–54.

Cullmann, O. *Jesus and the Revolutionaries.* Trans. G. Putnam. New York: Harper & Row, 1970.

————. *The State in the New Testament.* New York: Scribner's, 1956.

Dabrowski, E. "The Trial of Christ in Recent Research." In *Studi Evangelica* 4: 22–27. Ed. F.L. Cross. Berlin: Akademie Verlag, 1968.

Derrett, J. D. "Peter's Penny: Fresh Light on Matthew 17, 24–27." *Novum Testamentum* 6 (1963): 1–15.

Dibelius, M. "Rom und die Christen im ersten Jahrhundert." In *Botschafte und Geschichte,* 2: 177–228. Tübingen: Mohr, 1956.

Dodd, C.H. "The Historical Problem of the Death of Jesus." In *More New Testament Essays,* pp. 84–101. Grand Rapids: Eerdmans, 1968.

Edwards, G. R. *Jesus and the Politics of Violence.* New York: Harper and Row, 1976.

Enslin, M. S. "The Temple and the Cross." *Judaism* 20, 1 (1971): 24–31.

Epstein, V. "The Historicity of the Gospel Account of the Cleansing of the Temple." *Zeitschrift für die Neutestamentliche Wissenschaft* 55 (1964): 42–58.

Flourney, P.P. "What Frightened Pilate?" *Bibliotheca Sacra* 82 (1925): 314–20.

Flusser, D. "A Literary Approach to the Trial of Jesus." *Judaism* 20, 1 (1971): 32–36.

Gaechter, P. "The Hatred of the House of Annas." *Theological Studies* 8 (1947): 3–34.

Gaugler, E. "Der Christ und die staatlichen Gewalten nach dem Neuen Testament." *Internationale Kirchliche Zeitschrift* 40 (1950): 133–55.

George, A. "Jésus devant le problème politique." *Lumière et Vie* 20 (1971): 5–17.

Giblin, C.H. " 'The Things of God' in the Question Concerning Tribute to Caesar (Lk 20:25, Mk 12:17, Mt 22:21)." *Catholic Biblical Quarterly* 33 (1971): 510–27.

Gnilka, J. "War Jesus Revolutionär?" *Bibel und Leben* 12 (1971): 67–78.

Goppelt, L. "The Freedom to Pay the Imperial Tax (Mark 12,17)." In *Studia Evangelica* 2: 183–94. Ed. F.L. Cross. Berlin: Akademie Verlag, 1964.

————."Der Staat in der Sicht Neuen Testaments." In *Christologie und Ethik.* Göttingen: Vanderhoeck und Ruprecht, 1968.

Grant, F.C. "The Economic Significance of Messianism." *Anglican Theological Review* 6 (1924): 196–213, and 7 (1925): 281–89.

————. "The Impracticability of the Gospel Ethics." In *Aux sources de la tradition chrétienne,* pp. 86–94. Ed. O. Cullmann. Paris: Delachaux et Niestle, 1950.

————. "Method in Studying Jesus' Social Teaching." In *Studies in Early Christianity,* pp. 239–81. Ed. S.J. Case. New York: Century, 1928.

————. "On the Trial of Jesus: A Review Article." *Journal of Religion* 44 (1964): 230–37.

Guillet, Jacques. "Jésus et la politique." *Recherches de Science Religieuse* 59 (1971): 531–44.

Hall, J.G. "Swords of Offence." In *Studia Evangelica* 1: 499–502. Ed. K. Aland and others. Berlin Akademie Verlag, 1959.

Hamilton, N.Q. "Temple Cleansing and Temple Bank." *Journal of Biblical Literature* 83 (1964): 365–72.

Hauck, F. "ballo, ekballo." In *Theological Dictionary of the New Testament*, 1: 527–28. Ed. G. Kittel. Trans. and ed. G. Bromily. Grand Rapids: Eerdmans, 1964–1974.

———."mamonas." In *Theological Dictionary of the New Testament*, 4: 388–90. Ed. G. Kittel. Trans. and ed. G. Bromily. Grand Rapids: Eerdmans, 1964–1974.

Harrison, E.F. "Jesus and Pilate." *Bibliotheca Sacra* 105 (1948): 307–19.

Henderson, C.R. "The Influence of Jesus on Social Institutions." *Biblical World* 2 (1898): 167–76.

Hengel, M. *Property and Riches in the Early Church*. Trans. J. Bowden. Philadelphia: Fortress, 1974.

———. *Victory Over Violence*. Trans. D. Green. Philadelphia: Fortress, 1973.

———. *Was Jesus a Revolutionist?* Trans. W. Klassen. Philadelphia: Fortress, 1971.

———. "Review of S.G.F. Brandon's *Jesus and the Zealots*." *Journal of Semitic Studies* 14 (1969): 231–40.

Hoehner, H.W. "Why Did Pilate Hand Jesus Over to Antipas?" In *The Trial of Jesus*, pp. 84–90. Ed. E. Bammel. London: SCM, 1970.

Judson, H.P. "The Political Effects of the Teaching of Jesus." *Biblical World* 11 (1898): 229–38.

Kautsky, K. *Foundations of Christianity*. Trans. J.W. Hartmann. New York Monthly Review, 1972.

Kennard, J.S., Jr. *Render to God: A Study of the Tribute Passage*. New York: Oxford University, 1950.

Kittell, G. *Christus und Imperator das Urteil der Ersten Christenheit über den Statt*. Stuttgart: Kohlhammer, 1939.

Klassen, W. "Jesus and the Zealot Option." *Canadian Journal of Theology* 16 (1970): 12–31.

Klijn, A.F.J. "Scribes, Pharisees, High Priests, and Elders in the New Testament." *Novum Testamentum* 3 (1959): 259–67.

Lake, K. "Simon Zelotes." *Harvard Theological Review* 10 (1917): 57–63.

Liberty, S. *The Political Relations of Christ's Ministry*. London: Oxford University Press, 1921.

———. "The Importance of Pontius Pilate in Creed and Gospel." *Journal of Theological Studies* 45 (1944): 38–56.

Löwe, H. "War Jesus Revolutionär?" *Quatember* 33 (1969): 50–60.

MacGregor, W.M. "Christ's Three Judges." *The Expositor* 6/1 (1900): 407–14; 6/2 (1900): 59–68 and 119–29.

Manson, T.W. *Ethics and the Gospel.* New York: Scribner's, 1960.

———. "The Cleansing of the Temple." *John Rylands Library Bulletin* 33 (1951): 271–82.

Maurer, C. "Jesus Christus—Revolutionär oder Reaktionär?" *Reformatio* 21 (1972): 342–51.

Mendner, S. "Die Tempelreinigung." *Zeitschrift für die Neutestamentliche Wissenschaft* 4,7 (1956): 93–112.

Montefiore, H. "Jesus and the Temple Tax." *New Testament Studies* 10 (1964):60–61.

Paupert, J.M. *The Politics of the Gospel.* Trans. G. Roy. New York: Holt, Rinehart and Winston, 1969.

Richardson, A. *The Political Christ.* Philadelphia: Westminster, 1973.

Rist, M. "Caesar or God (Mark 12:13–17)? A Study in Form-Geschichte." *Journal of Religion* 16 (1936): 317–31.

Schlier, H. "Der Staat nach dem Neuen Testament." In *Besinnung auf das Neue Testament*, pp. 193–211. Freiburg: Herder, 1964.

Schnackenburg, R. *The Moral Teaching of the New Testament.* Trans. J. Holland-Smith and W. O'Hara. New York: Seabury, 1973.

Schrage, W. *Die Christen und der Staat nach dem Neuen Testament.* Gütersloh: Mohn, 1971.

Schreiber, J. "Das Schweigen Jesu." In *Theologie und Unterricht*, pp. 79–87. Ed. K. Wegenast. Gütersloh: Mohn, 1969.

Schultz, S. "Hat Christus die Sklaven Befreit? Sklaverei und Emanzipationsbewegungen in Abendland." *Evangelische Kommentar* 5 (1972): 13–17.

Schweizer, E. "Zum Sklavenproblem im Neuen Testament." *Evangelische Theologie* 32 (1972): 502–5.

Sherwin-White, A.N. "The Trial of Christ." In *Historicity and Chronology in the New Testament*, pp. 97–116.

Stauffer, E. *Christ and the Caesars.* Trans. K. and R.G. Smith. Philadelphia: Westminster, 1955.

Streeter, B.H. "On the Trial of Our Lord Before Herod—A Suggestion." In *Studies in the Synoptic Problem*, pp. 229–31. Ed. W. Sanday. Oxford: Clarendon Press, 1911.

de Surgy, P. "L'Evangile et la violence." *Lumière et Vie* 18, 9 (1969):87–110.

Taylor, V. *The Passion Narrative of St. Luke: A Critical and Historical Investigation.* Ed. O. Evans. London/New York: Cambridge University Press, 1972.

Thurman, H. *Jesus and the Disinherited.* Nashville: Abingdon, 1970.

Trocme, A. *Jesus and the Non-Violent Revolution.* Trans. M.H. Shank and M.E. Miller. Scottsdale, Pa.: Herald, 1973.

Trocme, E. *Jesus as Seen by His Contemporaries.* Trans. P. Wilson. Philadelphia: Westminister,1973.

Tyson, J.B. "Jesus and Herod Antipas." *Journal of Biblical Literature* 79 (1960): 239–46.

Vermes, G. *Jesus the Jew.* London: Collins, 1973.

Verrall, A.W. "Christ Before Herod." *Journal of Theological Studies* 10 (1909): 321–53.

Volkl, R. *Christ und Welt nach dem Neuen Testament.* Wurzburg: Echter Verlag, 1961.

Wendland, H.D. *Ethik des Neuen Testaments.* Göttingen: Vandenhoeck and Ruprecht, 1970.

Wilder, A. *Eschatology and Ethics in the Teaching of Jesus.* New York: Harper, 1939.

———. *Otherworldliness and the New Testament.* New York: Harper, 1954.

Wilson, W.R. *The Execution of Jesus: A Judicial, Literary, and Historical Investigation.* New York: Scribner's, 1970.

Wink, W. "Jesus and Revolution. Reflections on S.G.F. Brandon's *Jesus and the Zealots.*" *Union Seminary Quarterly Review* 25, 1 (1969): 37–59.

Winter, P. *On the Trial of Jesus.* Berlin: DeGruyter, 1961.

Yoder, J.H. *The Christian Witness to the State.* Newton, Kansas: Faith and Life Press, 1964.

———. *The Original Revolution.* Scottsdale, Pa: Herald, 1972.

———. *The Politics of Jesus.* Grand Rapids: Eerdmans, 1972.

Other Works Consulted

Bauer, W. *A Greek-English Lexicon of the New Testament and Other Early Christian Literature.* Trans. and adapted by W. Arndt and F. Gingrich. Chicago: University of Chicago Press, 1957.

Bondurant, J. *Conquest of Violence: The Gandhian Philosophy of Conflict.* Berkeley: University of California Press, 1967.

Fischer, L. *The Life of Mahatma Gandhi.* London: Cape, 1951.

Gandhi, M.K. *An Autobiography: The Story of My Experiments with Truth.* Trans. M. Desai. Boston: Beacon Press, 1957.

———. *Economic and Industrial Life and Relations.* 3 vols. Comp. and ed. V. Kher. Admedabad: Navajivan, 1957.

———. *Gandhiji and International Politics.* Comp. and ed. P. Chaudhury. Admedabad: Navajivan, 1970.

———. *Gandhi: Selected Writings.* Ed. R. Duncan. New York: Harper and Row, 1971.

Lenski, G., and J. Lenski. *Human Societies: An Introduction to Macrosociology*. 2nd ed. New York: McGraw-Hill, 1974.

Liddell, H., and R. Scott. *A Greek-English Lexicon*. Rev. H. Jones. Oxford: Clarendon Press, 1940.

Sharp, G. *The Politics of Nonviolent Action*. Boston: Sargent, 1973.

Index of
Names and Subjects

Index of
Scriptural References

OLD TESTAMENT

NEW TESTAMENT

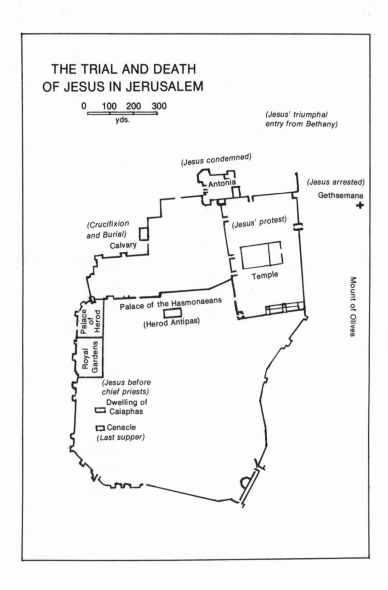

THE TRIAL AND DEATH
OF JESUS IN JERUSALEM

0   100   200   300
yds.

(Jesus' triumphal
entry from Bethany)

(Jesus condemned)

Antonia

(Jesus arrested)

Gethsemane

(Crucifixion
and Burial)

Calvary

(Jesus' protest)

Temple

Mount of Olives

Palace of the Hasmonaeans

Palace
of
Herod

(Herod Antipas)

Royal
Gardens

(Jesus before
chief priests)

Dwelling of
Caiaphas

Cenacle
(Last supper)

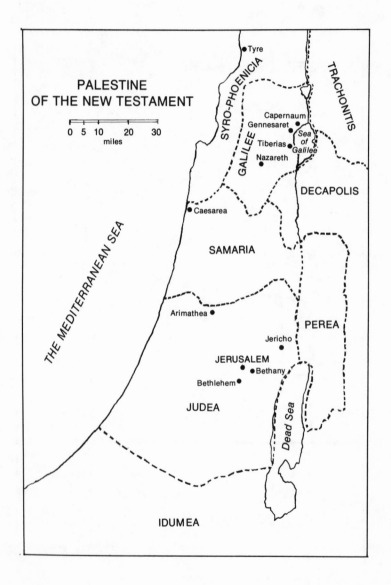

PALESTINE
OF THE NEW TESTAMENT

0 5 10   20   30
miles

Tyre

SYRO-PHOENICIA

TRACHONITIS

GALILEE

Capernaum
Gennesaret
Tiberias
Sea
of
Galilee
Nazareth

DECAPOLIS

THE MEDITERRANEAN SEA

Caesarea

SAMARIA

Arimathea

PEREA

Jericho

JERUSALEM
Bethany
Bethlehem

JUDEA

Dead Sea

IDUMEA